D1568269

EZRA POUND AND THE VISUAL CULTURE OF MODERNISM

Ezra Pound was deeply engaged with the avant-garde art scene in London and Paris during the early twentieth century. The effects of this engagement were not restricted to experiments in poetic form, however; they directly shaped Pound's social and political thought. In this book Rebecca Beasley tracks Pound's education in visual culture in chapters that explore his early poetry in the context of American aestheticism and middle-class education; imagism, anarchism and post-impressionist painting; vorticism and anti-democracy in early drafts of *The Cantos*; dadaist conceptual art, internationalism and Pound's turn to Italian fascism. In establishing a critical vocabulary profoundly indebted to the visual arts, Pound laid the basis for a literary modernism that is, paradoxically, a visual culture. Drawing on unpublished archive materials and little known magazine contributions, this study makes an important contribution to our understanding of Pound's intellectual development and the relationship between modernist literature and the visual arts.

REBECCA BEASLEY is Lecturer in English at Birkbeck College, University of London.

EZRA POUND AND THE VISUAL CULTURE OF MODERNISM

REBECCA BEASLEY

CAMBRIDGE
UNIVERSITY PRESS

CAMBRIDGE UNIVERSITY PRESS
Cambridge, New York, Melbourne, Madrid, Cape Town, Singapore, São Paulo

Cambridge University Press
The Edinburgh Building, Cambridge CB2 8RU, UK

Published in the United States of America by Cambridge University Press, New York

www.cambridge.org
Information on this title: www.cambridge.org/9780521870405

© Rebecca Beasley 2007

First published 2007

Printed in the United Kingdom at the University Press, Cambridge

A catalogue record for this publication is available from the British Library

ISBN 978-0-521-87040-5 hardback

For my parents, in gratitude and with love.

Contents

Illustrations

Acknowledgments

It is a great pleasure to be able to thank the many friends and colleagues who contributed to the writing of this book. The guidance of Ian F. A. Bell, Michael André Bernstein, Maud Ellmann, Tony Tanner, Clive Wilmer and Alex Zwerdling fundamentally shaped the work in its early stages, and Tim Armstrong, Nicola Bown, Katharine Craik, Markman Ellis, Anna Snaith and Tory Young generously commented on later versions of chapters. I have also benefited from the advice of Ann Banfield, Bernard Beatty, Joe Brooker, Peter Brooker, Gloria Carnivali, Stephen Clucas, Patricia Cockram, Jason Edwards, Tamara Follini, Peter Forshaw, Hilary Fraser, Simon Grimble, Thom Gunn, Nicholas Harrison, Alastair Horne, Anne Janowitz, Shulamith Deborah Kang, Matthew Kratter, Sally Ledger, Cheryl Leibold, Catherine Maxwell, David Peters Corbett, Elizabeth Pound, Omar Pound, Jeremy Prynne, John Rathmell, Laura Salisbury, Morag Shiach, Matthew Shinn, Noel Stock, Charles Tung, Dorothy Wang, Evelyn Welch, Peter White, Sue Wiseman and Richard Wollheim. I am grateful to David Ayers, John Beck, Ron Bush, Rod Edmond, Andrzej Gasiorek, Richard Gooder and John Schad for the opportunity to present and discuss parts of this work, and to the staff and students of the School of English and Humanities at Birkbeck for providing such an inspiring atmosphere in which to teach and research.

The research for this book was greatly facilitated by the staff of Cambridge University Library, the British Library, the Beinecke Rare Books and Manuscript Library at Yale and the Harry Ransom Humanities Research Center at the University of Texas, Austin. For assistance in obtaining illustrations, I am indebted to Maria Theresa Brunner of the Kunstmuseum Basel, DeAnn M. Dankowski of the Minneapolis Institute of Arts, Helen D'Monte representing the Wyndham Lewis Memorial Trust, Sarah Fahmy of Tate, London, Daniela Ferrari of the Museion Bolzano, Holly Frisbee of the Philadelphia Museum of Art, James Lafferty-Furphy of the Hunterian

Museum and Art Gallery, Naomi MacDonald of DACS, Magnus Malmros of the Moderna Museet, Stockholm, the Mary Cassatt Catalogue Raisonné Committee, Michael Scott of the Baltimore Museum of Art, Deborah Stultz of the Smithsonian Institution Scholarly Press, Luisa Càle, Bernard Dew, Jon Elek, Gloria Peck, Andrew Penman, Mary de Rachewiltz and Alison Rutherford.

Grants and fellowships from the following organisations made the research, writing and revision of the book possible: the Arts and Humanities Research Council, the British Academy, the University of California, Berkeley, the University of Cambridge, Birkbeck College, University of London, the University of Liverpool and the Harry Ransom Humanities Research Center. At Cambridge University Press, I am grateful to Ray Ryan for his commitment to this project, Maartje Scheltens, Jayne Aldhouse, Jodie Barnes and Clive Unger-Hamilton for their work on the manuscript, and to the manuscript's readers.

Grateful acknowledgement is given to New Directions Publishing Corporation and Faber and Faber Ltd for permission to quote from the following copyrighted works of Ezra Pound: *ABC of Reading* (all rights reserved), *The Cantos* (copyright © 1934, 1937, 1940, 1948, 1956, 1959, 1962, 1963, 1966, and 1968 by Ezra Pound), *Collected Early Poems of Ezra Pound* (copyright © 1976 by the Trustees of the Ezra Pound Literary Property Trust), *Ezra Pound and Dorothy Shakespear* (copyright © 1976, 1984 by the Trustees of the Ezra Pound Literary Property Trust), *Pound/Ford* (copyright © 1971, 1972, 1973, 1982 by the Trustees of the Ezra Pound Literary Property Trust), *Pound/Joyce* (copyright © 1967 by Ezra Pound), *Pound/Lewis* (copyright © 1985 by the Trustees of the Ezra Pound Literary Property Trust), *Pound/ The Little Review* (copyright © 1988 by the Trustees of the Ezra Pound Literary Property Trust), *Pound, Thayer, Watson and 'The Dial'* (copyright © 1994 by the Trustees of the Ezra Pound Literary Property Trust), *Ezra Pound and Music* (copyright © 1977 by the Trustees of the Ezra Pound Literary Property Trust), *Ezra Pound and the Visual Arts* (copyright © 1926, 1935, 1950, 1962, 1970, 1971, and 1980 by the Trustees of the Ezra Pound Literary Property Trust), *Gaudier Brzeska* (copyright © 1970 by Ezra Pound), *Guide to Kulchur* (copyright © 1970 by Ezra Pound). Quotations from previously unpublished works by Ezra Pound are copyright © 2007 by Mary de Rachewiltz and Omar S. Pound, and are used by permission of New Directions Publishing Corporation.

Earlier versions of chapters one, two and four appeared as 'Ezra Pound's Whistler', *American Literature*, 74 (2002), 485–516, 'Art as Propaganda for

Literary Modernism', *New Formations*, 43 (2001), 117–29, and 'Dada's Place in *The Cantos*', *Paideuma*, 30 (2001), 39–64. I am grateful to the editors of these journals for their permission to reprint material here.

My greatest debt is to my family. To my parents, to Ben and Lisa, and to Markman: thank you.

Abbreviations

GK	*Guide to Kulchur* (London: Faber and Faber, 1938)
HSM	*Hugh Selwyn Mauberley* (London: Ovid Press, 1920)
HTR	*How to Read* (London: Harmsworth, 1931)
J/M	*Jefferson And/ Or Mussolini: L'Idea Statale: Fascism As I Have Seen It* (London: Nott, 1935)
L	*The Letters of Ezra Pound: 1907–1941*, ed. D. D. Paige (New York: Harcourt, Brace, 1950)
L/DS	*Ezra Pound and Dorothy Shakespear: Their Letters: 1909–14*, ed. Omar Pound and A. Walton Litz (New York: New Directions, 1984)
L/FMF	*Pound/ Ford: The Story of a Literary Friendship*, ed. Brita Lindberg-Seyersted (New York: New Directions, 1982)
L/JL	*Ezra Pound and James Laughlin: Selected Letters*, ed. David M. Gordon (New York: Norton, 1994)
L/JQ	*The Selected Letters of Ezra Pound to John Quinn: 1915–1924*, ed. Timothy Materer (Durham, NC: Duke University Press, 1991)
L/MA	*Pound/ 'The Little Review': The Letters of Ezra Pound to Margaret Anderson – The Little Review Correspondence*, ed. Thomas L. Scott and Melvin J. Friedman, with the assistance of Jackson R. Bryer (New York: New Directions, 1988)
L/MC	*Ezra Pound and Margaret Cravens: A Tragic Friendship, 1910–1912*, ed. Omar Pound and Robert Spoo (Duke, NC: Duke University Press, 1988)
L/TW	*Pound, Thayer, Watson and 'The Dial': A Story in Letters*, ed. Walter Sutton (Gainesville, FL: University of Florida Press, 1994)
L/WCW	*Pound/ Williams: Selected Letters of Ezra Pound and William Carlos Williams*, ed. Hugh Witemeyer (New York: New Directions, 1996)
MA	*Machine Art and Other Writings: The Lost Thought of the Italian Years*, ed. Maria Luisa Ardizzone (Durham, NC: Duke University Press, 1996)
P	*Personæ: The Collected Poems of Ezra Pound* (New York: Boni & Liveright, 1926)
R	*Ripostes of Ezra Pound* (London: Swift, 1912)

RSWWII   *'Ezra Pound Speaking': Radio Speeches of World War II*, ed.
             Leonard W. Doob (Westport, CT: Greenwood Press, 1978)
SR   *The Spirit of Romance* (London: Dent, 1910)

Citations of *The Cantos*, 4th edn (London: Faber and Faber, 1987) are
inserted parenthetically after the quotation or reference in the form of
'canto number: page number(s)'.

Introduction

The 1930s were years of consolidation for Ezra Pound. His poetry became available to a wider public as its publication was taken over by major publishers, Faber and Faber in Great Britain, and Farrar and Rinehart in the United States. A new generation of poets and critics, including R. P. Blackmur, Basil Bunting, e.e. cummings, George Oppen, Allen Tate and Louis Zukovsky, looked to him as the vanguard of their literary revolution. His confirmed status was reflected in his literary criticism, which, always pedagogical, now explicitly took on the form of the textbook. 'How to Read', first serialised in the *New York Herald Tribune* in 1929, was published in book form in 1931; in 1934 it was supplemented with *ABC of Reading*, conceived as a 'text-book that can also be read "for pleasure as well as profit" by those no longer in school; by those who have not been to school; or by those who in their college days suffered those things which most of my generation suffered' (*ABCR*, ix). In 1938 *Guide to Kulchur* appeared, 'written for men who have not been able to afford an university education or for young men, whether or not threatened with universities, who want to know more at the age of fifty than I know today' (*GK*, [6]). Between them, these three works set out a programme of study and thought designed to provide the reader with 'instruments' and 'tools' with which to measure literary works and compare pieces of information (*ABCR*, 14; *GK*, 23).

Measure, compare – but first of all, *look*, is Pound's injunction in his textbooks, and in them we encounter a succession of figures distinguished by their optical perspicacity. There is the post-graduate student instructed by the biologist Louis Agassiz to look at a dead fish for three weeks; the fifteenth-century painter and medallist Pisanello, who drew horses so precisely that (Pound believed) Francesco Sforza, Duke of Milan, sent him to buy them; the sculptor Henri Gaudier-Brzeska who could 'see' the meaning of Chinese characters 'without any study'; and the critic of the future who will be able to tell the economic health of a period from a painting (*ABCR*, 1–2, 14, 5; *GK*, 27). The picture gallery is Pound's chosen analogy for his comparative mode of criticism: in *How to Read* the example of the National Gallery suggests that the 'best history of literature [. . .] would be a twelve-volume anthology' (*HTR*, 10), and in *ABC of Reading*, shading the art gallery into the laboratory, the quotations are presented as 'exhibits' (*ABCR*, 81).[1]

Pound advocates gaining knowledge by listening as well as by looking: in *ABC of Reading*, he remarks that the concerts he organised with Olga Rudge and Gerhart Münch in Rapallo during the winter of 1933 'demonstrate[d] the *How to Read* thesis in a medium nearer to poetry than painting is' (*ABCR*, 8; *EPM*, 337–40). But even though Pound believed music to be the more precise correlative to poetry and, indeed, he was engaged with music during this period in a way he no longer was with the visual arts, as an analogy it is nevertheless looking that is the preferred model of engagement, the art gallery that suggests a methodology, and the painting that is the equivalent of the verbal text. It is indicative that Pound capitalises 'look' four times in *ABC of Reading* (all in the first two chapters), a rate exceeded only by his capitalisation of 'know'; 'listen' is not capitalised once. The object of this book is to track how the visual sense and the visual arts came to occupy this key position in Pound's thought, and to explain the shifting ideological significance of their presence.

The terms of my title require some explanation here. It is a critical commonplace that early twentieth-century literature was in thrall to the visual arts: 'we are under the dominion of painting', wrote Virginia Woolf in 1925.[2] The notion of a 'visual culture of modernism' is, in this sense, an instantly recognisable concept. However, viewed from another perspective, from within the critical field of visual culture, the phrase is more problematic. Since its emergence in the last thirty years, visual culture has come to define itself through a very different set of theoretical precepts and objects of interest than those historically associated with modernism. For W. J. T. Mitchell, for example, 'the most obvious evidence' of interest in visual culture is 'the emergence of studies in film, television, and mass culture, alongside a new social/ political/ communicational order that employs mass spectacle and technologies of visual and auditory stimulation in radically new ways'.[3] While the 'new' is conventionally, though not unproblematically, understood as a constituent of modernism, the other elements of

---

[1] See also 'I Gather the Limbs of Osiris, [II]: A Rather Dull Introduction', *New Age*, 10 (1911), 130–1.

[2] Virginia Woolf, 'Pictures' (1925), in *The Essays of Virginia Woolf: 1925–1928*, ed. Andrew McNeillie (London: Hogarth Press, 1994), pp. 243–7 (p. 243).

[3] W. J. T. Mitchell, 'What is Visual Culture?', in *Meaning in the Visual Arts: Views from the Outside*, ed. Irving Lavin (Princeton, NJ: Institute for Advanced Study, 1995), pp. [207]–17 (p. [207]).

this definition have been typically associated with the not-modernisms, the avant-garde and postmodernism. In these discourses, it is precisely modernism's failure to engage with mechanical reproduction, mass culture and the socio-political order – in short, with the distinctive features of twentieth-century modernity – that is its defining trait. For critics such as Marshall Berman, Peter Bürger and Andreas Huyssen, modernism is the reactionary response to modernity – and Pound is frequently invoked as this argument's defining example. Berman, for example, defines modernity against 'a distinctive mode of aesthetic modernism, pervasive in our century – e.g. in Pound, Wyndham Lewis, and their many followers – in which modern people and life are endlessly abused, while modern artists and their works are exalted to the skies, without any suspicion that these artists may be more human, and more deeply implicated in *la vie moderne*, than they would like to think'.[4]

These influential anti-modernist critics revised the hegemonic conception of the relationship between modernity and its literary expression, rejecting self-conscious experiment as the marker of modernity in favour of art's critique of its own social status.[5] They thus attacked the very ground of modernism's self-definition as a radical movement. But in doing so, they also regenerated Anglo-American modernist studies, galvanising the discipline into moving beyond the exaltation of formal experiment for its own sake and conducting a sustained interrogation of early twentieth-century cultural production. The 'new modernisms' that have emerged are less hostile to modernity than their singular predecessor, even if they retain an equivocal relationship to technology and mass culture.[6] After two decades, the challenge of Bürger's 'historical avant-garde' has been assimilated, as is demonstrated by Ann Ardis's recent reappropriation of the once uncontentious phrase 'modernist avant-garde'.[7] The legacy of anti-modernism is a more nuanced history of literary activity in the early twentieth century, from which the radical and the reactionary have emerged with a considerably more complex relationship than was previously acknowledged.

[4] Marshall Berman, *All That is Solid Melts Into Air: The Experience of Modernity* (London: Verso, 1983), p. 141. See also Peter Bürger, *Theory of the Avant-Garde*, trans. Michael Shaw (Minneapolis, MN: University of Minnesota Press, 1984) and Andreas Huyssen, *After the Great Divide: Modernism, Mass Culture, Postmodernism* (Bloomington, IN: Indiana University Press, 1986), pp. 163, 167.
[5] Bürger, p. 49.
[6] 'The New Modernisms' was the title given to the first two conferences of the Modernist Studies Association, held on 7–10 October 1999 at Penn State University and 12–15 October 2000 at the University of Pennsylvania.
[7] Ann L. Ardis, *Modernism and Cultural Conflict: 1880–1922* (Cambridge: Cambridge University Press, 2002), pp. 7–8.

But even though the respective values of visual culture and of modernism no longer seem as opposed as they did ten years ago, in this study I want to preserve the tension between the two terms in order to pursue a particular argument. In her recent book on visual culture and the modernist novel, *The Eye's Mind: Literary Modernism and Visual Culture*, Karen Jacobs argues that the perspective of visual culture

allows us to see literature as responsive to a broader set of influences than the narrow and often purely formally conceived aesthetic sphere. Determinations about modernist politics have often been predicated on assessments of its form, equating its opacity with elitism and solipsism or, conversely, with the progressive project of defamiliarization and subversion [. . .]. These various valorizations of form, I believe, threaten to obscure equally important valorizations of the ideological content of modernist texts.[8]

Like Jacobs, I am drawn to visual culture as a means of expanding our thinking about modernism, and asking questions about the ideological content of modernist texts, as well as their form. But our approach is different; where Jacobs juxtaposes the terms modernism and visual culture to explore how modernist texts can be productively understood as responding to the visual culture of *modernity*, my title intends to register a visuality embedded within *modernism* itself, modernism understood here as the retrospectively applied literary critical category. My interrogation of modernism is informed by a recognition of its influence on the inter-war professionalisation of English studies, and its construction through an institutionalised version of its own terms. The canonisation of certain texts under the term 'modernism' in the mid-twentieth century was achieved by a criticism that emphasised 'spatial form', analysed by 'practical criticism' or 'close reading', and, above all, believed that the literary text could 'embody reality rather than merely refer to it'.[9] These terms were derived from modernism's own account of itself, an account, I want to emphasise, that drew heavily on modernism's encounter with the visual arts. Literary modernism is, paradoxically, a visual culture.

Pound contributed decisively to this formation of modernism, and from the very beginning of his career his engagement with the visual arts had a fundamental impact on his theorising of the literary. The nature of that impact has long been a source of debate. William Carlos Williams famously

[8] Karen Jacobs, *The Eye's Mind: Literary Modernism and Visual Culture* (Ithaca, NY: Cornell University Press, 2001), pp. 4–5.
[9] Joseph Frank, 'Spatial Form in Modern Literature', *Sewanee Review*, 53 (1945), 221–40, 433–56, 643–53; Wendy Steiner, *The Colors of Rhetoric: Problems in the Relation between Modern Literature and Painting* (Chicago, IL: University of Chicago Press, 1982), p. 24. See also Ardis, pp. 173–6, and Chris Baldick, *Criticism and Literary Theory: 1890 to the Present* (London: Longman, 1996), pp. 64–115.

denounced Pound as 'color blind', citing his preference for Francis Picabia and Fernand Léger over Picasso, Braque and Matisse as evidence of his lack of knowledge and taste, and at the end of his career Pound himself dismissed the idea that his association with artists had had 'anything to do with [him] as a writer'.[10] But literary critics have found much to say about Pound's writing on art, especially his advocacy of the distinctive critique of pre-war aesthetics mounted by Wyndham Lewis and the vorticist group, and his ardent support for contemporary sculpture. Richard Cork's and Timothy Materer's rigorous work on the vorticist Pound over the last thirty years has carved out a unique place for him in the period as a catalyst in the history of art, as well as of literature.[11] The ground for this portrait was well prepared by early studies by Walter Baumann, Donald Davie, Hugh Kenner and Hugh Witemeyer that deployed Pound's own spatial analogies, 'patterned energy', 'rose in the steel dust', 'vortex' and 'intaglio' to elucidate his experiments in poetic form.[12] In the new wave of Pound scholarship in the 1980s, the visual arts continued to play an important role: Harriet Zinnes's anthology of Pound's writing on the visual arts made available previously obscure articles, notably the 'Art Notes' column for the *New Age*, and Charles Altieri, Andrew Clearfield, Reed Way Dasenbrock, Michael North and Marjorie Perloff explored Pound's poetics through the lenses of cubism, collage, vorticism, classicist architecture and sculpture, and futurism, respectively. In 1984 the Tate Gallery held an exhibition of *Pound's Artists*, accompanied by a book of the same name that to date is the best single source of information about Pound's interaction with visual artists.[13]

[10] William Carlos Williams, 'Ezra Pound: Lord Ga-Ga!', *Decision*, 2.3 (1941), 16–24 (p. 21); Donald Hall, 'Ezra Pound: An Interview', *Paris Review*, 28 (1962), 22–51 (p. 30).

[11] See especially Richard Cork, *Vorticism and Abstract Art in the First Machine Age*, 2 vols. (London: Fraser, 1976) and Timothy Materer, *Vortex: Pound, Eliot and Lewis* (Ithaca, NY: Cornell University Press, 1979).

[12] See Hugh Kenner, *The Pound Era* (London: Faber and Faber, 1972), pp. 146–7, for a discussion of these terms. See also Walter Baumann, *The Rose in the Steel Dust: An Examination of* The Cantos *of Ezra Pound* (Bern: Francke, 1967); Donald Davie, *Ezra Pound: Poet as Sculptor* (London: Routledge & Kegan Paul, 1965); Hugh Kenner, *The Poetry of Ezra Pound* (London: Faber and Faber, 1951); Hugh Witemeyer, *The Poetry of Ezra Pound: Forms and Renewal, 1908–1920* (Berkeley and Los Angeles, CA: University of California Press, 1969).

[13] *EPVA*; Charles Altieri, *Painterly Abstraction in Modernist American Poetry: The Contemporaneity of Modernism* (Cambridge: Cambridge University Press, 1989); Andrew Clearfield, *These Fragments I Have Shored: Collage and Montage in Early Modernist Poetry* (Ann Arbor, MI: University of Michigan Research Press, 1984); Reed Way Dasenbrock, *The Literary Vorticism of Ezra Pound and Wyndham Lewis: Towards the Condition of Painting* (Baltimore, MD: Johns Hopkins University Press, 1985); Michael North, *The Final Sculpture: Public Monuments and Modern Poets* (Ithaca, NY: Cornell University Press, 1985); Marjorie Perloff, *The Futurist Moment: Avant-Garde, Avant Guerre, and the Language of Rupture* (Chicago, IL: Chicago University Press, 1986); *Pound's Artists: Ezra Pound and the Visual Arts in London, Paris and Italy* (London: Tate Gallery, 1985).

However, it was also in the 1980s, and indeed in these works, that the use of the visual arts as an interpretative framework for Pound's poetry began to be productively questioned. As the critical landscape was revivified by its encounter with post-structuralism and Marxism, and at the same time more sustained attention was given to Pound's politics and economics, discussion of Pound and the visual arts could no longer be restricted to analyses of formal interaction. Two statements from this period summarise the questions such studies raised. First, Charles Altieri wrote:

But if we concentrate simply on comparing the concepts or stylistic devices poets and painters share, we tend to reduce poetry to a narrow range of predicates and to subordinate it to values in fact best realized by the visual arts. Relations between the arts, especially in post-romantic cultures, are not likely to resolve into a series of discrete borrowings. We ought then to expect intricate networks of provocations and threats, permissions and fears as writers see what can be borrowed, who one becomes when one imitates, and what may be possible if one tries to transform what has been inherited into the characteristic thematic and performative dimensions of poetry.[14]

For Altieri the limitation of the formalist analyses he associates particularly with Kenner's criticism is that they leave out a consideration of ethics: he proposes instead a 'constructivist aesthetic', in which contemporaneous visual arts challenge Pound to develop a poetics in which he can balance, 'the aesthetic, the utopian, and the practical'.[15] A year later, Michael André Bernstein suggested a related programme:

What we require, I believe, is less a catalog of all of Pound's specific statements about various artists, with each utterance assigned a positive or negative prefix depending upon our own personal and currently sanctioned hierarchy of values, than a careful study of the place of those statements in the logic and texture of Pound's own work. The attempt to focus attention on *The Cantos'* network of artistic references – its invocation of masterpieces and privileged moments of cultural achievement – will yield only trivial results unless the inner dynamic linking Pound's various exampla and the actual role these play in the poem's argument become clearer in the process.[16]

Unlike Altieri, Bernstein is less interested in rethinking Pound's formal response to the visual arts than he is in mapping the ideological implications of Pound's allegiances and references. But what these proposed programmes

---

[14] Charles Altieri, 'Modernist Abstraction and Pound's First Cantos: The Ethos for a New Renaissance', *Kenyon Review*, 7 (1985), 79–105 (p. 79).
[15] Altieri, *Painterly Abstraction in Modernist American Poetry*, pp. 290, 470.
[16] Michael André Bernstein, 'Image, Word and Sign: The Visual Arts as Evidence in Ezra Pound's Cantos', *Critical Inquiry*, 12 (1986), 347–64 (p. 351).

share is an insistence that the visual arts be seen as part of the 'argument' of Pound's work, providing a model that is not restricted to the formal.

The last decade has seen a number of responses to these programmatic statements. Four works in particular have set out the parameters within which this study is conceived. Vincent Sherry's *Ezra Pound, Wyndham Lewis, and Radical Modernism* made the decisive move of associating Pound's and Lewis's prioritising of the visual sense and the terms of their visual rhetoric with a particular ideological tradition, an anti-democratic Continental philosophical tradition that also includes Julien Benda, Ortega y Gasset, Remy de Gourmont and Wilhelm Worringer. David Kadlec's more recent *Mosaic Modernism* focussed its discussion of Pound's aesthetic terminology particularly on the individualist anarchism Pound encountered in the pages of Dora Marsden's *Egoist*, whose privileging of immediacy and action Kadlec compellingly relates to the juxtapositional technique of *The Cantos*. In *Solid Objects*, Douglas Mao explained the modernist attraction to objects and 'thingly opacity' as an aspiration to a realm beyond the reach of ideology, minutely detailing the lacunae in Pound's theorising of individual production that rationalised his turn to fascism. Finally, Lawrence Rainey's *Institutions of Modernism* demonstrated with force and clarity how the detailed reconstruction of moments of cultural production could yield insights into the politics of form.[17]

This book traces the place of the visual and the visual arts in Pound's work, from his earliest writings, many of them unpublished, to the 1930s, by which time his interest had lessened: as Reed Way Dasenbrock has commented, though Pound 'continued to cite artists and works of art as touchstones or exemplars of civilization, [. . .] there is virtually no discussion of works qua art in the way there was in the decade from 1914 to 1924'.[18] In order to track and assess the associations Pound built between his literary project and contemporaneous visual culture, this study proceeds chronologically, measuring Pound's interaction with the visual arts, and his interpretations of particular works, against those of contemporary critics. In his first published article, written from within American aestheticism's

[17] Vincent Sherry, *Ezra Pound, Wyndham Lewis, and Radical Modernism* (New York: Oxford University Press, 1993) (see also Richard Sieburth's *Instigations: Ezra Pound and Remy de Gourmont* [Cambridge, MA: Harvard University Press, 1978], which anticipates elements of Sherry's argument); David Kadlec, *Mosaic Modernism: Anarchism, Pragmatism, Culture* (Baltimore, MD: Johns Hopkins University Press, 2000), pp. 54–89; Douglas Mao, *Solid Objects: Modernism and the Test of Production* (Princeton, NJ: Princeton University Press, 1998), pp. 140–93 (p. 164); Lawrence Rainey, *Institutions of Modernism: Literary Elites and Public Culture* (New Haven, CT: Yale University Press, 1998).
[18] Reed Way Dasenbrock, 'Pound and the visual arts', in *The Cambridge Companion to Ezra Pound*, ed. Ira B. Nadel (Cambridge: Cambridge University Press, 1999), pp. 224–35 (p. 225).

cult of beauty, Pound's professional investment in the visual arts is clear: the visual arts are to provide the model for an alternative mode of criticism from the philological tradition in which he had been educated. Analogies with works by Whistler, Waterhouse and Turner function as explanatory strategies in place of biographical information and textual scholarship, and extensive quotation (showing) rather than commentary (saying) introduces a methodology that looks forward to the close reading techniques developed in the 1920s. Pound continued to use the visual arts to invoke a transcendent poetics of beauty during his first years in London, but as he reconfigured the terms of his career through the movement tactics of imagism and vorticism in the context of the post-impressionist debates about aesthetic modernity, his interpretation of the visual arts began to focus on their ability to set his poetry to the task of contemporary critique. This, indeed, made contemporary art an important model not only for the form but also for the content of *The Cantos*, yet during this period Pound also began to seriously question the ability of painting and sculpture to foster the 'free circulation of thought' which had become his chief preoccupation.[19] The very materiality of painting and sculpture makes them luxury goods, he decides, and, disregarding the mass arts of photography and cinema, he argues that literature alone can lend itself to popularisation. The conceptual art of the dadaists forces a reconsideration of this question and during the 1920s Pound's aesthetics enter a final phase in which the prime criterion of artistic value is intelligence.

However, this is only part of the story, and while an account of the visual arts as a component of Pound's self-fashioning can explain the rationale for his engagement, it falls short of interpreting the politics of that engagement. Pound's aesthetic decisions cannot be separated from ideological considerations, and for that reason this study frequently ranges well beyond Pound's writing about art, both to lesser known or unpublished critical pieces by Pound, but also to contemporary debates that enable an evaluation of his decisions. In the first chapter, for example, consideration of the ideology of the department store and the professionalisation of university study leads to a reading of Pound's poetics of beauty as part of the middle classes' reconfiguration of the cultural landscape from an aristocracy to a meritocracy. In chapter two, a genealogical account of Pound's critical terminology leads us not only to the familiar formalist criticism of Laurence Binyon and Roger Fry, but also to the less familiar individualism of Huntly Carter, the art and drama critic of the *Egoist*. Although Pound was not committed to

---

[19] 'Things to Be Done', *Poetry*, 9 (1917), 312–14 (p. 312).

a single political position at this point, for critics at his other main publishing outlet, the socialist *New Age*, his criticism appeared to encode the *Egoist*'s individualist anarchism, a politics that linked Pound to the new art movements before he engaged with them himself. Chapter three is a sustained reading of the earliest drafts of *The Cantos* as what Pound termed a 'realist' text, in which the vorticist art of Lewis and Gaudier is admired as 'a historical method' that can represent the values of the individualist and oppose the verbalism of both German *Kultur* and British democracy.[20] The final chapter describes the intellectual and ideological trajectory of the post-war Parisian avant-garde at the time of Pound's stay in Paris from 1921 to 1924. The aesthetic choices William Carlos Williams professed not to understand are explained by the dadaists' lone commitment to an individualist and anti-nationalist programme, while Picasso led the embrace of post-war patriotic classicism. Yet the dadaist programme, with its dissolution of artistic categories into 'art in general', to use Thierry de Duve's term, would for Pound initiate the collapse between the aesthetic and the political that brokered his shift to Italian fascism.[21]

To return to Pound's early poetry and to issues of aesthetics is not to put aside the ethical questions that accounts of his later career inevitably make central. This study endeavours to provide a bridge between work on Pound's early career and the criticism on his later career that has had more to say about politics and history. My reading of Pound's early writings demonstrates how directly he was concerned with social and political questions during this supposedly aestheticist phase, and my account of Pound's intellectual activity in post-war Paris, in particular, helps to explain how he arrived in Paris as an individualist anti-nationalist, and left as a supporter of Mussolini – Tim Redman's otherwise excellent study of Pound's attraction to Italian fascism omits the Paris period entirely. I aim to contribute to the recovery of a history of modernism in which the revolutionary rhetoric of the avant-garde, appearing first in the visual arts and subsequently in literature, is not read simply as the posturing of the competitive young artist, but rather as having a particular political resonance. Modernist individualism should not be collapsed into late Romantic subjectivity. This mistake formed the basis of one of the most powerful critiques of modernism, that levelled by Georg Lukács, who argued that the modernists' 'rejection of modern reality is purely subjective', lacking 'both content and

[20] 'Ur-Cantos [III]: Autograph ms. and typescript', EPP, Beinecke, 69.3101.
[21] Thierry de Duve, 'Echoes of the Readymade: Critique of Pure Modernism', in *The Duchamp Effect*, ed. Martha Buskirk and Mignon Nixon (Cambridge, MA: MIT Press, 1996), pp. 93–129 (p. 95).

direction', unlike 'the bourgeois protest against feudal society, the proletarian against bourgeois society', in both of which 'the protest [. . .] was based on a concrete *terminus ad quem*: the establishment of a new order'.[22] On the contrary, modernist individualism did envision the establishment of a new order, hence its attraction to both communism and fascism, sometimes simultaneously. While Pound's engagement with contemporary art has tended to be interpreted as evidence of his aestheticist preoccupation with form, this study explores how the appeal of the visual arts lay primarily in their apparent immediacy, an immediacy valued first as an expression of subjectivity, then as the corollary of anarchist direct action, and, finally, the cult of efficiency that drew Pound to fascist Italy.

[22] Georg Lukács, *The Meaning of Contemporary Realism*, trans. John and Necke Mander (London: Merlin, 1963), pp. 30, 29.

CHAPTER I

American aestheticism: the origins of an interdisciplinary modernism

BEAUTY

When the September 1906 issue of the Philadelphia-based *Book News Monthly* appeared, it contained two articles by a new contributor, Ezra Pound, 'Fellow in Romance languages for the University of Pennsylvania', who was making his first appearance as a published critic. *Book News Monthly* was owned and published by John Wanamaker, 'America's most influential merchant of the early twentieth century', the owner of Philadelphia's first department store, and a self-professed book lover.[1] 'He had an insatiable thirst for books', reported a family member, 'He always gave us books for our Christmas and birthday gifts. He loved them so himself that I suppose he thought he could give nothing more precious, more delightful or more welcome.'[2] Although he effectively educated himself through reading, Wanamaker's chosen books, his biographers admitted, 'were not always those of a cultivated man'.[3] Favourites included devotional works and bible commentaries, such as G. Campbell Morgan's *The Hidden Years at Nazareth* and Josiah H. Penniman's *A Book about the English Bible*, political biographies, such as Ulysses S. Grant's *Personal Memoirs* and William Roscoe Thayer's *Theodore Roosevelt: An Intimate Biography*, and popular works by the novelist Florence Barclay and the essayist David Grayson. He 'adored' Eleanor H. Porter's *Pollyanna* stories and his favourite poet was James Whitcomb Riley, followed by Tennyson.[4]

---

[1] William Leach, *Land of Desire: Merchants, Power and the Rise of a New American Culture* (New York: Pantheon, 1993), p. xv. Pound's appearance in *Book News Monthly* was facilitated by the fact that Carlos Tracy Chester, the pastor of his parents' church and the dedicatee of *Exultations*, helped to edit it: see Noel Stock, *Ezra Pound's Pennsylvania* (Toledo, OH: Friends of the University of Toledo Libraries, 1976), p. 14.

[2] Russell H. Conwell, *The Romantic Rise of a Great American* (New York: Harper & Brothers, 1924), p. 160.

[3] Herbert Adams Gibbons, *John Wanamaker*, 2 vols. (New York: Harper & Brothers, 1926), 1: 207.

[4] Conwell, p. 162; Gibbons, 1: 208–11.

Book News Monthly was conceived, according to Wanamaker's biographers, 'to induce people not only to own and read books, but to take more interest in them'. It began in 1882 as a compendium of newspaper book reviews, but soon developed into a more substantial publication, and from 1906 Wanamaker took it under his own supervision.[5] 1882 had also seen the opening of the Wanamaker Book Store on the ground floor of the Philadelphia department store, and by 1887 Wanamaker was the largest retail bookseller in the United States.[6] *Book News Monthly* contributed to this success. It carried a large number of advertisements, some its own, but of course those which were ostensibly for publishers also advertised Wanamaker's stock, often explicitly. Through its regular columns and articles Wanamaker's could draw readers' attention to the availability and desirability of particular works and create demand for forthcoming books by running features on specific authors. It also offered samples of Wanamaker's goods in the form of serialisations.

The two articles offered by *Book News Monthly*'s new critic seemed unlikely to contribute to Wanamaker's profits in quite the same way. The second of the articles, it is true, was a review of a recently published work, *Le Secret des troubadours* by the French Rosicrucian, Joséphin Péladan. Péladan's book argued that the songs of the Provençal troubadours were encoded versions of the Albigensian heresy; Pound told the journal's readers that this was 'interesting reading' but ultimately lacking the 'absolute proof' required.[7] The first article, 'Raphaelite Latin', was a much more ambitious piece, but it was even more specialist in its appeal. It was a defence of Renaissance poetry written in Latin, 'the most neglected field in all literature', wrote the young scholar, and it argued for a new estimation of the work of Pietro Bembo, Baldassare Castiglione, Camillo Capilupi and Marcantonio Flaminio.[8] According to Pound, the neglect of their poetry was emblematic of the limitations of the prevailing system of academic scholarship, philology:

The scholars of classic Latin, bound to the Germanic ideal of scholarship, are no longer able as of old to fill themselves with the beauty of the classics, and by the very force of that beauty inspire their students to read Latin widely and for pleasure;

---

[5] Conwell, p. 166.   [6] Gibbons, I: 202.
[7] 'Interesting French Publications', *Book News Monthly*, 25 (1906), 54–5 (p. 55); Joséphin Péladan, *Le Secret des troubadours: De Parsifal à Don Quichotte* (Paris: Sansot, 1906). On Pound and Péladan, see Leon Surette, *The Birth of Modernism: Ezra Pound, T. S. Eliot, W. B. Yeats, and the Occult* (Montreal, PQ and Kingston, ON: McGill-Queen's University Press, 1993), pp. 122–42.
[8] 'Raphaelite Latin', *Book News Monthly*, 25 (1906), [31]-34 (p. [31]). Pound mistakes the first name of the latter, confusing him with his father, Giovanni Antonio Flaminio, and referring to him (using the Latin form) as Johannes Antonius Flamininus.

nor are they able to make students see clearly whereof classic beauty consists. The scholar is compelled to spend most of his time learning what his author wore and ate, and in endless pondering over some utterly unanswerable question of textual criticism.

'Beauty' is made to carry considerable weight in this short passage: the rhetorical grandeur of its repetition mocks the mundane biographical and philological concerns of the early twentieth-century scholar, and it sets the author firmly in opposition to academic scholarship. But its very repetition highlights two related difficulties for the critic adopting it as a critical category in the early twentieth century: what methodology is available to the critic who wants to demonstrate the beauty to be found in these recalcitrant poems? And how can he perform this task while maintaining the academic authority insisted on by the use of his fellowship title at the head of the article; how can he avoid incurring 'the abject and utterly scornful' label of '"dilettante"'?[9]

Two years later Pound would begin the preface to his second volume of poetry 'BEAUTY should never be presented explained', and his first published article prefigures that maxim (*AQFTY*, [6]). After some general historical and critical background, Pound simply presents his evidence of the poems' beauty, in the form of lengthy translations from the Latin texts. The high poetic diction of lines such as 'In thy gleaming hair doth Hesper, maiden loved/ Ever as a red rose shine/ O'er the front of thy brow', from Castiglione's elegy for Raphael ('De morte Raphaelis pictoris') is designed to radiate the beauty the article has identified: neither analysis nor justification are provided. To Pound, the beauty and value of the lines quoted is so self-evident that he is able to end his article on a deliberately bathetic note: 'The least one can say in praise is that the "surprising literary barrenness of this period" rather fades on closer inspection.'[10]

Although the style and subject matter of Pound's first work of criticism are incongruously academic for a general readership, its argument is markedly appropriate. Pound aims to convey the immediate appeal of this body of poetry, and he suggests that specialised study at university level is unnecessary, indeed an impediment, to its appreciation. The general reader of his article should be able to recognise the beauty of the lines he quotes without special training or guidance. The broader assumption of the article, that the cultivation and appreciation of beauty is of supreme importance, is

---

[9] 'Raphaelite Latin', p. [31]. For an account of the forces that sidelined the Latin works of the Renaissance, see Christopher S. Celenza, *The Lost Italian Renaissance: Humanists, Historians, and Latin's Legacy* (Baltimore, MD: Johns Hopkins University Press, 2004).
[10] 'Raphaelite Latin', pp. 33–4.

also appropriate to its publication context in Wanamaker's periodical. One of the defining innovations of the department store, after all, was its 'spread of an aesthetic to serve business needs'. Its business of selling goods could only be sustained by adding the 'diffusion of "desire"' to the perception of need, and the discourse of beauty was a central strategy in the sublimation of the commodity. In its drive to increase consumption, the department store sought to inspire the imagination by using strategies such as the new science of window dressing, catalogues illustrated in colour, and interiors filled with glazed and mirrored surfaces. The new visual advertising transformed the experience of buying goods.[11]

John Wanamaker had shown himself to be particularly talented at the importation of beauty into business, culling many of his innovations from visits to Parisian department stores, such as Bon Marché and Printemps.[12] In 1908, for example, he had an enormous showroom constructed in the New York Wanamaker store. 'The House Palatial', as it was called, was intended to represent 'the home of a family of taste and wealth' and included an 'Elizabethan library decorated with tiger skins, a Jacobean dining room, a Louis XIV salon, and even a large Italian garden off the dining room'.[13] Since 1881 the Philadelphia store had contained an art gallery, in which 'hundreds of the best modern paintings – most of them selected from Paris Salons and many world-famous – [were] hung for the enjoyment and education of the public'. The emphasis on the educative here is characteristic; Wanamaker's merging of art and business was in part the product of his genuine belief that his store should act as an educational institution. He claimed that his business had translated Herbert Spencer's theory that 'every industrial institution should be educational' into everyday life: the stores' 'stocks of merchandise are a liberal education for all who come in contact with them. One's eyes are the great gateways to knowledge', he wrote.[14] *Book News Monthly* carried a regular educational section, which since April 1904 had been a 'Home Reading Course in Literature'.

Although promoted as educational, the reading courses and art galleries were of course also designed to increase sales. The 'Home Reading Course in Literature' and the 'Books for the Study and Library' column provided the tuition necessary to acquire both culture and a material display of

[11] Leach, pp. 40, 37, 55–61, 44–5, 71–5, 44. See also Simon J. Bronner, ed., *Consuming Visions: Accumulation and Display of Goods in America, 1880–1920* (New York: Norton, 1989).

[12] Leach, p. 74.

[13] John Wanamaker Firm, *Golden Book of the Wanamaker Stores: Jubilee Year 1861–1911* (Philadelphia, PA: Wanamaker, 1911), p. 296; Leach, p. 81

[14] John Wanamaker Firm, pp. 73, 227.

culture, and they incorporated handy shopping lists of 'supplementary reading', complete with full publisher's details for ease of purchase.[15] The art galleries and the articles on art exhibitions in *Book News Monthly* had a more subtle, but no less effective influence, glossing the commercial activity of the department store with the purifying patina of beauty. To repeat Pierre Bourdieu's famous formulation: 'alongside the pursuit of "economic" profit, which treats the cultural goods business as a business like any other [. . .] there is also room for *the accumulation of symbolic capital'*.[16] While Pound's article may not have increased sales of Renaissance Latin poets in the Wanamaker Book Store, it did affirm the importance of cultivating beauty, beauty one could both experience and buy at Wanamaker's. As Wanamaker himself is reported to have remarked: 'What is not for sale is still for sale.'[17]

Just over a year later, Pound, now with the by-line 'Professor of Romance Languages in Wabash College, Indiana', returned to Renaissance Latin poetry in the pages of *Book News Monthly* with an article devoted to one poet in particular, Marcantonio Flaminio. It repeated the earlier article's argument against philology, and gave beauty an even more prominent place in its critical lexicon. This time, however, Pound was considerably more specific about its connotations. 'What is beauty and where shall one lay hold on it?', he began. In answer he compared Flaminio's poetry with that of a poet his readers were more likely to know, 'the utter poet John Keats'. He defined their similarities as follows:

All the old Pantheon revivified, each wood a nesting-place of nymphs; rose petals their meat, and dew their nectar; dreaming in a world of Pan pipes and fair shepherds, with no Spenserian moralizings to give their beauty the function of a mere covering; loving the wood-wild fairness for itself alone, and myrtle and rose and moonlight for themselves and not as poetic ornament; poetry with no strong optimism as Browning's to make it vital, or to cause it to be slandered with the name of prose in verse; a beauty so sweet, so unreal, that we may not have it with us always without cloying, save when by its poetic utterness it holds our memory as must all absolute things.[18]

---

[15] Frank H. Sweet, 'A Home Reading Course in Literature. Lesson XLIII. English. Period XII. The Victorian Era. Charles Kingsley' and Talcott Williams, 'Books for the Study and the Library', *Book News Monthly*, 25 (1907), 707–12, 704–6.

[16] Pierre Bourdieu, *The Field of Cultural Production: Essays on Art and Literature*, ed. Randal Johnson (Cambridge: Polity, 1993), p. 75.

[17] Qtd in Gibbons, II: 81.

[18] 'M. Antonius Flamininus and John Keats: A Kinship in Genius', *Book News Monthly*, 26 (1908), [445]-7 (pp. 445–6). See Ian F. A. Bell and Patricia A. Agar, 'Romantic Modernisms: Early Pound and Late Keats', *Paideuma*, 19.1&2 (1990), 93–105.

This is a virtuoso display of the appreciation of beauty, recreating the effect of the poetry in both the allusions and the rhythm of the prose. The beauty the readers are invited to rescue from critical oblivion is a pastoral beauty, characterised by lack of moral statement, lack of ornamentation, and – somewhat surprisingly in light of the poetry Pound himself is already producing – lack of vitality, the quality Pound associates here, as in later essays, with Browning's poetry, and with prose. But this is not only beautiful poetry, desirable as that is; it is presented as the epitome of poetry, the best the medium has to offer. This 'unreal', 'cloying', unvital verse is literally more *poetic* than other forms of the medium, it has a quality Pound calls 'poetic utterness'. It is implicitly more poetic than the work of Yeats and Rossetti, described later in the article, and explicitly more poetic than Browning's poetry.

Paradoxically, Pound's notion of 'poetic utterness' and the type of beauty that characterises it is thoroughly imbued with another medium: painting. As in 'Raphaelite Latin', the argument of this second article is made primarily by quotation; there is no technical analysis, and indeed, bar the quotations themselves, there is little in Pound's discussion to suggest that the manifestation of beauty he describes is poetic, or even verbal. In fact, Pound repeatedly comments on the quotations by turning to painterly analogy. So the classicists' 'tones are as Whistler's when he paints the mist at moth hour', one of Flaminio's *lusus pastorales* contains '"genre" painting', which 'none has done [. . .] in better harmony of line and color', and Pound's only comment following a twenty-line quotation from Flaminio's 'Hercules and Hylas' is to compare it with late Pre-Raphaelite painting: 'For this last picture, we must seek Waterhouse's "Foreboding in the Pool"' (*Hylas and the Nymphs* [1896]).[19] Allusion to contemporary, or near contemporary, painting appears to be central to Pound's communication of beauty in poetry: visual strategies are as important to Pound's recommendation of Flaminio's poetry as they are to Wanamaker's selling of household goods. But what is the effect of these advertisements? They attribute an immediacy to the poetry that is in direct opposition to the resolutely verbal and textual considerations of philology, 'such as syntax, metric, errors in

---

[19] 'M. Antonius Flamininus and John Keats', pp. 446–7. See II: VII ('Sic tibi perpetuam donet Venus alma juventam') and II: VI ('De Hercule, & Hyla'), in *Marci Antonii, Joannis Antonii et Gabrielis Flaminiorum Forocorneliensium carmina*, ed. Franciscus Maria Mancurtius [Francesco Mancurti] (Padua: Josephus Cominus [Giuseppe Comino], 1743), pp. 94, 68–70, and *SR*, 239–42; Pound's title for Waterhouse's painting appears to have been his own invention, since the painting has been consistently exhibited and reproduced as *Hylas and the Nymphs*: see Anthony Hobson, *The Art and Life of J W Waterhouse RA, 1849–1917* (London: Studio Vista, 1980), pp. 97–101.

typography, etc.'.[20] They invoke a transhistorical sense of beauty, whereby Flaminio's poetry is as desirable as the popular, but still fashionable paintings of Whistler and Waterhouse. But above all Pound's visual analogies bring Renaissance Latin poetry into the context of the highly visual culture of contemporary aestheticism.

AMERICAN AESTHETICISM

Despite their emphatically personal rhetoric, these articles are a vivid expression of the tensions permeating literary culture at the turn of the century, tensions that would have a formative influence on Pound's work and career, and on the trajectory of an emergent modernist culture. The assumptions and values contained in Pound's critical vocabulary and, in particular, his preference for a 'visual' criticism over a 'verbal' scholarship are products of both institutional change in the academy, and general cultural changes in attitudes towards the arts. The years of Pound's attendance at university and training as a poet were years of dissension over the role of education, the role of the arts, and the relationship between the two.

The rise of philological scholarship in North American language and literature departments was part of a general reassessment of the procedures of American intellectual and cultural life during the 1880s in the context of industrial expansion and a growing need for an educated managerial class. Originally derived from German models, philology connoted not only specialist linguistic research, but 'a total science of a civilization'. However, as René Wellek and Gerald Graff have discussed, the form of philology practised in the United States was of a narrower kind, emphasising the scientific, positivist precision of the study of Anglo-Saxon grammar, for example, or the history of English phonology, in opposition to the generalist liberal education that had hitherto characterised the departments' provision.[21] An important element in philology's success in North American universities was its ability to endow the teaching and research of language and literature with clearly discernible professional standards, in the form of a rigorous and scientific methodology and an output of demonstrable facts in the place of subjective interpretation.

Yet philology had its detractors from the beginning, with the conservative forces in universities defending a general curriculum that valued

---

[20] 'M. Antonius Flamininus and John Keats', p. [445].
[21] René Wellek, 'American Literary Scholarship' in *Concepts of Criticism*, ed. Stephen G. Nichols, Jr. (New Haven, CT: Yale University Press, 1963), pp. 296–315 (pp. 299, 300), Gerald Graff, *Professing Literature: An Institutional History* (Chicago, IL: University of Chicago Press, 1987), pp. 55–118.

appreciation over specialist research. By the 1890s, reactions against philology were widespread and calls for a less sterile, more 'literary' approach to the teaching of literature were increasingly voiced, in terms that positioned the philologists in turn as conservative. Henry E. Shepherd of the College of Charleston, for example, complained in the *Proceedings of the Modern Language Association* (its founding in 1883 itself a marker of the recent professionalization) that 'the trend of the Modern Language Association has been, thus far, almost exclusively in the direction of grammatical criticism and philological exegesis. The literary side of language has been subordinated or retired until it is almost faded out of memory in the confusion of tongues and the strife of phonetics. Nearly all the illustrating power, the aesthetic brilliance of literary culture, is lost upon the philological devotee.' Shepherd's essay was preceded in *PMLA* by 'A Plea for the Study of Literature from the Aesthetic Standpoint' by John P. Fruit, an instructor at Bethel College. 'The teacher of literature [. . .] ought to stand forth as the expounder of that "Beauty" which "is its own excuse for being," against utilitarian beauty', he wrote. 'We are in the thrall of utilitarian ideas and are being dwarfed into low and mean statures.'[22] Pound's view that 'the universities train scientific specialists for utility, and the fugitive fragrance of old song-wine is left to the chance misfit or the much-scorned *dilletante* [*sic*]' was thus far from an isolated complaint.[23]

The generalist creed gained strength from its intersection with late nineteenth-century aestheticism. Generalists like Charles Eliot Norton, Harvard's first Professor of Fine Art, cast their pedagogy in the mould of John Ruskin and Matthew Arnold, preaching a social gospel of art's redemptive power: as Graff remarks, 'they saw themselves as the upholders of spiritual values against the crass materialism of American business life, of which the "production" ethos of the philologists was for them only another manifestation'.[24] The craze for aestheticism, too, even in its most visible and undeniably materialist manifestation of domestic interior design, was couched in moral and spiritual terms drawn from Ruskin and William Morris. The American interpretation of the cult of beauty was therefore both structured against materialism, and at the same time invoked to promote material goods. The scholar-aesthete occupied a similarly double position: while he risked being confused with the dilettante, that reputation in itself did not necessarily entail the loss of his professional identity. The

[22] Henry E. Shepherd, 'Some Phases of Tennyson's "In Memoriam"', *PMLA*, 6.1 (1891), 41–51 (p. 41); John P. Fruit, 'A Plea for the Study of Literature from the Aesthetic Standpoint', *PMLA*, 6.1 (1891), 29–40 (p. 29).
[23] 'M. Antonius Flamininus and John Keats', p. [445].   [24] Graff, pp. 82–6, p. 85.

turn-of-the-century aesthete proved adept at turning the apparent disinterest of the dilettante into a professional attribute through precisely the same process of specialisation as that employed by the philologist: as Reginia Gagnier notes, 'even intellectuals, a sort of classless class above the concerns of the marketplace (as one says), had to specialize'. The aesthete's defining move, to claim a special place for art distinct from other aspects of human endeavour, can be read as a form of specialisation that markets art in a new and effective way. An identification with aestheticism, then, had the attraction of an 'engaged protest' against the 'utility, rationality, scientific factuality, and technological progress' of late nineteenth-century capitalist society, while simultaneously providing a fashionable and authoritative professional identity, that of aesthetic arbiter.[25]

Pound's rhetorical dependence on the term 'beauty' obviously draws on the discourse of aestheticism, even though his demand for 'absolute proof' in his review of Péladan composed at the same time indicates that he had not entirely repudiated the values of the philologist.[26] The fact that he interprets beauty in specifically visual terms is also aestheticist to a degree, insofar as the aestheticist creed is so frequently framed by visual analogy: one thinks of Walter Pater's famous descriptions of the aestheticist moment in the conclusion to *The Renaissance*, for example.[27] Current literary criticism repeats the association: 'Aestheticism', writes one critic, 'represents primarily an angle of vision that aims at the purification of vision Ruskin sought but which increasingly discovers the impossibility of such preternatural clarity of sight.'[28] There is good reason for aestheticism's association of beauty with the visual sense; the eye appears to offer the possibility of capturing the passing moment by wresting it from time and perceiving it in space. At the same time, however, the aesthetes themselves continually problematized this notion: the arrested moment is the deadened moment, its life inheres in its evanescence, hence aestheticism's simultaneous attraction to the temporal art of music, and, indeed, its frequent conflation of music and painting or sculpture, as in Pound's description of Flaminio's poetry as 'harmony of line and color'.[29]

---

[25] Reginia Gagnier, *Idylls of the Marketplace: Oscar Wilde and the Victorian Public* (Stanford, CA: Stanford University Press, 1986), pp. 11–12, 3.

[26] 'Interesting French Publications', p. 55.

[27] Walter Pater, *The Renaissance: Studies in Art and Poetry*, in *The Works of Walter Pater*, 8 vols. (London: Macmillan, 1900), I: 233–9 (p. 236).

[28] Jonathan Freedman, *Professions of Taste: Henry James, British Aestheticism, and Commodity Culture* (Stanford: Stanford University Press, 1990), p. 10.

[29] 'M. Antonius Flamininus and John Keats', p. 447.

But Pound's direct references to Whistler and Waterhouse indicate that the visual character of his analogies was not only theoretical, nor simply a reaction to the generalised visual culture of aestheticism; rather it found specific material objects in contemporary painting. That Pound's mind should so naturally turn to contemporary painting to provide examples of beauty reflects the relatively recent rise in cultural status of the visual arts in the United States. In his classic account of what he called 'the Brown Decades' between 1865 and 1895, Louis Mumford remarked that 'the emphasis of the whole society shifted to the industrial and plastic arts' and away from literature, as, following the Civil War, increased industrial prosperity provided the financial means, leisure and inclination for the country to invest in its cultural potential.[30] Greater numbers of American artists began to study abroad, in Rome, Munich and, above all, Paris, bringing European influences home and transforming the taste of collectors. From the 1870s the major cities established art museums and art schools: the intensity of commitment to the fine arts is well summarised by the dates of their foundation: the Metropolitan Museum of Art in New York and the Museum of Fine Arts in Boston in 1870, the Massachusetts Normal Art School in 1873, the Corcoran Gallery of Art in Washington and the San Francisco School of Design in 1874, the St Louis School and Museum of Fine Arts in 1875, the Pennsylvania Museum and School of Industrial Art in 1876, the Rhode Island School of Design in 1877, the Chicago Academy of Fine Art in 1879, the Detroit Institute of Arts in 1885, and the Cincinnati Art Museum in 1886. New art societies and specialist groups were forming too: the American Society of Painters in Water Color in 1866, the Society of American Artists in 1877, the Society of American Etchers in 1880, the Society of American Painters in Pastel in 1882, the National Sculpture Society in 1893, and the National Society of Mural Painters in 1895.[31]

A number of factors were instrumental in producing this explosion of activity, but one catalyst in particular has been consistently highlighted by contemporary commentators and recent art historians alike: the Centennial Exposition, held in Philadelphia over six months in 1876. Although it was primarily an industrial exhibition, following the model of the world fairs initiated by the Great Exhibition of 1851 at Crystal Palace, it was the

[30] Louis Mumford, *The Brown Decades: A Study of the Arts in America, 1865–1895*, 2nd rev. edn (New York: Dover, 1955), p. 33.
[31] Matthew Baigell, *A Concise History of American Painting and Sculpture* (New York: Harper & Row, 1984), p. 123, Nathaniel Burt, *Palaces for the People: A Social History of the American Art Museum* (Boston: Little, Brown and Company, 1977), pp. 75–85, 184, 203.

Centennial's enormous display of international art that attracted the most attention from visitors and journalists. In total, 3,646 paintings, sculptures and watercolours were exhibited in seventy-one galleries, and in addition there were large exhibitions of engravings and lithographs, photography, industrial and architectural designs, and ceramics and mosaics.[32] Almost ten million people visited the Centennial, twelve times the population of Philadelphia, with the result that, as one contemporary critic wrote, 'millions of our fellow-citizens from the forests of Maine, the prairies of Iowa, from the sunny lands of Florida, and the slopes of the Rocky Mountains, were for the first time in their lives brought face to face with the rare and beautiful things of the Old World'.[33]

The Centennial presented the visual arts to the American public on an unprecedented scale; however, its impact was ideologically diverse. Traditionally, it has been understood as a landmark in the education of North American taste, democratically exposing artists and the wider public alike to European influences.[34] More recently, attention has turned to the Centennial's influence on private collections, its contribution to what Lawrence Levine has called the 'sacralization of culture' during the last third of the nineteenth century, through which art and knowledge of art increasingly became the preserve of a wealthy elite.[35] Between the 1870s and the early 1900s the core of the United States' public collections was built up by private collectors like Charles Lang Freer, Isabella Stewart Gardner, John G. Johnson and John Pierpont Morgan. Following the Centennial, French art dominated most American collections, the Barbizons giving way to impressionism by the end of the century. Interest in the impressionists had been growing through the late 1870s and 1880s, with Paul Durand-Ruel's exhibition of about three hundred canvases at the American Art Association galleries in New York in 1886 generating massive publicity and

---

[32] The official statistics include only paintings, sculptures and watercolours: see John F. Weir, 'Plastic and Graphic Art: Painting and Sculpture', in *International Exhibition, 1876, Reports and Awards: Group XXVII*, ed. Francis A. Walker (Philadelphia, PA: Lippincott, 1877), pp. 1–35 (p. 4). An excellent source of contemporary information about the Centennial is Susan Hobbs's, *1876: American Art of the Centennial* (Washington, DC: National Collection of Fine Arts/ Smithsonian Institution Press, 1976).

[33] C. B. Norton (ed.), *Treasures of Art, Industry and Manufacture Represented in the American Centennial Exhibition at Philadelphia, 1876* (Buffalo, NY: Cosack & Co., 1877), [n. pag.].

[34] Lorado Taft, *The History of American Sculpture* (New York: Macmillan, 1903), p. 9; Charles H. Caffin, *American Masters of Sculpture* (Garden City, NY: Doubleday, Page & Company, 1913), p. v.

[35] Lawrence Levine, *Highbrow/ Lowbrow: The Emergence of Cultural Hierarchy in America* (Cambridge, MA: Harvard University Press, 1988), pp. 83–168, Aline B. Saarinen, *The Proud Possessors: The Lives, Times and Tastes of Some Adventurous American Art Collectors* (New York: Random House, 1958).

controversy. By 1900 the United States had become the most important market for impressionism, which had, in turn, become the dominant style in American painting.[36]

The visual arts, then, had a particularly powerful cultural presence in the United States during the last third of the nineteenth century. Painting and sculpture were redefined and reallocated for refined contemplation in the public museum; major private collections of American and, especially, European art were created; specialist art journals created a space for the professional art critic, initially conceived as an educator, but by the end of the century, as an arbiter of taste; the influence of Ruskin and the aesthetic movement was felt in the development of a preference for art that was spiritually uplifting, and also in the cult of 'the house beautiful' decorated in the latest fashion; drawing was introduced into public schools in recognition that a modern industrial nation needed to create not only the useful, but the beautiful. Aesthetic discourse in the United States could not help but be imbued, more explicitly than in Britain, with the paradoxical conception of art as an alternative to the commodity, to the materialist life, and at the same time, as the pre-eminent commodity, the major sign of wealth and status.

No artist of the period summed up this paradox as well as James McNeill Whistler. An expatriate since 1855, Whistler's home country knew him primarily by reputation, and it was only in the 1880s that his oil paintings began to be widely exhibited.[37] By that time, however, Whistler's theories were well known, especially his aim 'to produce effects similar to those of musical compositions' as indicated by his notorious titles, and his paintings were enthusiastically received and extensively imitated.[38] Whistler's reputation grew swiftly in the following years, as his *Arrangement in Yellow and White* exhibition toured New York, Baltimore, Boston, Philadelphia, Chicago and Detroit in 1883, newspapers reported his sensational 'Ten O'Clock' lecture in 1885, and American collectors began to acquire his work. The publication of his critical writings, *The Gentle Art of Making Enemies* (1890), developed the critical context for his paintings, the French government's purchase of *Arrangement in Grey and Black: Portrait of the Painter's Mother* (1871) for the Musée du Luxembourg in 1891 confirmed his international significance,

---

[36] H. Wayne Morgan, *New Muses: Art in American Culture, 1865–1920* (Norman, OK: University of Oklahoma Press, 1978), pp. 112–44.

[37] The information in this paragraph is primarily drawn from Nicolai Cikovsky, Jr. with Charles Brock, 'Whistler and America', in Richard Dorment and Margaret F. Macdonald (eds), *James McNeill Whistler* (London: Tate Gallery, 1994), pp. 29–38.

[38] 'American Art', *New York Evening Post*, 20 April 1878, p. 1, qtd in Cikovsky, p. 33.

and he was well represented at the Columbian Exposition in Chicago in 1893.[39] By the time of his death in 1903 he had become a figurehead for American painting: Arthur Jerome Eddy was representative in congratulating his nation for producing 'the greatest artist since the days of Rembrandt and Velasquez, – and greater than either in some respects'.[40]

Recent studies of Whistler's reception in the United States have demonstrated in absorbing detail the skill with which he performed the balancing act required of the late nineteenth-century artist, appearing to distance himself from materialism, while cultivating the necessary commercial contacts to sell his work.[41] Whistler's pronouncements on art and beauty starkly contrasted 'the taste of the tradesman' for the 'tawdry, the common, the gewgaw' with a dematerialised art 'occupied with her own perfection only'.[42] Not only did he position the love of art for art's sake as something to which one should aspire, he positioned his own art as a more appropriate object of aspiration than that of his realist contemporaries. His calm tonalist works, built up of subtle washes of colour, created idealised landscapes and cityscapes that could be read as a repudiation of the material world, and an expression of a refined sensibility and spirituality. The collection assembled by Whistler's patron, the former industrialist Charles Lang Freer, which also included Asian art and works by Whistler's followers, Thomas Dewing and Dwight Tryon, appealed to a typically late nineteenth-century belief structure that took in theosophy, Egyptian religion and Buddhism. Freer's advisor from 1901, Ernest Fenollosa, placed Whistler as the centrepiece in his own influential Spencerian scheme of history in which Eastern and Western cultures were being synthesised into a higher order.[43] His refinement of Freer's collection, and Freer's gift of the collection to the Smithsonian Institution, 'enshrin[ed] the "higher art," and particularly Whistlerian aesthetics, for future generations'.[44] This aesthetics was also disseminated less obviously, but more widely, through the system of art education Fenollosa developed with Arthur Wesley Dow, which advocated learning to draw by mastering the principles of abstract design, the 'composition', or '"putting

[39] Cikovsky, p. 35.
[40] Arthur Jerome Eddy, *Recollections and Impressions of James A. McNeill Whistler* (Philadelphia, PA: Lippincott, 1903), p. 63.
[41] See Sarah Burns, *Inventing the Modern Artist: Art and Culture in Gilded Age America* (New Haven, CT: Yale University Press, 1996) and Kathleen Pyne, *Art and the Higher Life: Painting and Evolutionary Thought in Late Nineteenth-Century America* (Austin, TX: University of Texas Press, 1996).
[42] James McNeill Whistler, *The Gentle Art of Making Enemies* (London: Heinemann, 1890), pp. 142, 136.
[43] Ernest F. Fenollosa, *Epochs of Chinese & Japanese Art: An Outline History of East Asiatic Design*, 2 vols. (London: Heinemann, 1912), II: 30–88.
[44] Pyne, p. 206.

together" of lines, masses and colors to make a harmony', rather than by copying from casts.[45] The approach and terminology are recognisably Whistlerian, down to the use of the musical term, 'harmony', to register the ideal aim of design.

While Whistler represented his devotion to art as a form of religious service, it was equally a calculated commercial strategy. The *Arrangement in Yellow and White* exhibition, in which floor, walls, furniture and attendants were dressed in yellow and white, attested to Whistler's perfectionism, but also guaranteed extensive newspaper publicity and encouraged sales. He learned to increase notice of his paintings by engaging in antagonistic exchanges in newspapers and magazines, and his control of his own characteristic image, complete with monocle, cane and white plume of hair, gave him, as we would say today, brand recognition.[46] Whistler was the archetype of the late nineteenth-century self-marketing aesthete, but he also set the pattern for the modernist artist: 'No other artist before the generation of the Expressionists so thoroughly conceived of the artistic enterprise as infusing every aspect of an artist's life', writes Robert Jensen, 'and no artist before the Italian Futurist F. T. Marinetti was so inventive and multifaceted a propagandist for his own art'.[47]

PHILADELPHIA: AN EDUCATION IN ART

Pound was fully engaged in the pervasive visual culture of his era. The Pound family moved to Philadelphia in 1889, when Ezra, or 'Ra', was three years old. It was thirteen years since the city had staged the Centennial Exhibition and, despite the art associations and museums that had sprung up in its wake, the pace of cultural innovation had slowed considerably and Philadelphia had gained a reputation for conservatism in comparison with New York and Boston.[48] Nevertheless, the city's heritage ensured that the visual arts retained a high profile. Wealthy Philadelphians, such as John G. Johnson and Peter A. B. Widener, as well as John Wanamaker, who lived less than a mile from Pound's home, built up significant private collections. Pound's memory of these figures was negative: he was later to inveigh against 'American collectors buying autograph MSS. of William

[45] Arthur Wesley Dow, *Composition: A Series of Exercises in Art Structure for the Use of Students and Teachers* (Garden City, NY: Doubleday, Page, 1913), p. 3.

[46] Cikovsky, p. 35; Burns, 221–31.

[47] Robert Jensen, *Marketing Modernism in Fin-de-Siècle Europe* (Princeton, NJ: Princeton University Press, 1994), p. 43.

[48] Penny Balkin Bach, *Public Art in Philadelphia* (Philadelphia, PA: Temple University Press, 1992), p. 86.

Morris, faked Rembrandts and faked Vandykes [*sic*]' instead of supporting living artists, apparently forgetting that Wanamaker had published his own early work.[49]

Philadelphia's most prestigious contribution to the visual arts was the Pennsylvania Academy of the Fine Arts, founded in 1805 and a pioneer in the collection and exhibition of American art. The Academy's systematic acquisition of major works by living American artists from 1880 gave Pound the opportunity to view some of the most important contemporary examples of innovation in American painting: works by Winslow Homer, William Merritt Chase, Childe Hassam and Theodore Robinson, amongst many others, were acquired while he lived in Philadelphia. The Academy held an annual exhibition, student exhibitions, and a large number of special exhibitions. During 1906–7 Pound could have attended nineteen exhibitions at the Academy, including *Artists of the Glasgow School*; *Exhibition of Photographs Arranged by the Photo-Secession*; *Jules Guerin: The Châteaux of the Loire and Other Subjects*; *Maria Oakey Dewing: Paintings* and *Ernest Lawson: Paintings*. An art journal to which Pound subscribed claimed that even in 1905 'when one wishes to consider American art as a whole one goes to Philadelphia'.[50]

The Academy's renowned teaching was particularly associated with the realist tradition of Thomas Eakins who had taught there until 1885. During Pound's time in Philadelphia the instructors included Henry McCarter, who had studied under Puvis de Chavannes, one of Pound's early enthusiasms, Thomas Anshutz, one of Eakins's former students and a mentor of the Ash Can School, Hugh Breckenridge, and William Merritt Chase, also a former student of Eakins, but by this point painting in a style strongly influenced by the French impressionists and Whistler's later work.[51] Chase's career was culminating in national and international recognition, and his teaching had become legendary. In his classes at the Academy, in life

[49] 'Affirmations, III: Jacob Epstein', *New Age*, 16 (1915), 311–12 (p. 312). See also 'Dr. Williams' Position', *Dial*, 85 (1928), [395]-404 (p. 397).

[50] *Black Mirror*, 5 (1905), p. 27. The Academy later developed a good East Asian collection, but its main expansion took place after Pound had left Philadelphia. See Ira B. Nadel, 'Constructing the Orient: Pound's American Vision', in *Ezra Pound and China*, ed. Zhaoming Qian (Ann Arbor, MI: University of Michigan Press, 2003), pp. 12–30.

[51] See Frank H. Goodyear, Jr., 'A History of the Pennsylvania Academy of the Fine Arts, 1805–1976', in *In This Academy: The Pennsylvania Academy of Fine Arts* (Philadelphia, PA: Pennsylvania Academy of the Fine Arts, 1976), pp. 12–49, 'Hugh H. Breckenridge [obituary]', *Art Digest*, 12.4 (1937), 15, Leslie Katz, 'The Breakthrough of Anshutz', *Arts Magazine*, 37.6 (1963), 26–29, 'Two Philadelphians', *Art Digest*, 13.7 (1939), 27, Margaret Vogel, *The Paintings of Hugh H. Breckenridge, 1870–1937* (Dallas, TX: Valley House Gallery, 1967), and Sally Webster, 'Thomas Anshutz: The Philadelphia Connection', *Arts Magazine*, 54.3 (1979), 138–40.

drawing, painting from the figure and still life, he emphasised technique over subject matter, and a 'carefully careless' style. One of his favoured students, Charles Sheeler, recalled Chase's 'gift for transmitting his enthusiasm for painting to his students [. . .]. What a waste of time, the hours required for sleep, when one should be painting around the clock! The excitement caused by the gleam of light on brass and copper was in our blood and they were feverish, impatient hours while we tried to set it down on canvas.'[52]

Pound appears to have known something of the teaching at the Academy, using what he calls a 'Breckenridge phrase', 'the lyric of color', in an early unpublished essay, and jotting a note, 'Breckenridge. Sunday Ft Washington', on a scrap of paper now filed among his college work. The connection to Breckenridge was Pound's friend Frank Reed Whiteside, who had studied at the Academy and remained in touch with Breckenridge.[53] Pound had other, looser, connections to the Academy too: William Carlos Williams's close friend Charles Demuth, who was taught by Breckenridge during this period, and William Brooke Smith, a painter who attended the School of Industrial Art, to whose memory Pound dedicated his first volume of poetry, *A Lume Spento*.[54] Smith knew the Academy students Charles Sheeler and Morton Schamberg, and described the latter to Pound as 'one of Mr. Chase's bright & shining lights'.[55] H. D. remembered Smith as 'an art student, tall, graceful, dark, with a "butterfly bow" tie, such as is seen in

[52] Keith L. Bryant, Jr., *William Merritt Chase, A Genteel Bohemian* (Columbia, MO: University of Missouri Press, 1991), pp. 226, 186, 193.

[53] Untitled typescript on Browning, [p. 1], EPP, Beinecke, 86.3711. See Dorothy Alden Hapgood, 'A Student's Tribute', *Art Digest*, 12.6 (1937), p. 27: 'During his career as a teacher [Breckenridge] stressed color, and had for the past several years been working on a book, now nearly completed, dealing with the theory of color.' The book was not published, but its typescript is included in Breckenridge's papers at the Smithsonian Institution. Pound's note refers to the Darby School in Fort Washington, founded by Breckenridge and Anshutz in 1898. I have found no further evidence connecting Pound to Breckenridge or the Darby School. The note is filed in 'Scraps, unidentified material: ms. notes', EPP, Beinecke, 87.3737. See Stock, *Ezra Pound's Pennsylvania*, pp. 56, 78.

[54] Demuth met Williams while he was studying at the Drexel Institute of Art, Science and Industry; he transferred to the Academy in 1905, taking classes there until 1910. Hugh Witemeyer notes that Demuth 'came to know both EP and WCW in Philadelphia in 1903–05' (*L/WCW*, 23), though Betsy Fahlman has them meeting first in Paris during Demuth's visit to Europe between December 1912 and spring 1914. Pound saw Demuth in London in December 1913, but it is probable they were acquainted before, since Pound later remarked to John Quinn 'I saw some of his stuff in 1909 or 10 before I was interested in mod. art.; I didn't then make much of it, but now think it must have been good' (*L/JQ*, 213). Williams does not seem to have known Brooke Smith (*L*, 165), and did not meet Sheeler until 1923. See William Carlos Williams, *The Autobiography of William Carlos Williams* (New York: Random House, 1951), pp. 52, 171, Betsy Fahlman, *Pennsylvania Modern: Charles Demuth of Lancaster* (Philadelphia, PA: University of Pennsylvania Press, 1983), pp. 16–17, and Barbara Haskell, *Charles Demuth* (New York: Whitney Museum of American Art/ Harry N. Abrams, 1987), pp. 16–17, 35–6.

[55] Sheeler presumably met Smith at the School of Industrial Art, which he attended between 1900 and 1903, and from which Smith graduated in 1905. Schamberg and Sheeler attended the Academy from

the early Yeats portraits', and as this description suggests, he appears to have presented a pattern of the aestheticist artist to Pound. Brooke Smith's correspondence was significant enough for Pound to have read one of his letters to H.D.: it was, she said, 'poetic, effusive, written, it appeared, with a careful spacing of lines and unextravagant margin'.[56]

Three of these letters remain, two written in 1907 (4 April and 1 October) and one probably composed in 1906. They are written in a self-consciously Paterian, decadent style, littered with 'throbbing pulses', 'golden veil[s]', 'violet mist[s]', and a 'whole world of jade and sapphire'.[57] Their language and their subject matter testify that Smith and Pound founded their friendship on art, and a specifically aestheticist conception of art. They display the self-fashioning of the aesthete: in two of the three letters, Smith thanks Pound for sending him copies of his poetry, and in one he refers to their discussion of Pound's style: 'It makes me feel that perhaps I did not make myself well understood when I criticised the lack of color in your verse. I didn't mean that lack of color was lack of loveliness, for you know me to love the quiet, still things best, and the days of fading flower and falling leaf best of all.' In another, written after Pound had left Philadelphia for his post at Wabash College, Smith discusses his own art, describing time spent with Schamberg and Sheeler in Gloucester, Massachusetts: 'I worked entirely in oils but only do small things because I had only my small sketch box with [me] [. . .]. This has been a happy time for me, and my work is much better. I see it full of flaws but that very fact shows me that things are better. I have already sold two of the Gloucester things – some fishing boats against a gray sky and another of the big rocks, the sea & splashing surf.' Pound owned one of Smith's watercolours.[58]

While it is fruitless to speculate on Smith's style of painting, the early work of Schamberg, Sheeler and Demuth builds up a remarkably coherent portrait of the style practised in Philadelphia by the Academy-educated artists. Paintings like Schamberg's *Study of Spanish Peasant* and *Charles Sheeler and Nina Allender*, both undated but presumed to have been produced during Schamberg's attendance at the Academy, and *The Regatta*

1903 to 1906. See James J. Wilhelm, 'The Letters of William Brooke Smith to Ezra Pound', *Paideuma*, 19 [1990], 163–8 (pp. 164–5), Abigail Booth, 'Catalogue of the Exhibition and Biographical Notes', in *Charles Sheeler* (Washington, DC, Smithsonian Institution Press, 1968), pp. 10–31 (p. 10), Ben Wolf, *Morton Livingston Schamberg* (Philadelphia, PA: University of Pennsylvania Press, 1963), p. 20.

[56] H.D., *End to Torment: A Memoir of Ezra Pound*, ed. Norman Holmes Pearson and Michael King (New York: New Directions, 1980), pp. 13–14.

[57] Wilhelm, 'The Letters of William Brooke Smith to Ezra Pound', p. 164.

[58] Wilhelm, 'The Letters of William Brooke Smith to Ezra Pound', pp. 164, 165; Stock, *Ezra Pound's Pennsylvania*, p. 33.

(1907), which may have been painted during the stay in Gloucester with Brooke Smith, show the influence of Chase's teaching in their informality, their loose brushwork and their concern with the representation of light.[59] Demuth's *Self Portrait* (1907) also draws attention to its brushwork, though its more finished surface and darker palette relate it more closely to Eakins's and Anshutz's realism than Chase's impressionism.[60] Charles Sheeler's early work is also heavily indebted to the Academy's influence; the influence of Chase in particular can be seen in his *Beach Scene* (c. 1906). Like the early work of Demuth and Schamberg, it gives little indication of the precisionist style for which all three artists would later become known: as Sheeler later remarked, 'From the casual portrayal of the momentary appearance of nature learned in art school, to the concept of a picture as having an underlying architectural structure to support the elements in nature which comprise the picture, was a long journey with many stop-overs along the way.'[61]

Pound tried oil painting himself: he later told Dorothy Shakespear, 'I couldn't draw a pig but it was entertaining just the trying [*sic*] to prepare a palette. I can't remember which book on Whistler jaws so about the palette. It may have been "Mempes" [*sic*]' (*L/DS*, 248). It was indeed Whistler's pupil Mortimer Menpes whose memoir, *Whistler as I Knew Him* (1904), described Whistler's 'highly scientific' arrangement of the pigments on his palette in great detail.[62] It is telling that it was less the painting itself than the imitation of Whistler's artistic procedures that appealed to Pound. Although his literary studies at university were characterised by their focus on specifically linguistic issues, his construction of his own literary persona was far broader, drawing on the interdisciplinarity of aestheticism, its collapse of the individual arts into an all-encompassing 'beauty'. Pound's reading of aestheticism not only gave him a theory of art, it also provided a way of articulating his vocation to himself and others. The visual spectacle of the aesthete was central to his self-fashioning, as it was for his contemporaries: Schamberg was known for his 'Whistlerian exquisiteness', Demuth was 'the quintessential dandy, fastidious in dress and detached in manner', and Pound, known at college as 'Lily Pound', sported a Whistlerian beret

---

[59] See Wolf, pp. 43–4, 60–3.   [60] Fahlman, p. 26.

[61] Carol Troyen and Erica E. Hirshler, *Charles Sheeler: Paintings and Drawings* (Boston, MA: Museum of Fine Arts, Boston, 1987), p. 3; Charles Sheeler, 'A Brief Note on the Exhibition', in *Charles Sheeler: Paintings, Drawings, Photographs* (New York: Museum of Modern Art, 1939), pp. 10–11 (p. 10). See also John Driscoll, 'Charles Sheeler's Early Work: Five Rediscovered Paintings', *Art Bulletin*, 62 (1980), 124–9.

[62] Mortimer Menpes, *Whistler as I Knew Him* (London: Black, 1904), pp. 69–70.

and scarf, substituting his signature with a gadfly, in imitation of Whistler's butterfly.[63]

It was during his last year at the University of Pennsylvania that Pound wrote his first art criticism, preserved as two typescripts with pen and pencil corrections in the Ezra Pound Papers at Yale. The first, a document of six pages entitled 'Art', is a review of exhibitions in Philadelphia during November and December 1906. The second, ten pages long and untitled, is a more general account of Pound's aesthetic philosophy that makes extensive reference to Whistler's *The Gentle Art of Making Enemies*. It refers to 'Art' as 'last months criticism', so was composed no later than January 1907. 'Art' appears not to have been published; in the untitled article Pound writes that 'the Editor in chief turned down my last months criticism in order to keep me out of a libel suit'. Nor has a published record of the second essay been found, although the text explicitly states that both articles were written for publication: 'A while ago a painter friednd suggested that as I seemed a good deal more capable to criticise current art than most of those who were trying to do so, that I should take the department of art on some daily The Half Hour has offered me a place for my utterances.'[64] However, Noel Stock's description of the *Half Hour* suggests that it was a less substantial publication than Pound's comments imply. Stock writes: '*The Half Hour* was printed about this time at the author's (or perhaps his father's) expense. It was small (about 4 by 3 inches) and contained few pages. There was only one issue.'[65] No extant copy of this issue is known.

Although unpublished, these two essays provide important information about the origins of Pound's aesthetics. The first two pages of 'Art' briefly review four exhibitions: the *Fifth Annual Exhibition of the Pennsylvania Society of Miniature Painters* at the Academy, the Academy's own Fellowship exhibition, the Art Club's *Eighteenth Annual Exhibition of Oil Paintings*

---

[63] Wolf, p. 30; Haskell, p. 21; Humphrey Carpenter, *A Serious Character: The Life of Ezra Pound* (London: Faber and Faber, 1988), pp. 35, 38, H.D., pp. 14, 23.

[64] Untitled typescript on Whistler, pp. 4, 2, EPP, Beinecke 86.3710. In quoting from these essays, I have retained Pound's spellings, typographical errors, and material he crossed out. Angled brackets denote Pound's own manuscript annotations. Jo Brantley Berryman quotes briefly from the untitled typescript in her *Circe's Craft: Ezra Pound's* Hugh Selwyn Mauberley (Ann Arbor, MI: UMI Research Press, 1983), p. 98.

[65] Noel Stock, *The Life of Ezra Pound* (Harmondsworth: Penguin, 1974), p. 45. Stock's description was based on information provided by Frank Ankenbrand, Jr., who boarded with Pound's parents during 1928–9 (letter to the author, 2 February 2006; Stock, *Pound's Pennsylvania*, p. 33).

and Sculpture, and the T-Square Club's *Thirteenth Annual Exhibition of
Architecture and the Allied Arts*. Of the latter, Pound remarks 'Interest
chiefly technical', but nevertheless 'no young architect – nor indeed any
one ~~who thinks of building or decorating~~ who intends to build or decorate
~~their own homes~~ can afford to miss this sort of show'. He praises 'the
influence of the Greek on [E. H.] Blashfield's designs', but is less impressed
by Albert Beck Wenzell. Wenzell's work, '~~he nearly always lacks the master
touch and yet his peofle~~ [people] ~~are the, sort one likes to meet, this means
for him of course the scorn of the artist and the sympathy of the mass~~'.
He is even more critical of the designs for the City Hall monument
to William McKinley: 'at each end of the arc are two symbolic figures
in classic attire and on the pedestal in the centre Wm. McKinley
with "vest" of great dimensions. one hand in his "Pants" pocket.
looking like the immortal Pickwick stepped into the Iliad [. . .].
~~For this sort of artistis (the word is not polite in English) there is no muck
vile enough to be raked.~~'[66]

Pound's criticism of the McKinley designs pales in comparison with
his comments on the *bête noire* of this essay: Mary Cassatt. Although
Pound terms the Art Club's exhibition generally a 'rather interesting
exhibit', he is extremely critical of Cassatt, who was exhibiting *Après le
bain* (1901), now known as *The Sun Bath*, '~~one of her usual horrors, which
no jury is ever impolite enough to turn down, and no critic <sufficiently>
impolitic to antagonise~~' (fig. 1). His main objection is that Cassatt has not
earned her success, that American critics are too easily impressed by artists
with European connections: 'she is usurping attention that rightly belongs
to other artistrs who are doing better work in a less glaring manner. After
the bluff of having gotten into European exhibits. no american critic dares
to hold her to account for pictoreal idiocy. Anyone who has ever seen
a Paris salon knows the tremendours amount of rot. there is no other
title. that gets into it.' Drawing on his recent research trip to Europe, he
concludes authoritatively, 'altho this last summer the distinct genious of
Carriere towered above the rest of the exhibit, the average picture in the
<comparatively unheard of> Madrid exhibit was of a higher grade of
interest'.[67]

Pound also attempts to justify his dislike of Cassatt's work on aesthetic
grounds. In an effort to present a 'level judgment', he relates that he asked
'Mr. Mc.F. whose art views are broad and sufficiently different from my
own', for his opinion of Cassatt. Mr. Mc.F.'s answer, 'Saveing certain color

[66] 'Art', pp. [1]-[2], EPP, Beinecke, 86.3710.
[67] 'Art', pp. 1, 4, 5; Suzanne G. Lindsay, *Mary Cassatt and Philadelphia* (Philadelphia, PA: Philadelphia Museum of Art, 1985), p. 91.

1 [Mary Cassatt, *The Sun Bath* (1901)]

harmonies I can see nothing in her work', provokes Pound to compare the 'harmony of her last canvass' to 'certain chintxz curtains a misguided relative sent me in undergraduate days', where at least 'the harmony was there free and unaccompanied by Miss C̶a̶s̶s̶a̶t̶t̶s̶ horrible distortions of humanity'. Even his fellow undergraduates, Pound thinks, would have felt compelled to react to such poor taste: 'I did not han̶d̶g the curtains', he writes, 'as I did not want my windows broken with greater frequency than usual'.[68]

On the last page of the essay Pound turns to the 'laws' of painting, but he is ultimately unable to provide a statement of aesthetics that supports his criticism of *The Sun Bath*. Framing his argument in terms of the traditional opposition of colour and line and the 'mythical repartee of Titian and Michael Ann̶gelo' on that topic, Pound asserts that 'the function of the painter is neither to rival the cemera [camera] in exactness of reproduction of line and mass. Nor is it simply the filling of space with k̶color (though this is a closer̶s̶ <closer> approach to it), for here h̶e̶ ̶c̶a̶n̶ his work drifts into that of the oriental rug maker. whose ~~work~~ <results> he can never excell.' Pound appears to be drawn to the side of Michelangelo and the colourists, but he is aware of the contemporary complication of that position, a complication he articulates by reference to the 'oriental rug maker'. For Pound, like Pater before him, the Oriental carpet exemplifies the aesthetically pleasing object which is, however, categorically not art: 'We have our color on the walls and floor and want something ~~something~~ different in our picture ~~frams~~ frames', Pound writes, and in a final attempt to define that 'something different', he concludes, 'Manifestly the painters art is in a blending of these two things, design and color; in selection; and in ~~that~~ harmony which is ever the essential of beauty.'[69]

Pound revisits this argument in his second essay, this time making a firm distinction between what he calls the 'art of <u>painting</u>', which he defines as 'the art of filling a given space with color and lines with harmony of color, with rythm of line, and ballance of light and shade, ballance of color, ballance of mass', and, on the other hand, 'a totaly different art. i.e. that of the expression of ideas', produced by 'designers and draughts men' like G. F. Watts, whose paintings, while beautiful, can lead one to forget 'the lack – o even of the truths of form'.[70] Pound is on the verge of expressing a formalist aesthetics here, but in both essays his general theory is problematised by his reactions to individual artists. He evidently likes Watts's painting and dislikes Cassatt's, but his definition of 'the art of painting', and his stated preference for it over 'the expression of ideas' risks elevating her work over his. His formalism precludes consideration of the reasons that make Cassatt's painting uncongenial to him – her institutional affiliations and her subject matter. And, at present, he lacks the vocabulary and critical framework to make technical distinctions between different examples of 'color harmonies'.[71]

In fact, technical considerations have no place in Pound's early formalism. What this second essay makes clear is that Pound is using a formalist language and a superficial knowledge of recent art criticism to explore what are essentially the central questions of Kantian aesthetics, questions about the definition of beauty and aesthetic judgement. The aesthetic theory developed here may be exemplified by individual works of art, but it is not derived from their study. Echoing Pater once again, Pound writes that 'it seems to me that the acme of all artistic expression is that wherein all a mans former being ~~bus~~ bursts into the flame of a perfect line a harmony of color . . . or where his own life kisses vitality into tehe clay and for him in

---

[69] 'Art', p. 6, Pater, I: 133.   [70] Untitled typescript on Whistler, p. 3.   [71] 'Art', p. 4.

tehe instant of keen joy. He is as the legendary sculptor olf old whose statu e became flesh and blood and loved him.' There is a tension between the thoroughgoing expressivism of this statement and the earlier formalism, 'the art of filling a given space with color and lines with harmony of color', but fundamentally both artistic expression and appreciation are a matter of sensibility or, to use Pound's term, 'genius':

> I count not that may a knower of art, that has some luck in picking a good canvass and more in picking one that will sell. That man has an art education (or a Talent – one or two of us have genious but that is another matter.) who can get a morning's enjoyment from a horse chestnut and a single blossom of honey suckle, watching the varing harmonies of brown and white as the strength of the sunlight varies or the angle of reflection is changes and from studying the variations of the line of beauty in the different stamenae of the flower: Or who lacking chance to wander in the winds over free grass, can look up to the cloud blown sky above him, tho he be in the verriest tenement, and can in his imagination cut squares and oblongs from that sky in such manner that his frame is filled with ballance of blue and white.[72]

The connoisseur, with his minute knowledge of the history of individual artworks, is attributed no knowledge of art as Pound defines it. The connoisseur's knowledge is tainted by its commercial role, its use in establishing the sale value of art. Pound's discussion is so far from being interested in the technical details that absorb the connoisseur that he frequently, as here, slips from discussing painting to describing the natural world. His discussion is even transferable between media: 'there is absolutely nothing new in this note but there is a lot here that everybody ought to know before they thy [try] to look at pictures (or books)'.[73] The correlation with the articles he would soon publish in *Book News Monthly* is clear: the appreciation of beauty is to be valued more highly than scholarship.

Several sources for Pound's first foray into art criticism can be traced. First, there is the course in literary criticism at the University of Pennsylvania that Pound took with Josiah Penniman during the first term of the 1906–7 academic year, which introduced him to key texts on aesthetics. Josiah Penniman, the same Josiah Penniman who would in 1919 publish one of John Wanamaker's favourite books, *A Book about the English Bible*, was Dean of the College Faculty, later Provost of the University, and a scholar of Elizabethan drama.[74] The course was notoriously the only one Pound failed: 'In 1907 I achieved the distinction of being the only student flunked

---

[72] Untitled typescript on Whistler, pp. 8, 5.   [73] Untitled typescript on Whistler, p. 9.
[74] Josiah H. Penniman, *The War of the Theatres* (Philadelphia, PA: University of Pennsylvania Press, 1897).

in J. P.'s course in the history of literary criticism', he wrote in 1930. 'So far as I know I was the only student who was making any attempt to understand the subject of literary criticism and the only student with any interest in the subject.'[75]

Pound's lecture notes bear out his dislike of Penniman's course. During the 7 November lecture on Francis Bacon and Ben Jonson, for example, Pound covered his sheet of paper in doodled faces, and scrawled 'have to amuse my self somehow' across the page.[76] But the beginning of the course, at least, proved more interesting. In line with the recommendations of contemporary textbooks on literary criticism, it began with an introduction to aesthetics, since 'the principles of literature [. . .] are but special applications of the broader principles which lie at the base of all the arts', in the words of one of the works on the course reading list.[77] The required reading for the first week was Aristotle's *Poetics*, Horace's *Art of Poetry*, and Longinus's *On the Sublime*, all works Pound returned to in his later criticism. Pound's record of this first lecture is insubstantial, but the note 'Art. Crit. Mike & Titan' registers this as Pound's source of information about the 'mythical repartee' of the two artists.[78]

According to Pound's typed list of the authors covered, Penniman's course ended with Pater, though there is no record of which works were recommended, nor are there any lecture notes relating to Pater. In fact, although Mary Ellis Gibson has shown how deeply Pound's early work is indebted to Pater, and Pater's influence certainly pervades Pound's art criticism, it is unclear how direct that influence was. On the penultimate page of the second piece of art criticism Pound appears not to recognise Pater's most famous statement, the statement which he would later include (correctly attributed) in his definitions of vorticism:

> "All art constantly aspires ~~toward the~~.   towards the condition of
>   music" and in music nothing happens
>   Mackail quoting somebody else.[79]

[75] Qtd in Emily Mitchell Wallace, 'Youthful Days and Costly Hours', in *Ezra Pound and William Carlos Williams*, ed. Daniel Hoffman (Philadelphia, PA: University of Pennsylvania Press, 1983), pp. 14–58 (p. 24).
[76] 'College Notes: Literary Criticism ms. notes', EPP, Beinecke, 87.3732.
[77] Charles Mill Gayley and Fred Newton Scott, *An Introduction to the Methods and Materials of Literary Criticism* (Boston, MA: Ginn & Company, 1899), p. 80. The other general work on literary criticism recommended by Penniman, W. Basil Worsfold's *The Principles of Criticism: An Introduction to the Study of Literature*, rev. edn (London: Allen, 1902), made the same point.
[78] 'Art', p. 6.
[79] Pound's notes for the penultimate lecture are dated 23 January [1907]; Mary Ellis Gibson, *Epic Reinvented: Ezra Pound and the Victorians* (Ithaca, NY: Cornell University Press, 1995), pp. 28–38;

The extent to which Pound's early art criticism is indebted to Ruskin is also difficult to determine. From the second half of the nineteenth century to the early twentieth century Ruskin's influence so deeply pervaded the way one thought about art, and moreover, the way that one looked at one's environment, that his ideas formed the invisible aesthetic norm. Ever the iconoclast, Pound's references to Ruskin before the Great War are uniformly hostile for precisely this reason, but that by no means suggests that he was not profoundly influenced by Ruskin from an early stage. Gibson points out that the title and initial metaphor of Pound's early poem, 'Rex', are drawn from 'Of King's Treasuries' and his admiration for Turner during this period surely led him to Ruskin, if it was not directly inspired by him.[80] But the art criticism is ostensibly written in direct opposition to Ruskin's: Pound begins the second, untitled, typescript by telling his readers 'If any of you are by chance seeking to know what others have said concerning art, in order that your views may be orthodox [. . .] I beseech you by such gods as you may happen to believe in "Do not let a professor of English refer you to Ruskins Modern Painters and think you can read it safely untill you have read the First part of Whistler's "Gentle Art of Making Enemies" which is the most perfect introduction and interpretation of the "Great Critic's" maunderings inthe realm of paint.' On the next page, Pound writes that 'in justice to my hearers I started to study the subject of art criticism historically. I am appalled at the ungodly ignorance that has paraded as instruction in art. At the crass botching in Ruskin, in the words of Hammerton and other pervertors of taste.'[81]

'Vortex. Pound.', *Blast*, 1 (1914), 153–4 (p. 154), 'Vorticism', *Fortnightly Review*, 96 (1914), [461]–71 (p. 461); Untitled typescript on Whistler, p. 9. Pound quotes from J. W. Mackail, 'Introduction', in Maurice Maeterlinck, *Aglavaine and Selysette; A Drama in Five Acts*, trans. Alfred Sutro (London: Richards, 1897), pp. v–xxiii (p. xi).

[80] Gibson, p. 62. I suggest a date of 1907 for this poem: its use of Browning and the references to Monet, Michelangelo and Fra Angelico place 'Rex' in close proximity with the 1906–7 art criticism and the poetry written in July 1907, discussed below. On Pound and Ruskin, see Michael André Bernstein, 'Image, Word and Sign: The Visual Arts as Evidence in Ezra Pound's *Cantos*', *Critical Inquiry*, 12 (1986), 347–64; Robert Casillo, 'The Meaning of Venetian History in Ruskin and Pound', *University of Toronto Quarterly*, 55 (1986), 236–60; Michael Coyle, *Ezra Pound, Popular Genres, and the Discourse of Culture* (University Park, PA: Pennsylvania State University Press, 1995); Peter Nicholls, 'Ruskin's Grotesque and the Modernism of Ezra Pound and Wyndham Lewis', in Giovanni Cianci and Peter Nicholls (eds), *Ruskin and Modernism* (Basingstoke: Palgrave, 2001), pp. 165–80; Clive Wilmer, 'Sculpture and Economics in Pound and Ruskin', *PN Review*, 24.6 (1998), 43–49 and Hugh Witemeyer, '"Of Kings' Treasuries": Pound's Allusion to Ruskin in *Hugh Selwyn Mauberley*', *Paideuma*, 15 (1986), 23–31.

[81] Untitled typescript on Whistler, pp. 1, 2. Pound was taking courses with several members of the English faculty in 1906–7, so the 'professor of English' could have been Clarence Griffin Child, Penniman, Felix Schelling, Cornelius Weygandt, or indeed another member of the department, since Pound was taking 'Current Criticism', taught by the department rather than a single teacher. See Wallace, p. 23 and Wilhelm, *The American Roots of Ezra Pound*, p. 152.

Pound's claim that he had started a historical study of art criticism is tantalising, though a sceptical reader would point out that the two critics mentioned in that context, Ruskin and Philip Hamerton, are both conspicuous presences in Whistler's *Gentle Art of Making Enemies*, and Pound may not have explored further than Whistler's reprinting of their critical remarks about his own works.[82] Whistler's quotations highlight Hamerton's outdated taste and his pedantic approach to criticism. Ruskin, Whistler's key antagonist, is represented as dogmatic, inconsistent, prosy and moralistic, his critical opinions mocked in the account of the famous libel trial Whistler brought against him in 1878, in response to his description of Whistler as a 'coxcomb' asking 'two hundred guineas for flinging a pot of paint in the public's face', in the form of *Nocturne in Black and Gold: The Falling Rocket* (1875).[83] Although the trial's discussion of art and aesthetics ranged widely, the fundamental disagreement between the protagonists concerned the way in which the commercial value of a work of art was determined, and it was this that interested Pound most. Whistler's 'imposture', Ruskin thought, was in selling paintings produced in a few days, with little effort, for too high a price, a price that was substantially higher than that which the purchaser could earn in the same time. Whistler's response to this line of argument succinctly expressed the conception of art, and of the relationship between artist and artwork, held by the young impressionists and the aesthetes: the price, he said, bought not the labour of two days, but 'the knowledge of a lifetime'.[84] For Pound, this was an 'immortal answer', one he could use to justify his own creative work, and indeed the approach to literature he had recently laid out in *Book News Monthly*. 'The "Time element" in art is another myth', he wrote, 'it is worse it is a barbaric relic of unmitigated ignorance. The best thing we can say of a lyric poem is that it seems spontaneous.'[85] Although Ruskin's writings had played a large part in shaping the generalist position Pound had taken up in his criticism, here Pound associates him with the bookish morality of the philologist. Whistler, on the other hand, provides Pound with a means of theorising the spontaneous response to beauty, rebutting the 'abject and utterly scornful' charge of '"dilettante"' by insisting on the necessity of knowledge.[86]

[82] Whistler, pp. 1–19, 78–89, 91–105, 295–331.
[83] Qtd as 'Prologue' to Whistler, p. [1], from John Ruskin, *Fors Clavigera*, in *The Works of John Ruskin*, ed. by E. T. Cook and Alexander Wedderburn, 39 vols. (London: Allen, 1903–12), XXIX: 146–69 (p. 160).
[84] Whistler, pp. 4–5.   [85] Untitled typescript on Whistler, p. 8.   [86] 'Raphaelite Latin', p. [31].

Whistler's criticism was the most important influence on Pound's second piece of art criticism, and it represents the beginning of a lifelong engagement with Whistler's work. Not only did Pound adopt Whistler's critical vocabulary of 'arrangements' of 'line, form, and colour' to describe vorticist art and, later, the music of George Antheil, Pound's reading of Whistler created fundamental elements of his theoretical architecture: his conception of art as a science, his justifications of abstract design, and his belief in the authenticity and dynamism of unfinished art.[87] More obviously, but no less importantly, he provided Pound with a congenial model of an anti-academic critic-practitioner: a spokesperson for the avant-garde, who simultaneously cultivated an impression of artistic individualism.

Whistler also stands behind Pound's ambivalent view of criticism. Although over the course of his career Pound would write criticism on a remarkably wide array of topics, including painting, sculpture, architecture, music, politics and economics, as well as many different forms of literature, he repeatedly argued that only the practitioner had the authority to write criticism. This was Whistler's uncompromising stance in his 'Ten O'Clock' lecture, and one of his key complaints against Ruskin: 'what greater sarcasm can Mr. Ruskin pass upon himself than that he preaches to young men what he cannot perform!'[88] Pound derides art criticism even while he is writing it, remarking that 'even as a boy I was fond of wandering in the galleries without the customary printed guide as to what I would be PERMITTED to admire, and that even then I had some luck in finding the great pictures for myself'.[89] The pedagogical and moral impetus of mid-nineteenth-century art criticism is the target here, as it is of a number of the quotations from *The Gentle Art of Making Enemies* Pound copies into the essay. Pound's experiments with a formalist approach to criticism are an attempt to emulate Whistler's disavowal of the social function of art: 'There is no moral element in his chiaroscuro', he quotes from Whistler's own quotation from *The Richmond Eagle*, and comments indignantly 'is a man expected to paint pictures or moral philosophy'.[90] Although Pound presents this rhetorical question so confidently that its question mark is omitted, he struggles to keep up with Whistler's formalism. The specifically American emphasis on aestheticism as a key to a 'higher life' is felt

---

[87] Qtd in Linda Merrill, *'A Pot of Paint': Aesthetics on Trial in Whistler v. Ruskin* (Washington, DC: Smithsonian Institution Press, 1992), p. 144; Ian F. A. Bell, *Critic as Scientist: The Modernist Poetics of Ezra Pound* (London: Methuen, 1981), pp. 9–11, 18–19.
[88] Whistler, p. 34.   [89] Untitled typescript on Whistler, p. 2.
[90] Whistler, p. 102; Untitled typescript on Whistler, p. 7.

in his expressivist leanings, perhaps derived from his reading of drawing manuals in the Dow-Fenollosa tradition. One such work is Henry Rankin Poore's *Pictorial Composition and the Critical Judgment of Pictures*, the book Antony Ozturk has identified as that which Pound claimed had 'started [him] on the idea of comparative forms before [he] left America'.[91]

If Pound's identification with Whistler and his close attention to the 1878 trial appears anachronistic it was an anachronism he shared with his contemporaries. Pound's avowed model for his art criticism, the *Black Mirror: The Journal of the Colorists*, was aimed at the impressionist avant-garde, and claimed Whistler as an authority. 'The BLACK MIRROR does not appear as often as we would wish', wrote Pound in 'Art', 'I can not hope to imitate the crispness of tone of that pamphlet whose tone I confessedly follow as near as may be considering the descrepancy of i betwween the brilliancy of its editors and my own stumblinmg.'[92] Seven issues of the New York-based journal appeared irregularly between 1903 and 1912, promoting the transcendent claims of the artist against those of the dealer, the critic and the academy. Artists favoured by the editors included Breckenridge, William Glackens, Childe Hassam, Robert Henri, Maurice Prendergast, and Cassatt, who was described as 'perhaps the best example of the colorist, pure and simple, we have seen in New York'.[93]

Pound's adoption of the discourse of aestheticism in his art criticism, and to a more limited extent, in his first literary criticism, is the adoption of the dominant mode of art appreciation in 1906, but it is also a calculated rejection of the values he was being taught at university. While his university studies emphasised historical specificity and the technical analysis of language, Pound's early criticism promotes the appreciation of beauty, conceived as a transhistorical and interdisciplinary category, in which all the arts can act as enlightening analogies for each other. Aestheticism also provides Pound with a valuable framework within which to negotiate his own burgeoning career. As Jonathan Freedman has noted, aestheticism was embraced by the new middle classes as a means by which they could 'challenge the cultural hegemony of the established gentry elite'.[94] It provided

---

[91] Anthony Ozturk, 'Ezra Pound and Visual Art', unpublished PhD thesis, Oxford University (1987), p. 12; Donald Hall, 'Ezra Pound: An Interview', *Paris Review*, 28 (1962), 22–51 (p. 31). Henry Rankin Poore, *Pictorial Composition and the Critical Judgment of Pictures: A Handbook for Students and Lovers of Art*, 6th rev. edn (New York: Baker & Taylor, 1903).

[92] 'Art', p. 5.

[93] *Black Mirror*, 3 (1904), p. 28. These artists were all included in the 'Mentions 1903–1904' list, *Black Mirror*, 2 ([1]904), p. [2]. Chase's name was one of those added to the list in the magazine's fourth number, in 1905.

[94] Freedman, p. 112.

both social respectability and the opportunity to assert one's artistic individualism, showing the way towards a cultural meritocracy that would underlie much of Pound's future criticism, and indeed modernism itself.

'THE LYRIC OF COLOR'

Seven months after composing these first two critical essays on art, Pound wrote a document that developed his thoughts on beauty and colour specifically in relation to poetry. It is untitled, consists of eight typed pages with corrections in pen and pencil, and is dated 'July 31 07' on the final page. It refers to a further seven-page typescript of prose and poetry, 'In Praise of the Masters', and a two-page typescript of a poem, 'Fra Angelico: For the Annunciation'. The untitled document has been examined by George Bornstein and Mary Ellis Gibson, who have focussed on its discussion of Browning, and Gibson has also commented on, and edited, 'In Praise of the Masters', which contains a dramatic monologue spoken by Rembrandt, clearly modelled on Browning's 'Fra Lippo Lippi'.[95] But as well as providing an important commentary on Pound's early reading of Browning, these works constitute a sustained exploration of a poetics based on the model of painting.

The untitled essay begins by describing the limitations of the poems on Rembrandt and Fra Angelico:

> I regret ~~tht~~ that to balance these two expressions of what is more properly poet's painting I have not at hand and appreciatiin [an appreciation] of painters painting. The passion ~~a~~ of saying in the ~~ly~~ lyric of color alone <all that is to be said> (Breckenridge phrase), the lyric of color. and make that carry its message. thru its own beauty and not thru accidental chances of subject which flashes at the bypasser,
>
> I would like and will I ~~t~~hope in future voice praise of color for its, well not its own sake, but color itself for ~~itse~~ the exalting power of its own beauty and for its power, on canvass to lead us deeper into the mystery and wonder of gods own coloring, whereof we but begin to understand the subtlety of shade and blending. and but stumble mid arcane of lights and atmosphere. To praise the royal line who say color is the only field on which the painter runs alone. And here tis meet should be his valor shown.
>
> Altho Whistler has done much to writing these things openly.
>
> For surely one can not rest till he has at least some appreciation of all divers beauty. of all the masques of Beauty
>
> In pauca I would say for paint what Arthur Symons has said for music in his Spiritual Adventure "Christian Trevalyan" who understood sounds as having a

[95] George Bornstein, 'Pound's Parleyings with Robert Browning', in *Ezra Pound Among the Poets*, ed. Bornstein (Chicago: Chicago University Press, 1985), pp. 106–27, Gibson, pp. 60–2, 35–8, 219–22.

seperate existence above mere human passion, a beauty of their own, a feeling not to be injured by the player. or as he said in his own praise "I believe I have hurt fewer tones than any other musician" This would I for color, but it comes not yet.[96]

The distinction between 'expressions of [. . .] poet's painting' and 'appreciatiin of painter's painting' is ambiguous, but in the context of the essay Pound appears to be distinguishing between poetry that is inspired by other poets' writings about painting, as the poems he refers to here are inspired by Browning's dramatic monologues about Renaissance painters, and poetry that is inspired by paintings themselves. He is especially compelled by painting that experiments with colour, rather than narrative painting (which 'carr[ies] its message [. . .] thru accidental chances of subject'), imagining a future project which is an equivalent of the 'passions of abstract sound' experienced by Symons's fictional pianist, Christian Trevalga.[97] The central ideas of this passage are closely related to the definitions of painting and beauty Pound had explored in his unpublished critical essays seven and eight months earlier, but on this occasion he aligns beauty with colour almost without qualification, only baulking at the idea of a purely formalist appreciation of colour, 'color for its [. . .] own sake', and insisting instead on a spiritual or mystical referent, 'the exalting power of its own beauty and for its power [. . .] to lead us deeper into the mystery and wonder of gods own coloring'.

   The typescript continues by addressing issues of originality and poetic influence. Pound asks whether 'when one stumbles of a flaming blade that pierces him to extacy' he should 'hide it' for fear of looking like a 'copyist' or 'blind follower' of his predecessors who have written poetry on the same subject. The question has direct implications for the type of poetry one should write. 'Is it', asks Pound, 'more original to cry some great truth higher and more keen, to add a candle to the daylight that none can see, or to reverse some million proverbs that the mob may laugh to see the worthies butt-end up displayed to common view?'[98] Should one, in other words, write poetry that repeats a 'great truth' that has already been expressed but is disregarded or not appreciated, or should one write satire? Eventually the reason behind these questions becomes apparent: Browning has already written the poem Pound wants to write. 'Just ɵ my luck, confounded and delightful that after I had threshed these things out for myself I I find

---

[96] Untitled typescript on Browning, [p. 1].

[97] Arthur Symons, 'Christian Trevalga', in *Spiritual Adventures* (London: Constable, 1905), pp. 83–113 (p. 90). Pound misquotes from p. 111: 'I am certain that I have hurt fewer sounds than any other pianist.'

[98] Untitled typescript on Browning, [p. 2].

"Baulustions [*sic*] Adventure' helds them better said, and said some sooner.'
Pound directs his reader to Browning's *Works*, 'MacMillan edit. p. 661',
in which Balaustion argues that poetic originality is not affected by the
existence of closely related works, 'no good supplants a good,/ Nor beauty
undoes beauty.'[99]

Having justified the inevitability of his poetry's engagement with earlier
works, Pound can preface his poem, 'In Praise of the Masters', with an
explanation of Browning's particular relevance:

> Oh yes. I have studied Browning. but one does not imitate by using a sonnet
> of Dantesque form . . I had been reading Shelly within the week. but so far as I
> know Shelly has written not poem for painting. Tho you may d find my opening
> line form at the beginning of "Queen Mab". Nor do I remember a single line for
> the masters, (of Italy or elsewhere . . The cor cordium was atuned to the winds
> and the sun light. and his kin art was music, as Brownings is <that of the brush>
> the brush.[100]

This quotation shows that Pound conceives of this project in the first place
as a poem about painting, thus dictating his use of Browning, rather than
as an imitation of Browning for its own sake. In the prose accompanying
'In Praise of the Masters', apparently a draft of a covering letter, Pound
explains that the poems are intended to raise awareness of the Old Masters
for a generation who are only interested in contemporary art, 'I continualy
hear the philistine hiccuping "What is there in the old masters" and I
continualy hear the modern discople of Monet sneer that the old fellows
are very much over estimated', 'I had watched these old masters make
pale some very beautiful modern things. Notably Morphine by Matignon
and a Carriere. Both of which are wonderfully beautiful.'[101] To this end, he
included, or intended to include, tcn illustrations for the poems, instructing
his potential editor 'But ten old masters just for once would do the magazine
no harm and might make a star make-up . . Now unless you either know
Rembrandt and Rapael [*sic*] and Leonardo and Fra Angelico or unless you
have patience to study the prints enclosed and then read the verses and
then go back to the prints. You may as well send the thing back [. . .]
(I suppose Gowans and Gray [publishers] might lend you the plates of
most of the pictures . . they ought to be full page.'[102]

---

99 Untitled typescript on Browning, [p. 5]; Robert Browning, 'Balaustion's Adventure', in *The Poetical Works of Robert Browning*, 2 vols. ed. Augustine Birrell (New York: Macmillan, 1901), I: 627–65 (p. 661). See Bornstein, pp. 109–112.
100 'In Praise of the Masters', [p. 1], EPP, Beinecke, 86.3712.
101 *La Morphine* (1905) by Albert Matignon.
102 'In Praise of the Masters', [pp. 6, 7, 5–6]. 'In Praise of the Masters' is written in capitals on the bottom of the first page of the typescript, and I follow the Beinecke and Gibson in adopting this

Pound was pleased with these two poems, 'I know I have hit a real thing', he wrote in the draft covering letter, and to his mother he declared, 'Have done two rather good things one for Rembrandt and the other for Fra Angelico. [. . .] it is some satisfaction to do a decent thing once and a while. even if it dont buy pork and gasoline.'[103] In fact, these are very derivative works. In 'In Praise of the Masters', Pound's Rembrandt closely echoes Browning's Fra Lippo Lippi, touring the reader around his paintings and speaking, as Mary Ellis Gibson observes, 'something like Browning's knottiest language'.[104] The poem ends:

> But beauty?? what in hell's eggs are you
> grumbleing and mumbling o beauty for
> i paint what i see sir<,>. danme, lights and no lights
> folk as they come to me. your spindle shanked
> goddesses, where do you find em
> I see no such a running o our ways.
>
> Paint what i see sir. taint such as<'>ll
> be pleasin your finiky lordship. small beans to me sir
> No stick in my craw, take what I find
> But tis ~~thu~~ truth sir.
> Egad tis the truth sir. an't stick[105]

Like 'Fra Lippo Lippi', 'In Praise of the Masters' is a manifesto for realism in painting, and, by association, in poetry too. Pound would continue to associate this realist mode with Rembrandt and Browning, and just over a year later wrote to William Carlos Williams about his use of 'the short so-called dramatic lyric' in terms that echo this poem: 'I catch the character I happen to be interested in at the moment he interests me, usually a moment of song, self-analysis, or sudden understanding or revelation. And the rest of play would bore me and presumably the reader. I paint my man as I *conceive* him. Et voilà tout!' (*L*, 3–4). This realist mode deliberately eschews the finish of beauty.

Although the Browningesque dramatic lyric has come to be seen as the dominant and most successful form in Pound's early work, in 1907 it was only one mode of Pound's poetry, and, it seems, not the mode he regarded most highly. In the draft cover letter he writes, 'Most anyone who

---

title to refer specifically to the seven-page typescript. But Pound surely meant it to refer to the collection of two poems and ten illustrations he sent, or intended to send, to a periodical editor. The poem about Rembrandt follows on the next page of the typescript and, unlike the poem about Fra Angelico, does not carry its own title.

[103] Letter to Isabel Weston Pound, [July 1907], EPP, Beinecke, 59.2654.

[104] Gibson, p. 36.   [105] 'In Praise of the Masters', [p. 3].

knows Rembrandt at all. will be able to fath om the first of these poems. Wherein he speaketh. The second is a deeper thing.'[106] This second poem, 'Fra Angelico: For *The Annunciation*' is written in the medievalized and incantatory style of the Pre-Raphaelites, and like its companion poem, it is programmatic. But its programme is not the realism of Rembrandt; Pound threads a refrain through the poem which exclaims 'HOW WONDER-FUL IS ART/Art and art's mother, life' replacing the final word with another each time the refrain is repeated: 'love', 'solitude', 'mystery', 'holiness'. In comparison to Rembrandt's rejection of 'beauty' in favour of a vigorous, down-to-earth realism, the speaker in 'Fra Angelico: For *The Annunciation*' evokes art as a religion.[107]

The two poems correspond to two discernible categories in the poetry of Pound's earliest volumes. The poems of 'Hilda's Book' (written 1905–7), *A Lume Spento* (1908), the San Trovaso notebook (mainly written in 1908) and *A Quinzaine for This Yule* (1908) have been conveniently categorised by Mary Ellis Gibson in terms of two competing traditions, the Keatsian, which 'flows for Pound through Keats, Tennyson, Swinburne, and the Pre-Raphaelites to the Georgian aesthetes, including the later Yeats' and 'that represented by Browning, by Landor and Beddoes, possibly by Wordsworth, and by the "harder" language of Yeats's middle period'.[108] The latter tradition has been critically favoured, following Pound's example: in *Personae*, the 1926 collected edition of 'all Ezra Pound's poems except the unfinished "Cantos"', Pound retained the poems written in the Browning tradition but omitted almost all those belonging to the Keatsian.[109] When they reappeared in *A Lume Spento and Other Early Poems* in 1965 Pound famously referred to the volume as 'a collection of stale creampuffs'.[110] But Pound and his critics have underplayed the significance of those cream puffs. Despite the fact that Pound saw Browning's 'kin art' as 'that of the brush', it is the poems of the neglected Keatsian line which engage most fully with the visual culture in which Pound was immersed. Read alongside Pound's earliest essays they constitute a consistent effort to establish a poetics of beauty, a poetics which would resurface, clothed in a remarkably similar range of imagery, in *The Cantos*.[111]

106 'In Praise of the Masters', [p. 7].
107 'Fra Angelico: For *The Annunciation*', EPP, Beinecke, 89.3812, [pp. 1–2].   108 Gibson, p. 66.
109 *Personæ: The Collected Poems of Ezra Pound* (New York: Boni & Liveright, 1926), [n. pag.], Thomas F. Grieve, *Ezra Pound's Early Poetry and Poetics* (Columbia, MO: University of Missouri Press, 1997), pp. 37–48.
110 'Foreword (1964)', *A Lume Spento and Other Early Poems* (New York: New Directions, 1965), p. [7].
111 'In Praise of the Masters', [p. 1].

During the early stages of his career, it was by no means clear to Pound that the poems to emerge from the Browning side of his poetic inheritance were his strongest. Although he had completed most of the poems that made up the most stylistically diverse of the early volumes, *A Lume Spento*, before leaving the United States, he did not at that point choose to continue his work in the Browning tradition of the dramatic lyric; instead, over the next six months he perfected his Keatsian style. This is the dominant style of the poems that make up the San Trovaso notebook, which Pound compiled in Venice in the summer of 1908, and those he added to the nine chosen from the notebook to be published as *A Quinzaine for This Yule* in December of the same year. On 7 January Pound wrote to his parents comparing his new book with *A Lume Spento*, and while he rightly notes that it 'lacks the more obvious rigor and virility of A.L.S.', he also claims that 'the workmanship is finer and more finished and a great many people prefer it'.[112]

The 'finish' of Pound's second book is indeed striking. This volume presents a surprisingly uniform expression of Pound's poetic credo in a series of programmatic poems. The poet is constructed as an outsider: in 'Purveyors General' the speaker tells how she or he has wandered the world and 'chaos' 'seeking new things/ And quaint tales' for 'you, the Home-stayers'; in 'Lucifer Caditurus', Lucifer wonders whether to brave 'all fears/ Of chaos or this hell the Mover dreams' and break God's 'bonds/ That hold the law' or continue as 'an huckster of the sapphire beams'; in 'Sandalphon', the angel 'watching/ ever the multiplex jewel, of beryl and jasper and sapphire', is alone and immortal in the 'ash wood' (*AFQTY*, 10, 16, 18). The speakers do not have full understanding or experience of their message: in 'Prelude: Over the Ognisanti', the speaker hears only 'shades of song re-echoed/ Within that somewhile barren hall, my heart', Lucifer realises that God '*knows* what is to me yet dim', and Sandalphon can only 'marvel and wonder' at his immortality (*AFQTY*, [7], 16, 18). The poet-speaker's dislocation is not only spatial: he or she speaks between times, at twilight and, above all, dawn. These poems are by no means simply experiments, or copies of outmoded models, they are refinements of a central argument and range of imagery. In short, these poems are Pound's attempt at 'poetic utterness'.[113]

At the heart of *A Quinzaine for This Yule* and the San Trovaso notebook is Pound's esoteric theory of the genesis of art. It is most clearly expressed in a draft of an essay following the short poem, 'Shalott', in the San Trovaso notebook. It begins:

---

[112] Letter to Isabel Weston Pound, 7 January [1909], EPP, Beinecke, 59.2659.
[113] 'M. Antonius Flamininus and John Keats', p. 446.

All art begins in the physical discontent (or torture) of loneliness and partiality.

It is <was> to fill this lack that man first spun shapes out of the void. And with the intensity <intensifying> of this longing gradually came unto him power, power over the essences of the dawn, over the filaments of light and the warp of melody.

And I?

Of the dawn's reflexion as you see here, feeling the flowing of the essences of beauty [here color chiefly, as I remember] until they gradually grouped themselves into form.

Of such perceptions rise the ancient myths of the origin of demi-gods. Even as the ancient myths of metamorphosis rise out of flashes of cosmic consciousness. (*CEP*, 322)

Pound repeats this theory of art in 'That Pass Between the False Dawn and the True', 'Masks', 'In that Country', 'Purveyors General' and 'Anima Sola'. 'Lucifer Caditurus' and 'Prelude: Over the Ognisanti' draw on these ideas too. It is formal qualities that define art for Pound, rather than, for example, ideas or context: he refers to art in terms of 'shapes', 'filaments of light', 'warp of melody', 'essences of beauty', 'color'. Apprehension of these elements is described in terms of 'perceptions', momentary 'flashes' of understanding, in an otherwise chaotic and indecipherable cosmos. These predominantly visual metaphors reappear in the preface to *A Quinzaine for This Yule*, where Pound's alter ego, 'Weston St. Llewmys', informs his readers that 'Beauty should never be presented explained', and that one should approach it through 'these doors – Marvel and Wonder', which give way to 'a slow understanding (slow even though it be a succession of lightning understandings and perceptions) as of a figure in a mist' that finally 'gives to each one his own right of believing, after his own creed and fashion' (*AQFTY*, [6]). The terms in which these ideas are expressed are recognisably Whistler's and William Brooke Smith's, and the metaphorical fashioning of Pound's poetry in terms of visual perception derives from the interdisciplinary lexicon of his aestheticist milieu. His speakers 'dip [their] brushes' and 'choose [their] hues' or 'paint the rainbow at sunset'. The poet's subject matter is given as 'the sunset shadow', 'the rose's bloom', 'the sapphire seas' and the 'mighty hues out-worn/ Weaving the Perfect Picture.'[114] Pondering his vocation in 'In that Country', the speaker wonders whether it is better

---

[114] Untitled poem fragment, notebook (1899–1907), p. 162, EPP, Beinecke, 114.4878; 'Swinburne: A Critique', *CEP*, 261; 'The Decadence', *CEP*, 44; 'That Pass Between the False Dawn and the True' *CEP*, 29. Compare Whistler, pp. 139, 143.

To hover astral o'er some other soul
And breathe upon it thine own outpouring passion
Of how this line were wrought or how from chaos
The God outwrought the sprinkled dust of stars
Or say what blending
Of hue on hue on hue would make the ending
Of such a sketch.   (*CEP*, 248)

The text's reference to itself, 'this line', connotes the line of both painter and poet, but by the end of the quotation the ambiguity has been collapsed into the exclusively pictorial metaphors of 'hue' and 'sketch'. Even 'Nel Biancheggiar', Pound's homage to the concert pianist Katherine Heyman, turns her music into colour, reproducing Dante Gabriel Rossetti's painting, *The Blue Bower* (1865).[115]

Pound's self-reflexive metaphors are by no means exclusively visual, he refers to his poetry using the musical metaphors of 'chords', 'harmonies' and 'songs', too. But his portrayal of beauty in visual terms has a particular force because, unlike its portrayal in aural terms, it is deployed comparatively. These poems compare different modes of perception, drawing on the Romantic designation of the poet as seer. This trope is explored most explicitly in one of the San Trovaso notebook poems that Pound wrote for a painter he met in Venice in August 1908, Italico Brass. The poem was not included in *A Quinzaine for This Yule*, but, according to the table of contents in the San Trovaso notebook, Pound originally intended it to conclude the volume (*CEP*, 317). 'For Italico Brass' begins:

From boat to boat the bridge makes long its strand
And from death's isle they on returning way
As shadows blotted out against far cloud
Hasten for folly or with sloth delay.
When thou knowst all that these my hues strive say
Then shalt thou know the pain that eats my heart.
Some see but color and commanding sway
Of shore line, bridge line, or how are composed
The white of sheep clouds ere the wolf of storm
That lurks behind the hills
        shall snap wind's leash
And hurl tumultuous on the peace before.
But I see more.   (*CEP*, 253)[116]

---

[115] Ozturk, p. 30.

[116] The poem is dated 'Aug. 7' [1908]. It was first published in *A Lume Spento, 1908–1958* (Milan: [Scheiwiller], 1958). Italico Brass was a painter who lived near Pound when he was staying in the San Trovaso quarter of Venice in 1908 and this poem seems to describe Brass's painting *Il Ponte del Redentore*. See Ozturk, p. 14.

Pound's painter-speaker distinguishes himself from those who see only colour and line in nature (or his painting, the referent is not clear), where he sees 'more'. A purely formalist mode of seeing is inadequate, superficial, and self-deluding, for what the artist sees is not only something different, but specifically morbid: the boats returning 'from death's isle' perceived as 'shadows', with his painting expressing 'pain'. The second stanza suggests that the superficiality of the formalist vision is specifically related to the seduction of colour:

> Some as I say
> See but the hues that gainst more hues laugh gay
> And weave bright lyric of such interplay
> As Monet claims is all the soul of art.
> *But I see more.* (*CEP*, 254)

This poem expresses Pound's reservations about impressionism, or at least about Monet's impressionism, and the superficial formalism he associates with it. It would be misleading to suggest that Pound had developed a coherent critique of impressionism; his comments on the impressionists elsewhere are either implicit or in passing, and his criticisms tend to target Monet specifically, rather than impressionism in general.[117] Monet appears to have become a straw man for Pound's increasing reservations about art in which the 'lyric of color' predominates, but it is perhaps less Monet's painting itself that Pound critiques than his popularity and his scientific approach to painting, widely perceived by detractors as inappropriately materialist.[118] As the *Black Mirror* pointed out, there are substantial similarities between Monet's work and Whistler's, 'In the reproductions the Thames Series and the Nocturnes can scarcely be told apart', yet Pound's appreciation of Whistler remained unaffected.[119] In fact, Pound sees Whistler's painting, and also Turner's, as producing precisely the effect 'For Italico Brass' suggests Monet's does not. Moreover, Pound associates their achievement with his own in *Quinzaine for This Yule*: the following passage is drawn from Pound's letter to his parents justifying his stylistic departure in that volume:

There are two kinds of artist
1. Waterhouse who painted perhaps the most beautiful pictures that have ever been made in england.
   but you go from them & see no more than you did before. The answer is in the picture.
2. Whistler & Turner. – to whom it is theoretically necessary to be "educated up". when you first see their pictures you may say "wot-t-'ell". but when you leave

---

[117] See 'In Praise of the Masters', [p. 6], 'Rex', [p. 1], EPP, Beinecke, 88.3782.
[118] Pyne, p. 236. [119] *Black Mirror*, 5 (1905), pp. 37, 39.

the pictures you see beauty in mists, shadows, a hundred places where you never dreamed of seeing it before.
The answer to their work is in nature.
—

The artist is the maker of an ornament or a key as he chooses.[120]

According to Pound, while Waterhouse creates a beauty that, like Monet's, is only self-referential, Whistler's and Turner's paintings have the potential to transform one's view of the world. For Pound, this is a new distinction; in 'Raphaelite Latin', Whistler and Waterhouse were undifferentiated in their creation of beauty, now they are firmly categorised, and indeed placed in a hierarchy, as makers of either an 'ornament' or a 'key'. Pound appropriated the term 'key', henceforth central to his critical vocabulary, from Whistler's essay, 'The Red Rag', but their different usage of the word is significant. Whistler, arguing against naturalism, states that the artist should 'treat a flower *as his key, not as his model*', but for Pound, the individual Whistler painting is the key to the flower, and indeed, to all flowers.[121]

This revision of Whistler's argument, and the terms of the letter in general, show Pound moving decisively away from the aestheticism and formalism that had characterised his commentaries on art two years before. His firmer commitment to art that is not only beautiful in itself, but also enables the perception of beauty elsewhere, has several implications. It shifts aesthetic attention away from the artwork itself towards the experience of art. This in turn implies that the value of the artwork will no longer be determined by its own qualities, such as use of paint or use of language or, to turn to another critical paradigm, its beauty, its 'harmonies', its 'lyric of color', but rather by the experience it inspires. And, finally, it attributes an educative impulse to art. Although there is no suggestion yet that Pound is concerned with the 'moral element in [Whistler's] chiaroscuro', the distinction he makes in this letter opens up the possibility for Whistler and, more appropriately, Turner, to be surreptitiously harnessed to a potentially Ruskinian programme.[122] Over the next few years, Pound would become increasingly preoccupied with the social relevance of the arts and, although he would by no means abandon his commitment to aesthetic beauty and a notion of 'poetic utterness', their interest would be temporarily eclipsed by less anachronistic concerns. Chief among these was a concerted investigation into the signifying power of language and form, an investigation that would underpin Pound's engagement with contemporary visual art and, subsequently, the politicisation of his poetics.

[120] Letter to Isabel Weston Pound, 7 January [1909]. In 1910 he rewrote the point in *The Spirit of Romance*, substituting Burne-Jones for Waterhouse (p. 162).
[121] Whistler, p. 128.   [122] Untitled typescript on Whistler, p. 7.

CHAPTER 2

Imagism, vorticism, and the politics of criticism

NOMINALISM AND VISUAL PRIORITY

Between February 1914, when his first piece of art criticism, 'The New Sculpture', was published in the *Egoist*, and February 1915, when he completed his 'Affirmations' series in the *New Age*, Pound built up a body of criticism that set out defining criteria for the modernist aesthetic project. These criteria were wrought from a profound engagement with the sculpture, painting and woodcuts of Jacob Epstein, Henri Gaudier-Brzeska, Wyndham Lewis and Edward Wadsworth, but were applied to literature as well as the visual arts. The critical terminology Pound developed during this period was immensely influential in placing a technical vocabulary deeply indebted to early twentieth-century art criticism at the heart of twentieth-century literary criticism. Without Pound's translation of terms between artistic fields, the most familiar characterisations of modernism, as, for example, 'a new era [. . .] in which art turns from realism and humanistic representation towards style, technique, and spatial form', would have been literally unthinkable.[1] Pound's adoption of an art critical terminology was an attempt to register the aesthetic qualities of literature that he thought were neglected by the philological tradition in which he had trained. It was also a means of defining his own professional standpoint, that of the Whistlerian artist-critic, whose authority derived from his superior intellectual and perceptual capabilities, rather than his formal training or position in the establishment. Pound's formalist criticism was a criticism for a meritocracy, and in prioritising intelligence, rather than knowledge of classical languages or access to research libraries, it proved well suited to the expanding educational field. This formalism is, therefore, not politically neutral: its middle class meritocratic values are closely related to the individualism central to Pound's political beliefs throughout his career. During the period

---

[1] Malcolm Bradbury and James McFarlane (eds), *Modernism, 1890–1930* (Harmondsworth: Penguin, 1976), p. 25.

49

addressed by this chapter, Pound's criticism encodes the anarchism of the *Egoist* circle, espousing in particular a deep distrust of the democratic State, a distrust that would be hardened by the experience of the Great War. This chapter traces the growth of Pound's interest in contemporary art and its impact on his critical vocabulary in both his literary criticism and his art criticism.

Pound's art criticism was the culmination of a broader exploration of signification with which he had been occupied long before February 1914. His commitment to a poetics of beauty in his very earliest poetry and criticism was an attempt to signify beyond the limitations of language. Between 1908 and 1914 Pound's criticism segued from the aestheticism that characterised his American and Venetian work, to a more characteristically modernist nominalism which led him to ground his poetics on a principle of verbal insufficiency. With words figured as an inadequate but necessary gesture towards some more primary 'thing', to use a favourite modernist word, the poet-critic might compensate for the failure of words by drawing on the supposedly more natural languages of music or painting. Pound initially draws on both these alternative languages. But, as Vincent Sherry has demonstrated, the influence of a strain of continental thought that privileged the discriminating eye over the empathetic ear moved Pound, and many of his contemporaries, towards a critical language in which visual metaphors represent the modern intelligence and the aural is aligned with the Romantic sensibility.[2] The critical language Pound adopted was not wholly drawn from continental philosophy, however. It was also directly indebted to the new terminologies developed to describe post-impressionist, futurist and cubist art.

During his first years in London, Pound appeared to put aside the critical project begun in the pages of *Book News Monthly*, concentrating instead on establishing his credentials as a poet. But when he published two substantial critical works in 1910 and 1911–12, it became clear that he had by no means abandoned the questions he had raised about literary criticism between 1906 and 1908; on the contrary, he was now in a position to suggest possible answers. Both *The Spirit of Romance*, written over 1909 and 1910 as lectures for the Regent Street Polytechnic, and published in book form in 1910, and 'I Gather the Limbs of Osiris', serialised in the *New Age* in 1911–12, take up the anti-philological stance of the *Book News Monthly* articles, but they also begin to set out the potential elements of a replacement. *The Spirit of Romance* begins the search for a new vocabulary. 'The history

---

[2] Sherry, *Ezra Pound, Wyndham Lewis, and Radical Modernism*, pp. 5, 25.

of literary criticism', Pound explains, 'is the history of a vain struggle to find a terminology which will define something', and his first chapter tries replacing the outworn terms, 'romantic' and 'classic', with 'an uncorrupted terminology from architecture', using '*Doric, Romanesque* and *Gothic*' to 'convey a definite meaning' (*SR*, 3, 4). In 'I Gather the Limbs of Osiris', Pound shifts the focus from terminology to methodology, proposing a 'New method in Scholarship', that of the 'Luminous Detail'.[3]

In both cases, Pound emphasises the provisional nature of the relationship between that which is written on the page and the knowledge it aims to convey. Not all words, or groups of words, communicate equally efficiently. This is a lesson a student of philology could not fail to learn, but though the insight was the product of Pound's university training, the solution was not. For, as Victor Li has remarked, Pound's project was less 'a study of the socio-historical formation (and deformation) of languages, and more an ahistorical account of the eternal values embodied in literary masterpieces', a work of 'linguistic idealism'. Li lists three assumptions of idealist accounts of language: '(1) language is secondary to some primary reality an epiphe-nomenon to some prior ontological necessity [. . .] (2) language's role is to represent or communicate aspects of that reality; and (3) language is most effective when it can communicate the real in the most unmediated and transparent way possible'.[4] Pound sums up these assumptions succinctly in his definition of poetry as 'a sort of inspired mathematics, which gives us equations, not for abstract figures, triangles, spheres, and the like, but equations for the human emotions' (*SR*, 5).

Pound's insistence on the secondary nature of language and the primacy of 'the real' leads him to represent the latter in aural or, especially, visual terms. Thus, the experiment of using an architectural vocabulary not only aspires towards an 'uncorrupted' terminology, but a more concrete one, one that displays the abstract qualities of the 'romantic' or 'classic' in a 'definite', in this case, visual, referent. The 'Luminous Detail', similarly, is characterised as a 'fact' that is 'swift and easy of transmission' and 'gives us intelligence of a period', 'a sudden insight'. As the prevalence of light metaphors suggests, this is a theory that privileges knowledge gained as if by looking, rather than reading. The light-giving detail is 'illuminating' in the way that 'a few days in a good gallery are more illuminating than years would be if spent in reading a description of these pictures', Pound writes. And, confessing that he 'dislike[s] writing prose', Pound tells his readers

---

[3] 'I Gather the Limbs of Osiris, [II]: A Rather Dull Introduction', p. 130.
[4] Victor P. H. Li, 'Philology and Power: Ezra Pound and the Regulation of Language', *Boundary 2*, 15 (1986–7), 187–210 (pp. 188, 189).

that in this series of essays, he has substituted a verbal method with one that is metaphorically visual: 'I have, if you will, hung my gallery, a gallery of photographs, of perhaps not very good photographs, but of the best I can lay hold of.'[5]

Such abstract speculations about the representational power of language were widespread during this period, drawing a variety of inflections from figures as diverse as the Cambridge logicians, Bertrand Russell and Ludwig Wittgenstein, their antagonist, the vitalist Henri Bergson, political radicals following Nietzsche and anarchist philosophy, and poets associated with the symbolist movement. They pervade three distinct theories of poetry that directly influenced Pound between the publication of *The Spirit of Romance* in June 1910 and the invention of imagism in August 1912: those of the American chemist, Hudson Maxim, the French symbolist, Remy de Gourmont, and the British Bergsonian, T. E. Hulme. All three posit poetry as a more ideal language, and all, to various degrees, locate poetry's greater power of suggestion in its allegedly heightened appeal to the visual sense.

Pound reviewed Hudson Maxim's *The Science of Poetry and the Philosophy of Language* for *Book News Monthly* in 1910.[6] The book is a sustained effort to establish 'a practical method for literary criticism and analysis, and a standard of uniform judgment for determining the relative merits of literary productions' using a scientific approach. For Maxim, poetry consists of 'elemental constants' that can be revealed by the logical analysis of certain 'incontrovertible facts' governing language development, principally, the 'fact' that metaphor is 'the master instrument of human speech', evidence of the superior imagination and intellect that separates man from 'the brute', and that therefore the best poetry is that which most efficiently communicates 'the unfamiliar, the abstract' through the 'familiar, the concrete': 'poetry is largely an act of visualization'. Drawing on the work of Herbert Spencer, Maxim's is a Social Darwinist theory of language, in which poetry's ability to enable the 'visualization' of abstract concepts marks it out as the most advanced form of language.[7]

Maxim's argument clearly corroborated the ideas about language and poetry Pound had very recently published in *The Spirit of Romance*, and his pithy remark that 'poetry obeys the law of conservation of energy' is an important source for Pound's account of the Luminous Detail's economy

---

[5] 'I Gather the Limbs of Osiris, [II]: A Rather Dull Introduction', pp. 130–1.

[6] Letter to Isabel Weston Pound, 7 October 1910, EPP, Beinecke, 59.2665: 'The "Science of Poetry" hardly worth reviewing. I sent off some copy on it to Book News which they may print if they can read it.'

[7] Hudson Maxim, *The Science of Poetry and the Philosophy of Language* (New York and London: Funk & Wagnalls Company, 1910), pp. ix, xi, 24, 37, 41.

and energy the following year.[8] Ian Bell is surely right that 'the tenor and the axioms of Pound's London period owed far more than he was willing to admit to Maxim's work [. . .]. Maxim established principles that Pound was to advocate insistently for the next twenty years.'[9] Pound's reading of Maxim's book prepared the ground in particular for his later encounter with Fenollosa's essay on 'The Chinese Written Character as a Medium for Poetry', also a Social Darwinist theory of language that evaluated poetry in terms of its powers of visualisation. But Pound's review gives little sense of this. Although he agrees with Maxim that 'poetry *does* admit of scientific analysis and discussion', he points out that Maxim's definition of poetry as 'the expression of imaginative thought by means only of the essentials of thought', while 'sane', is not specific to poetry, but 'applies to painting, sculpture and the equations of analytical geometry'.[10] Pound repeats this point in a second essay on Maxim's book, 'The Wisdom of Poetry', apparently written for the *Forum* in 1910, but not published there until 1912.[11] Although Pound comments on Maxim's relative disregard for poetry's aural elements, his own explanations of poetry also repeatedly turn to visual analogy, whether of the circle described by analytic geometry, 'Greek sculpture', 'the Japanese grotesque', 'the art of Beardsley', or the Rembrandt portrait that teaches us 'to consider the exact nature of things seen'.[12]

Just over a year after reading Maxim's *The Science of Poetry*, Pound first encountered Remy de Gourmont's *Le Problème du style*, which Richard Sieburth and Vincent Sherry have shown was decisive in moving Pound towards a system of values predicated on the primacy of vision.[13] For Gourmont, as for Maxim, abstract ideas must be transformed into visual images

---

[8] Maxim, p. 36.

[9] Ian F. A. Bell, *Critic as Scientist: The Modernist Poetics of Ezra Pound* (London and New York: Methuen, 1981), p. 27. See also Bell's 'The Real and the Ethereal: Modernist Energies in Eliot and Pound', in *From Energy to Information: Representation in Science and Technology, Art and Literature*, Bruce Clarke and Linda Dalrymple Henderson (eds) (Stanford, CA: Stanford University Press, 2002), pp. 114–25.

[10] 'The Science of Poetry', *Book News Monthly*, 29 (1910), 282–3 (pp. 282–3). Pound slightly misquotes the sentence: Maxim writes, 'poetry is the expression of imaginative thought by means only of the essentials to the thought' (p. 43).

[11] See *L/MC*, 55: on 2 November 1910 Pound wrote to his patron Margaret Cravens, 'There's a sort of vitriolic essay of mine in the Forum, next month.' 'The Wisdom of Poetry' is the only article Pound published in the *Forum* during his career, but it did not appear until April 1912, when it referred to Maxim's 1910 work as 'causing some clatter about a year ago', suggesting that the beginning of the article, at least, was revised. See 'The Wisdom of Poetry', *Forum*, 47 (1912), 497–501 (p. 497).

[12] 'The Wisdom of Poetry', pp. 500, 498.

[13] Pound first mentions Gourmont in a letter to his mother on 21 February 1912, EPP, Beinecke, 60.2669: 'Flint, in return for being resurrected, has put me on to some very good contemporary French stuff: Remy de Gourmont, de Régnier, etc.' Sieburth argues that Pound first read Gourmont in 1912, see *Instigations*, pp. 2, 11–12, 173, n. 26; Vincent Sherry thinks Pound 'had probably read *Le Problème du style* by the end of the preceding year', see *Ezra Pound, Wyndham Lewis, and Radical Modernism*, p. 49.

to be effectively communicated: 'An idea is only a stale sensation, an effaced image. To reason with ideas is to assemble and combine into a labored mosaic faded cubes that have become almost indistinguishable', he writes. But if one is in the category of people Gourmont terms 'visual', as opposed to 'emotive', 'abstract words themselves become symbolically manifest in figures, in gestures: the infinite will summon up a vision of the sea, of the constellations of the sky, or even a representation, inevitably arbitrary and absurd, but visual, of interplanetary space'. Gourmont's typology leads him to associate the good writer with the painter: 'Almost all painters write well; it is inevitable; they relate that which they see and search for the words, one at a time, which translate their vision, just as they do with colours, before painting.'[14]

Pound did not initially adopt Gourmont's exclusive association between writing and seeing; if Vincent Sherry is correct in seeing Gourmont's influence on the sixth instalment of 'I Gather the Limbs of Osiris', published on 4 January 1912, then Pound's insistence that 'we do not all of us think in at all the same sort of way or by the same sort of implements' constitutes a repudiation of Gourmont's argument, as Sherry indeed notes. 'Certain people think with words, certain with, or in, objects', Pound writes, 'others realise nothing until they have pictured it; others progress by diagrams like those of the geometricians; some think, or construct in rhythm, or by rhythms in sound; others, the unfortunate, move by words disconnected from the objects to which they might correspond, or more unfortunate still in blocks and *clichés* of words; some, favoured of Apollo, in words that hover above and cling close to the things they mean [. . .]. It is the artist's business to find his own *virtù*.'[15] At this stage, Pound, unlike Gourmont, uses the rhetoric of visual perception only metaphorically, as is evident in 'The Wisdom of Poetry' when he concludes a very similar statement about the variety of individuals' thought processes with 'perception by symbolic vision is swifter and more complex than that by ratiocination'. 'Symbolic vision' here includes thinking in 'musical sounds' as well as in 'objects themselves', 'pictures' and 'diagrams'.[16]

It was above all T. E. Hulme who gave Pound's visual metaphors literal meaning. Hulme's influence on Pound has long played a central role in genealogies of modernism, even though it was strongly contested by Pound,

[14] Remy de Gourmont, *Le Problème du Style: Questions d'Art, de Littérature et de Grammaire* (Paris: Mercure de France, 1902), pp. 69, 33, 68–9, 34–5, English translations mine, Sieburth, *Instigations*, p. 62, Sherry, *Ezra Pound, Wyndham Lewis, and Radical Modernism*, p. 21.
[15] 'I Gather the Limbs of Osiris, VI: On Virtue', *New Age*, 10 (1912), 224–5 (p. 224).
[16] 'The Wisdom of Poetry', p. 497.

who claimed that 'the critical LIGHT during the years immediately pre-war in London shone not from Hulme but from Ford (Madox etc.)'.[17] Nevertheless, it is necessary to return to this well-trodden area, because while Ford may have contributed 'critical LIGHT', it was Hulme who made the theoretical connections that would underpin not only imagism, but the broader critical frameworks of modernism with which this study is concerned. Hulme, through his reading first of French symbolist theory and subsequently his study of Bergson, advanced a nominalist theory of language, in which visual imagery was understood as having a compensatory power, and poetry was conceived as the chief repository of that power. Although aspects of this argument reached Pound via Maxim, Gourmont, and slightly later, Dora Marsden and Ernest Fenollosa (the figure Pound preferred to credit), it was Hulme who brought these connections to Pound's notice first and most insistently. It is no accident that Hulme also provided the context for Pound's first published art criticism.

In April 1909 Pound had joined the poetry group Hulme had formed with F. S. Flint in secession from the Poets' Club. While the practical models for the new style of poetry they envisioned were Japanese and French symbolist verse, Bergson, via Hulme, provided the theory. From July 1909 Hulme had become Bergson's chief English expositor, effectively introducing him to the British public in four articles on 'the new philosophy' in the *New Age* between July and December, eleven more in 1911 and 1912, a series of four lectures in London during the winter of 1911, followed by one in Cambridge in February 1912, and an authorised translation of Bergson's 'Introduction à la métaphysique' published in New York in 1912 and London in 1913.[18]

According to Martin Jay, Bergson's philosophy was one of the launching pads for 'the denigration of the visual' in twentieth-century French thought. Bergson's 'trenchant critique of ocularcentrism had a profound and widespread effect', Jay writes, on a family tree that includes phenomenologists, existentialists, Surrealists and post-structuralists, as well as the

---

[17] 'This Hulme Business', *Townsman*, 2 (1939), p. 15. The other key primary documents for this debate are Pound's 'Prefatory Note' to 'The Complete Poetical Works of T. E. Hulme' (*R*, 59), and F. S. Flint's 'The History of Imagism', *Egoist*, 2 (1915), 70–1. Influential secondary accounts include Michael H. Levenson, *A Genealogy of Modernism: A Study of English Literary Doctrine, 1908–1922* (Cambridge: Cambridge University Press, 1984), pp. 103–36, Wallace Martin, *The New Age Under Orage: Chapters in English Cultural History* (Manchester: Manchester University Press, 1967), pp. 145–81, Cyrena N. Pondrom, *The Road from Paris: French Influence on English Poetry, 1900–1920* (Cambridge: Cambridge University Press, 1974), pp. 8–38, Herbert N. Schneidau, *Ezra Pound: The Image and the Real* (Baton Rouge, LA: Louisiana State University Press, 1969), pp. 3–73.

[18] See 'A Bibliography of Hulme's Works', in T. E. Hulme, *Collected Writings of T. E. Hulme*, ed. Karen Csengeri (Oxford: Clarendon Press, 1994), pp. 478–83 (pp. 478–80).

symbolists and modernists who were his contemporaries.[19] In the three works responsible for his early English reputation, *Essai sur les données immédiates de la conscience* (1889) (translated as *Time and Free Will* in 1910), *Matière et mèmoire* (1896) (translated as *Matter and Memory* in 1911), and *L'Evolution créatrice* (1907) (translated as *Creative Evolution* in 1911), Bergson pursued the immensely influential argument that the hegemony of spatial over temporal perception in post-Renaissance metaphysics had falsified understanding of time, memory and life itself. Mental life did not consist of a series of discrete moments, he argued, but was an indivisible whole existing in 'real duration' (*durée réelle*).[20]

Yet, from the very beginning of his career as a Bergsonian, Hulme promoted a peculiarly visually-oriented interpretation of Bergson's philosophy, emphasising the potential of the visual image to mediate between real duration and the spatially-inclined consciousness. Here I depart slightly from Vincent Sherry's account, which presents Hulme's emphasis on the visual sense as a progression, from 'categorically unvisual' representations of intuitive empathy in his early essays, to a 'challenge to Bergson' in his later writing.[21] Hulme is in fact consistent in his emphasis: it was in only his third essay concerning Bergson, published on 19 August 1909, that he made the important, and now famous, connection between poetry and the visual image, arguing that poetry is 'not a counter language, but a visual concrete one. It is a compromise for a language of intuition which would hand over sensations bodily. It always endeavours to arrest you, and to make you continuously see a physical thing, to prevent you gliding through an abstract process.'[22] Where Bergson emphasises the non-spatial character of real duration, Hulme draws attention to the spatial 'image' by which one attempts to access it.

Although Hulme's investment in this argument results in an emphasis on the visual sense that skews the aural predilections of Bergson's philosophy, the description itself is by no means an invention or falsification. Hulme here draws closely on Bergson's analysis of the perceptual image, first discussed in 'Introduction à la métaphysique', where Bergson writes that the image 'keeps us in the concrete' and 'many diverse images [. . .] may [. . .] direct consciousness to the precise point where there is a certain intuition

---

[19] Martin Jay, *Downcast Eyes: The Denigration of Vision in Twentieth-Century French Thought* (Berkeley and Los Angeles, CA: University of California Press, 1993), p. 207.

[20] Henri Bergson, *Essai sur les données immédiates de la conscience* (Paris: Ancienne Librarie Germer-Baillière et Cie, 1889), p. 94, English translation Bergson, *Time and Free Will: An Essay on the Immediate Data of Consciousness*, trans. F. L. Pogson (London: Swan Sonnenschein, 1910), p. 125.

[21] Sherry, *Ezra Pound, Wyndham Lewis, and Radical Modernism*, pp. 37–8.

[22] T. E. Hulme, 'Searchers after Reality – II: Haldane', *New Age*, 5 (1909), 315–16 (p. 315).

to be seized'.[23] In *Essai sur les données immédiates de la conscience* Bergson had defined the poet as 'he with whom feelings develop into images, and the images themselves into words which translate them while obeying the laws of rhythm', and, as Mark Antliff has shown, this aspect of Bergson's thought was being applied to symbolist poetry as early as 1907 by the neo-symbolist Bergsonian Tancrède de Visan.[24] In his 1911 review of de Visan's *L'Attitude du lyrisme contemporain* Hulme stated unequivocally that 'the spirit which finds expression in the Symboliste movement in poetry is the same as that represented by Bergson in philosophy. [. . .] life is a continuous and unanalysable curve which cannot be seized clearly, but can only be felt as a kind of intuition.' Like de Visan he understood symbolism as 'an attempt by means of successive and accumulated images to express and exteriorise such a central lyric intuition'.[25]

The importance of Hulme's emphasis is that it turns Bergson's theory of knowledge into a theory of aesthetics, shifting attention away from the character of what we cannot know, towards the structures by which we try to understand the unknowable. Hulme highlights Bergson's nominalism, where words are understood as part of the conceptual ordering process that falsifies reality, and he consistently asserts the compensatory ability of visual perception. He therefore also tends to represent artistic creation of all kinds in terms of visual apprehension, and does so most explicitly in the posthumously published 'Bergson's Theory of Art', probably composed in 1911 or 1912. Although Bergson 'has not created any new theory of art', writes Hulme, 'by the acute analysis of certain mental processes he has enabled us to state more definitely and with less distortion the qualities which we feel in art:

To use the metaphor which one is by now so familiar with – the stream of the inner life, and the definite crystallised shapes on the surface – the big artist, the creative artist, the innovator, leaves the level where things are crystallised out into these definite shapes, and, diving down into the inner flux, comes back with a new shape which he endeavours to fix. He cannot be said to have created it, but to have discovered it, because when he has definitely expressed it we recognise it as true. Great painters are men in whom has originated a certain vision of things which

[23] H. Bergson, 'Introduction à la métaphysique', *Revue de métaphysique et de moral*, 11 (1903), 1–36 (p. 7), English translation Bergson, *An Introduction to Metaphysics*, trans. T. E. Hulme (London: Macmillan, 1913), p. 14.
[24] Bergson, *Essai sur les données immédiates de la conscience*, p. 11, English translation Bergson, *Time and Free Will*, p. 15; Mark Antliff, *Inventing Bergson: Cultural Politics and the Parisian Avant-Garde* (Princeton, NJ: Princeton University Press, 1993), pp. 23–7, 42, 49–50.
[25] T. E. Hulme, '[Review of] *L'Attitude du Lyrisme Contemporain*. By Tancrède de Visan', *New Age*, 9 (1911), pp. 400–1.

has become or will become the vision of everybody. Once the painter has seen it, it becomes easy for us all to see it.[26]

There is a characteristic elision here between artistic creation in general and painting in particular, an elision that occurs a number of times in this essay and is testimony to the seductive power of the visual analogy over Hulme. But it *is* an elision, and it should remind us that, although the theories of Maxim, Gourmont and Hulme all encourage Pound towards a criticism that privileges the visual sense, this is quite distinct from moving him towards an engagement with the visual arts. Nevertheless, they are related: when a spectacular array of new painting and sculpture appeared in London in the first two decades of the century, a literary criticism that already prioritised the immediacy of the visual sense found a material referent.

THE LANGUAGE OF FORM

Before examining Pound's response to modernist art, the preceding account of literary critical influences must be supplemented by a brief survey of contemporary trends in art criticism. Hulme's description of 'great painters' who teach us to see 'a certain vision of things' was a response to a turn-of-the-century transformation in the way the visual arts were understood. During the last third of the nineteenth century, the popular belief that the visual arts spoke a universal language began to decline, and a growing sense that they were composed in a language of their own, in which one had to be educated, took its place. Whistler had made this point in his essay 'Whistler v. Ruskin', as had Pater in 'The School of Giorgione'.[27] Although Whistler argued that his paintings did not require the mediation of any critic, the lack of narrative in impressionist works highlighted the necessity of the art critic's guidance and an approach to art criticism that went beyond recounting the work's content and interpreting its moral stance. In addition, during the same period the rediscovery of the Italian primitive painters and the growth of interest in Japanese and Chinese art provided examples of works that did not conform to the hitherto hegemonic history of art as a history of representational ability, in which artists gradually developed the skill to reproduce nature perfectly. A *Times* review of the

[26] T. E. Hulme, 'Bergson's Theory of Art', in Hulme, *Collected Writings*, pp. 191–204 (p. 194). This essay was first published posthumously in 1922 as 'The Note-Books of T. E. Hulme', ed. Herbert Read, in *New Age*, 30 (1922), 287–8, 301–2, 310–12. Pound may have attended this lecture: see Stock, *The Life of Ezra Pound*, pp. 134–5.
[27] Whistler, pp. 25–34; Pater, I: 130–53. See Kate Flint, *The Victorians and the Visual Imagination* (Cambridge: Cambridge University Press, 2000), pp. 197–235.

1910 Japan-British Exhibition in Shepherd's Bush is representative in noting that 'our increasing knowledge and love of the primitive Italian painting has prepared our minds for the beauty of Oriental art' and understanding that although Chinese and Japanese painting was not characterised by progress towards an increasingly complete illusion 'these artists knew exactly what they wanted to do, and did it just as completely as Titian in the "Bacchus and Ariadne"'.[28]

Likewise, Hulme's examples of artists and artworks in 'Bergson's Theory of Art' (to Constable, Sickert, Giotto, Botticelli, and Laurence Binyon's book on Chinese and Japanese art, *The Flight of the Dragon*) were chosen for their challenge to dominant modes of perception: 'Nobody before Constable saw things, or at any rate painted them, in that particular way', he writes for example.[29] Pound also categorised art in terms of its ability to educate one's visual sense when he praised Whistler and Turner as makers of 'keys' rather than ornaments. By the time he wrote 'The Wisdom of Poetry' between 1910 and 1912, art's defining function was no longer to communicate beauty, but 'to strengthen the perceptive faculties and free them from encumbrance, such encumbrances, for instance, as set moods, set ideas, conventions'.[30]

The pre-eminent interpreter of East Asian art in Britain was Pound's friend Laurence Binyon, whom he met in February 1909.[31] Binyon was Assistant Keeper of Prints and Drawings at the British Museum and a successful poet, and the previous year he had published the highly praised *Painting in the Far East*, the first English-language overview of the subject.[32] When Ernest Fenollosa visited London in September 1908, he wrote to Binyon to ask for guidance through the British Museum's collection of Chinese and Japanese art, having heard 'most pleasant things said of you by Mr. Freer, and other mutual friends'. That Christmas, Charles Lang Freer himself congratulated Binyon on *Painting in the Far East*: 'in writing this

---

[28] 'Japanese Pictures at the Japan-British Exhibition', *Times*, 16 May 1910, p. 4, col. c. See Andrew Thacker, '"Mad after foreign notions": Ezra Pound, Imagism and the Geography of the Orient', in *Geographies of Modernism: Literatures, Cultures, Spaces*, ed. Peter Brooker and Andrew Thacker (London: Routledge, 2005), pp. 31–42.

[29] Hulme, *Collected Writings*, pp. 194, 199, 203, 196.

[30] Letter to Isabel Weston Pound, 7 January [1909], *SR*, 162; 'The Wisdom of Poetry', p. 498.

[31] Woon-Ping Chin Holaday, 'Pound and Binyon: China via the British Museum', *Paideuma*, 6 (1977), 27–36, Zhaoming Qian, *Orientalism and Modernism: The Legacy of China in Pound and Williams* (Durham, NC: Duke University Press, 1995), pp. 9–18

[32] Laurence Binyon, *Painting in the Far East* (London: Arnold, 1908), p. vii. In 1912 Binyon was put in charge of the newly created Sub-Department of Oriental Prints and Drawings. See *Times*, 26 December 1912, p. 7, col. g.

book you have done great service to "Painting in the East" and have placed all of its English-reading lovers and students under deep obligation'.[33]

A month after their first meeting, Binyon invited Pound to his lectures on 'Art and Thought in East and West', the first two of which, at least, Pound attended: he described the first, given in the small theatre of the Albert Hall at 5:30 on 10 March, as 'intensely interesting'.[34] Although transcripts of a number of Binyon's lectures survive, those relating to this series do not. However, Binyon lectured relatively frequently on this and related topics, and his notes show that sections of material recur between lectures. In the lectures Pound attended it is likely that Binyon described the Chinese scroll, *Admonitions of the Instructress to Court Ladies*, at that time thought to be the work of the fourth-century artist Gu Kaizhi, and that his discussion of Western art and poetry included observations on Blake, Rembrandt and Wordsworth.[35] More significantly for this discussion, Binyon probably began his first lecture by setting out his revisionist reading of Eastern art based on the 'Six Principles', the sixth-century theory of painting by Xie He (referred to by Binyon as Hsieh Ho), an art critic and painter of the Southern Qi. This is how he began most of his lectures and all three of his major publications during this period, *Painting in the Far East*, the *Guide to an Exhibition of Chinese and Japanese Paintings* at the British Museum (1910), and *The Flight of the Dragon* (1911), which Pound would later praise in *Blast*.[36] In *Painting in the Far East*, for example, Binyon argues that, contrary to the cliché that Eastern art is 'sensuous rather than intellectual' and therefore should 'excel in colour rather than form', 'the painting of Asia is throughout its main tradition an art of line [. . .]. The spaces to be coloured are flat spaces, and the instinct of the artist is to invent a harmony of colours which intensifies and gives added charm to the harmony of line.' Like the *Times* reviewer, he compares this approach with that of early Italian painting, in which even 'the colour of quite minor, insignificant, and provincial masters pleases us' because 'the painting of those early periods was as yet unconfused and undistracted by the problems of chiaroscuro'. But he also points out that the very antithesis of colour and form is problematic:

---

[33] Ernest Fenollosa, Letter to Laurence Binyon, 10 September 1908, Charles Freer, Letter to Laurence Binyon, 'Christmas 1908', LBP, British Library, vol. 4.

[34] Letter to Isabel Weston Pound, 15 March [1909], EPP, Beinecke, 59.2659. Pound records attending the second lecture in a letter to his father on 17 March 1909, EPP, Beinecke, 59.2659: 'Have just come from hearing Binyon lecture and meeting Sturge Moore'. See the *Times*, 11 February 1910, p. 8, col. f and 10 March 1910, p. 13, col. e.

[35] LBP, British Library, vols. 26–33; Richard M. Barnhart et al., *Three Thousand Years of Chinese Painting* (New Haven, CT: Yale University Press, 1997), pp. 48–50; Zhaoming Qian, *The Modernist Response to Chinese Art* (Charlottesville, VA: University of Virginia Press, 2003), pp. 7–8.

[36] Barnhart et al., pp. 1–2, 4; 'Chronicles', *Blast*, 2 (1915), 85–6 (p. 86).

'the phrases have no meaning except in so far as the idea of harmony or rhythm underlies both'. In the Six Principles, he explains, 'it is Rhythm that holds the paramount place; not, be it observed, imitation of Nature or fidelity to Nature'.[37]

Binyon's terminology was influential in establishing a language that could describe non-mimetic art, or, more precisely, art that did not fit preconceived ideas of mimetic art. The emphasis on pictorial rhythm, in particular, was taken up by other art critics, for whom it echoed the Bergsonian vocabulary circulating at the same time. As early as May 1910 art critics reviewing the Japan-British exhibition recommended the 'admirable "Painting in the Far East"' and used Binyon's vocabulary: works were praised for design 'so balanced and so precise that it seems a kind of poetic geometry, like the greatest Renaissance architecture', and a tenth-century painting was admired for a 'rhythm more free and complicated than any that Fra Angelico ever achieved'.[38] *The Flight of the Dragon* was even more influential. Written for a public that Roger Fry's *Manet and the Post-Impressionists* exhibition had recently introduced to formal experiments in Western art, Binyon abandoned the historical and geographical approach of *Painting in the Far East*, in favour of a structure that highlighted formal and technical issues. In the chapter on 'Rhythm' Binyon wrote that

Every statue, every picture, is a series of ordered relations, controlled, as the body is controlled in the dance, by the will to express a single idea. A study of the most rudimentary abstract design will show that the units of line or mass are in reality energies capable of acting on each other; and, if we discover a way to put these energies into rhythmical relation, the design at once becomes animated, our imagination enters into it; our minds also are brought into rhythmical relation with the design, which has become charged with the capability of movement and of life. In a bad painting the units of form, mass, colour, are robbed of their potential energy, isolated, because brought into no organic relation.[39]

Here Binyon develops his previous remarks about rhythm into a formalist vocabulary that effectively marks the difference between the compositional values of Chinese and Japanese art and the mimetic values dominating Western art since the Renaissance, while creating a means to understand it. Phrases such as 'ordered relations' and 'units of line or mass' had been

---

[37] Binyon, *Painting in the Far East*, pp. 2, 8, 12–13, 19, 8–9. See also *Guide to an Exhibition of Chinese and Japanese Paintings in the Print and Drawing Gallery* (London: British Museum, 1910), p. 9 and *The Flight of the Dragon: An Essay on the Theory and Practice of Art in China and Japan, Based on Original Sources* (London: Murray, 1911), pp. 11–14.

[38] 'Japanese Pictures at the Japan-British Exhibition', p. 4, col. c, 'Japanese Pictures at the Japan-British Exhibition: II', *Times*, 6 June 1910, p. 9, col. a.

[39] Binyon, *The Flight of the Dragon*, pp. 17–18.

present in nineteenth-century design manuals and guides to painting, as well as the art criticism of the more technically astute professional critics, but Binyon's timely intervention demonstrates how a technical vocabulary could translate the otherwise quite literally foreign language of East Asian art.[40] This would become an invaluable tool for those who found the new post-impressionist art equally foreign.

In *The Flight of the Dragon*, Binyon was responding to recent developments in art criticism associated above all with Roger Fry. Fry, as Elizabeth Prettejohn has discussed, was practising a formalist criticism long before his post-1910 polemics on behalf of post-impressionism; formalist criteria were recognized as the 'routine marks' of the professional art critic, especially one whose speciality was early Italian art.[41] According to Fry's own testimony of 1920, it was a desire for 'structural design', absent, he thought, from the prevailing avant-garde of impressionist painting, that drove him to the Italian primitives, and when he first saw Cézanne's work in 1906, he 'gradually recognised that what I had hoped for as a possible event of some future century had already occurred, that art had begun to recover once more the language of design and to explore its so long neglected possibilities'. It was to account for his attraction to art that subordinated imitation to what he later called the 'architectonic idea' that Fry wrote one of his most important essays, 'An Essay in Æsthetics', published in the *New Quarterly* in 1909.[42]

Although Fry rarely makes an appearance in accounts of Pound's intellectual history, the similarity between their aesthetic concerns during this period is striking. Pound's strident denunciations of Fry and the Bloomsbury group have effectively masked an initial commonality that has in turn obscured the trajectory of his early thinking about art. In 'An Essay in Æsthetics' Fry is motivated by largely the same questions as Pound in the slightly later 'The Wisdom of Poetry': 'Can we', Fry asks, 'arrive at any conclusions as to the nature of the graphic arts, which will at all explain our feelings about them, which will at least put them into some kind of relation with other arts, and not leave us in the extreme perplexity, engendered

[40] See Elizabeth Prettejohn, 'Aesthetic Value and the Professionalization of Victorian Art Criticism, 1837–78', *Journal of Victorian Culture*, 2 (1997), 71–94 and Kate Flint, 'The English Critical Reaction to Contemporary Painting, 1878–1910', unpublished PhD thesis, Oxford University (1983), chapter 7.

[41] Elizabeth Prettejohn, 'Out of the Nineteenth Century: Roger Fry's Early Art Criticism, 1900–1906', in Christopher Green (ed), *Art Made Modern: Roger Fry's Vision of Art* (London: Courtauld/ Merrell Holberton, 1999), pp. 31–44 (p. 31).

[42] Roger Fry, 'Retrospect', in Fry, *Vision and Design* (London: Chatto & Windus, 1920), pp. 188–99 (p. 190). See also Roger Fry, 'The New Gallery', *Athenaeum*, 4081 (1906), 56–7 (p. 56).

by any theory of mere imitation?' Like Pound, Fry wants to describe not only the form of his chosen medium, but also its particular psychological significance relative to other types of art. The essay is avowedly indebted to formalist accounts of art and treatises on design; Fry praises Denman W. Ross's *A Theory of Pure Design* (1907) and delineates the 'emotional elements of design' at considerable length. Like Pound, Fry remarks that art can give 'greater clearness of perception', and also like Pound, who sees the poet as the 'advance guard of the psychologist on the watch for new emotions', Fry refuses an out-and-out formalism and insists on the significance of 'the emotional aspect' of art.[43]

Both writers would retain this central qualification to formalism in their writings about art: as critics they were committed to providing analysis of the formal elements of artworks, not for their own sake, but because they believed that form, even more than content, could express and anal- yse the universal human emotions. Fry, it is true, comes somewhat closer to the more thoroughgoing formalism Clive Bell would introduce in his 1912 formulation 'significant form', agreeing that formal relations inspire a particular kind of 'aesthetic emotion' and insisting on the separation of the reaction to 'pure form' from the reaction to 'associated ideas'.[44] Pound's aesthetics maintain a closer relation between life and art, though during the initial establishment of imagism his proleptic echo of Fry's aversion to 'associated ideas' signifies a temporarily closer affinity with formalism: in the first part of 'Status Rerum', published in January 1913, Pound criticises Yeats for believing 'in the glamour and associations which hang near the words', preferring the method of Ford Madox Ford, who 'would strip words of all "association" for the sake of getting a precise meaning'.[45]

The aim of the foregoing discussion has been to demonstrate that when critics and public were confronted with what was, from 1910, termed post-impressionist art, elements of the formalist vocabulary that would become strongly associated with Fry and Bell had already been devel- oped in other contexts, especially the contexts of East Asian art and early Italian painting. Between 1910 and 1914, when Bell's *Art* was published,

---

[43] Roger Fry, 'An Essay in Æsthetics', *New Quarterly*, 2 (1909), 173–90 (pp. 173, 185, 186, 179, 181); 'The Wisdom of Poetry', p. 500; Denman W. Ross, *A Theory of Pure Design: Harmony, Balance, Rhythm* (Boston, MA and New York: Houghton, Mifflin, 1907).

[44] Clive Bell, 'The English Group', in *Second Post-Impressionist Exhibition* (London: Ballantyne, 1912), pp. 21–4 (p. 23); Roger Fry, 'A New Theory of Art', *Nation*, 14 (1914), 937–9 (p. 938); see the famous footnote Fry added to his 1900–1901 essay on Giotto on its republication in 1920: 'Giotto: The Church of S. Francesco at Assisi', in *Vision and Design*, pp. 87–116 (p. 87). Christopher Green provides a comprehensive overview of Fry's aesthetic theory in his 'Into the Twentieth Century: Roger Fry's Project Seen from 2000', in Green, pp. 13–30.

[45] 'Status Rerum, [I]', *Poetry*, 1 (1913), 123–7 (p. 125).

that vocabulary was extended and refined as critics and artists sought to position themselves in relation to the emerging post-impressionist canon. Although works by Cézanne, Denis, Van Gogh, Gauguin, Matisse and Signac had been exhibited in London before (notably at the International Society's annual exhibitions from 1908 and in the 1910 exhibition of *Modern French Artists* at the Brighton Public Art Galleries), and several journals and newspapers reported on the Paris exhibitions, Fry's 1910 *Manet and the Post-Impressionists* provided a more concentrated review. The attention it received in the national press, not only in reviews but also in letters, articles, cartoons and parodies, ensured that its account of contemporary trends in the visual arts was disseminated well beyond the visitors to the exhibition.[46]

Despite the availability of a formalist vocabulary, the explanatory framework initially constructed for *Manet and the Post-Impressionists* was more expressivist than formalist. In the single essay that introduced the exhibition catalogue, Desmond MacCarthy summarised post-impressionism as enabling 'the individuality of the artist to find completer self-expression in his work than is possible to those who have committed themselves to representing objects more literally'. 'In no school', he emphasised, 'does individual temperament count for more.' MacCarthy compared post-impressionism to art produced by children and 'primitives', which does not 'represent what the eye perceives' yet can be 'extraordinarily expressive': Van Gogh's work was explained as the product of a 'morbid temperament [that] forced him to express in paint his strongest emotions'. Cézanne was described as aiming for 'the coherent, architectural effect of the masterpieces of primitive art'; Gauguin's paintings, too, while committed to 'the fundamental laws of abstract form' were described as 'bring[ing] back into modern painting the significance of gesture and movement characteristic of primitive art'. The 'general effect' of Matisse's work was of 'a return to primitive, even perhaps of a return to barbaric, art'.[47]

The expressivist rhetoric is generally attributed to Fry's temporary engagement with German art criticism, and the influence of Julius Meier-Graefe's *Modern Art* (1908) in particular. As Jacqueline Falkenheim has described in detail, Fry began to revise this representation of post-impressionism almost immediately in articles in the *Nation* in November and December 1910 that deployed a classicist vocabulary to replace the

[46] See J. B. Bullen (ed), *Post-Impressionists in England* (London: Routledge, 1988), pp. 3–13, 494–6.

[47] [Desmond MacCarthy], 'The Post-Impressionists', in *Manet and the Post-Impressionists* (London: Ballantyne, 1910), pp. 7–13 (pp. 7, 10, 11).

Romanticism of Meier-Graefe.[48] But the catalogue's expressivism had already provided ammunition for the exhibition's detractors, who used it to represent post-impressionism as politically subversive, barbaric, and a glorification of the 'insanity' and 'egoism' of its artists.[49] *The Times* remarked that 'like anarchism in politics', post-impressionism was 'the rejection of all that civilization has done, the good with the bad'.[50] The *Daily Express* condemned Gauguin's 'primitive, almost barbaric, studies of Tahitian women – bizarre, morbid, and horrible', and Matisse's 'epileptic landscape [. . .] quite without form'. Robert Ross, in the *Morning Post*, was more sympathetic to Gauguin, but found Cézanne 'neither coherent nor architectural', and called Van Gogh's *Young Man with Cornflower* (1890) and *Crows over Wheatfield* (1890) 'the visualised ravings of an adult maniac'. The academic painters Charles Ricketts and William Blake Richmond and the watercolourist and conservative critic Ebenezer Wake Cook, all responding in letters to Ross's article, argued that post-impressionism was 'the analogue of the anarchical movements in the political world, the aim being to reduce all institutions to chaos; to invert all accepted ideas on all subjects', the product of 'morbid and suffering egotism', 'childish, not childlike', and the result of a peculiarly French decadence: 'In France we have had [Baudelaire's] *The Flowers of Evil*, Satanism, and the Black Mass; and many people enjoy a morning in the Morgue', wrote Wake Cook, 'the Grafton Galleries has been turned into a Morgue for "Modernity" art'.[51]

Despite the violence of these criticisms, both critical and public opinion changed remarkably quickly. When the exhibition closed in January 1911, the *Daily Graphic* noted that while 'a considerable proportion of the spectators used to shout with laughter in front of Van Gogh's *Girl with the Cornflower* [*Young Man with Cornflower*], or Gauguin's *Tahitians*', now 'the general attitude was one of admiration and of regret that an exhibition which has furnished so much food for discussion must close'.[52] The increasingly sympathetic responses in the press had begun to develop

[48] Roger Fry, 'The Grafton Gallery – 1', *Nation*, 8 (1910), 331–2, 'The Post-Impressionists – 2', *Nation*, 8 (1910), 402–3; Jacqueline V. Falkenheim, *Roger Fry and the Beginnings of Formalist Art Criticism* (Ann Arbor, MI: UMI Research Press, 1980), pp. 18–25.

[49] Bullen, *Post-Impressionists in England*, pp. 14–15.

[50] '"Post-Impressionist" Painting', *Times*, 7 November 1910, p. 12, col. c.

[51] 'Paint Run Mad: Post-Impressionists at Grafton Galleries', *Daily Express*, 9 November 1910, p. 8; Robert Ross, 'The Post-Impressionists at the Grafton: The Twilight of the Idols', *Morning Post*, 7 November 1910, p. 3; E. Wake Cook, 'The Post-Impressionists [letter]', *Morning Post*, 19 November 1910, p. 4; C. Ricketts, 'Post-Impressionism [letter]', *Morning Post*, 9 November 1910, p. 6; W. B. Richmond, 'Post-Impressionists [letter]', *Morning Post*, 16 November 1910, p. 5; Wake Cook, p. 4, all rpt. in Bullen, *Post-Impressionists in England*, pp. 100–20.

[52] 'An Art Victory: Triumphant Exit of the Post-Impressionists', *Daily Graphic*, 16 January 1911, p. 15.

extended explanations for post-impressionism's importance. Some followed Fry's lead, placing post-impressionism in a classicist tradition and adopting his formalist terminology. Laurence Binyon, for example, who was in fact deeply critical of the works themselves, nevertheless saw that the trajectory of the movement potentially supported his own aesthetic opinions: 'European art has become so cumbered with its complex endeavour to represent the complete effect of a scene [. . .] that nine painters out of ten forget the first business of art, which is with rhythmical design', he wrote. The ideas behind post-impressionism could therefore be seen as 'a healthy reaction, a movement in the right direction'.[53] But a number of supporters preferred to develop the expressivist framework, reappropriating the detractors' association between post-impressionism and revolution or anarchism. Holbrook Jackson wrote that post-impressionism was part of the same 'impulsion towards an altogether new interpretation of life' advocated in the anarchist writings of Mikhail Bakunin and Max Stirner, while Frank Rutter dedicated his *Revolution in Art: An Introduction to the Study of Cézanne, Gauguin, Van Gogh, and Other Modern Painters* to 'the rebels of either sex all the world over who in any way are fighting for freedom of any kind' and compared Cézanne and Gauguin to Karl Marx and Peter Kropotkin.[54]

By the time the *Second Post-Impressionist Exhibition* opened in October 1912, critical opinion had largely warmed to the three protagonists of *Manet and the Post-Impressionists*, Cézanne, Gauguin and Van Gogh. But neither Gauguin nor Van Gogh was included in the *Second Post-Impressionist Exhibition*, the only artist represented posthumously was Cézanne, enshrined as the progenitor of modern art. The catalogue notes promoted the classicism of post-impressionism, to the extent that Fry made 'the Classic spirit' the 'distinguishing characteristic of the French artists seen here', by which he meant 'that they do not rely for their effect upon associated ideas, as I believe Romantic and Realistic artists invariably do'. Bell repeated the point in his introduction to the English section of the exhibition that included work by Vanessa Bell, Frederick Etchells, Spencer Gore, Duncan Grant and Wyndham Lewis. For Bell, Lewis's work embodied the purest version of his understanding of art as 'significant form': 'whatever else may be said of it', he remarks, it 'is certainly not descriptive. Hardly at all does it depend for its effect on association or suggestion. There is no reason why a mind

[53] Laurence Binyon, 'Post-Impressionists', *Saturday Review*, 12 November 1910, pp. 609–10.
[54] Holbrook Jackson, 'Pop Goes the Past', *T. P.'s Weekly*, 16 December 1910, p. 829, Frank Rutter, *Revolution in Art: An Introduction to the Study of Cézanne, Gauguin, Van Gogh, and Other Modern Painters* (London: Art News Press, 1910), [n.pag.], p. 18.

sensitive to form and colour, though it inhabit another solar system, and a body altogether unlike our own, should fail to appreciate it.'[55]

The English section received little press, but the critics who did cover it struggled to appreciate Lewis's work. Lewis's contributions, which included *Creation* (1912), *Mother and Child* (1912), and part of the *Timon of Athens* project, were recognisably related to Picasso's cubist works, the most controversial of the exhibition.[56] Bell's and Grant's works tended to be read in relation to the more popular painting of Matisse. But whether positive or negative, criticism of the *Second Post-Impressionist Exhibition* was markedly more confident in its discussion of the formal constituents of the works. In *The Times*, for example, a discussion of Matisse's *Madame Matisse en madras rouge* (1907) alluded to the 'simplification' of the model's face and form 'by means of the flatness and the rough, strong containing lines', and P. G. Konody in the *Observer* described Picasso's 'amazing and utterly unintelligible tangle of interesting straight and curved lines and planes'.[57] 'Rhythm' was the term that predominated, especially in analyses of Matisse's paintings and sculptures: Fry, in a remark that highlights Binyon's influence, wrote in the catalogue that 'in his markedly rythmic [*sic*] design, he [Matisse] approaches more than any other European to the ideals of Chinese art'. 'Rhythm was the magic word of the moment', Frank Rutter recalled, 'the pictures of Matisse had lots of Rhythm.'[58]

The vocabulary described here was not confined to reviews of Fry's two post-impressionist exhibitions. It also structured the presentation and reception of the other important exhibitions of modern European art that were held in Britain over the next few years, such as *An Exhibition of Pictures by Paul Cézanne and Paul Gauguin* (1911), the exhibitions of the Camden Town Group (1911–12), *Exhibition of Drawings by Pablo Picasso*

[55] Roger Fry, 'The French Group', in *Second Post-Impressionist Exhibition*, pp. 25–9 (p. 28); Bell, 'The English Group', p. 22.

[56] Anna Gruetzner Robins, *Modern Art in Britain, 1910–1914* (London: Barbican/Merrell Holberton, 1997), p. 89; Walter Michel, *Wyndham Lewis: Paintings and Drawings* (London: Thames and Hudson, 1971), pp. 429–30. Only two of the works Lewis exhibited are known to have survived: *A Feast of Overmen* (1912) (also known as *The Creditors*) and *The Thebaid* (1912), both part of the *Timon of Athens* project: see Paul Edwards, 'Wyndham Lewis's *Timon of Athens* portfolio: The emergence of vorticist abstraction', *Apollo*, 148.439 (N.S.) (1998), 34–40. *Creation* was reproduced in the catalogue of the *Second Post-Impressionist Exhibition* and *Mother and Child* was reproduced in the *Sketch*: see Paul Edwards, *Wyndham Lewis: Painter and Writer* (New Haven, CT: Yale University Press, 2000), pp. 77–8 and Lisa Tickner, 'A Lost Lewis: the *Mother and Child* of 1912', *Wyndham Lewis Annual*, 2 (1995), 2–11.

[57] 'A Post-Impressionist Exhibition: Matisse and Picasso', *Times*, 4 October 1912, p. 9; P. G. Konody, 'Art and Artists – More Post-Impressionism at the Grafton', *Observer*, 6 October 1912, p. 6, rpt. in Bullen, *Post-Impressionists in England*, pp. 361–5, 368–72.

[58] Fry, 'The French Group', p. 27; Frank Rutter, *Art in My Time* (London: Rich & Cowan, 1933), p. 132.

(1912), *Post-Impressionist and Futurist Exhibition* (1913), *Exhibition of the Work of English Post Impressionists, Cubists and others* (1913–14), the exhibitions of the Grafton Group (1913–14), *Twentieth-Century Art: A Review of Modern Movements* (1914) and the exhibitions of the Allied Artists' Association between 1909 and 1914. The speed with which this vocabulary was assimilated is apparent from the reception of the Sackville Gallery's *Exhibition of Works by the Italian Futurist Painters* in March 1912. The thirty-five paintings were accompanied by a substantial catalogue that included three manifestos to explain the futurists' ideas.[59] But although the futurists provided their own terminology and critical framework, it was largely rejected in favour of that now associated with Fry and Bell's post-impressionism.

In 'The Exhibitors to the Public' the futurists argued that although they were on a parallel road to that of 'the Post-impressionists, Synthetists and Cubists of France', they were 'absolutely opposed to their art' because French painters 'obstinately continue to paint objects motionless, frozen, and all the static aspects of Nature'. It was precisely the return to form Fry and Bell so admired in post-impressionist painting that the futurists announced was a retrograde step. The futurists' aim was to render 'the *dynamic sensation* [. . .] the particular rhythm of each object, its inclination, its movement, or, to put it more exactly, its interior force', by including what they called 'force-lines' in the picture. By this means their painting would demonstrate that 'every object influences its neighbour, not by reflections of light (the foundation of *impressionistic primitivism*), but by a real competition of lines and by real conflicts of planes, following the emotional law which governs the picture (the foundation of *futurist primitivism*)'.[60]

The futurists' charge that the post-impressionist focus on form was not original is obviously true. Indeed, Fry and Bell suggest the same: in Bell's famous words, '"Significant Form" is the one quality common to all works of visual art', the 'Sta. Sophia and the windows at Chartres, Mexican sculpture, a Persian bowl, Chinese carpets, Giotto's frescoes at Padua, and the masterpieces of Poussin, Piero della Francesca, and Cézanne'.[61] In his generally positive review of the futurist exhibition, Fry, therefore, writes that he 'cannot accept without qualification their rash boast of complete and absolute originality, even supposing that such a thing were in itself desirable'.

---

[59] *Exhibition of Works by the Italian Futurist Painters* (London: Sackville Gallery, 1912). See Gruetzner Robins, pp. 56–63, Anne Coffin Hanson, *Severini futurista, 1912–1917* (New Haven, CT: Yale University Press, 1995), pp. 17–20, and Caroline Tisdall and Angelo Bozzola, *Futurism* (London: Thames and Hudson, 1977), pp. 37–59.

[60] Umberto Boccioni, et al., 'The Exhibitors to the Public', in *Exhibition of Works by the Italian Futurist Painters*, pp. 9–19 (pp. 9, 12, 14).

[61] Clive Bell, *Art* (London: Chatto & Windus, 1914), p. 8.

Nevertheless, he is relatively positive about the futurists' 'psychological painting', and picks out Gino Severini as the most talented: 'he has a genuine and personal feeling for colors and pattern, and the quality of his paint is that of an unmistakable artist. His "Pan Pan" is a brilliant piece of design, and really does, to some extent, justify the curious methods adopted, in that it conveys at once a general idea of the scene and of the mental exasperation which it provokes.'[62]

It is noticeable here that Fry discards the futurists' terms in favour of his own, and in fact the general critical reaction to the futurist exhibition was to a certain extent controlled by the lessons of post-impressionism, the futurists' disavowals notwithstanding. P. G. Konody, writing in the *Pall Mall Gazette*, commented that 'the exponents of Post-Impressionism and Cubism have trained our faculties to accept the new and the revolutionary without going into hysterics of indignation', but to a critic with such training, futurist art appears as 'the pictorial rendering of confused nightmares', 'chaos', 'kaleidoscopic pattern'.[63] C. H. Collins Baker, in the *Saturday Review*, also registered the failure of futurist art in terms of the new precepts: 'Art as a manifestation of developed mentality is not chaotic, kaleidoscopic, watery; it is concentrated and selective.'[64] Even Frank Rutter, who would include two works by Severini in his *Post-Impressionist and Futurist Exhibition* the following year, complained that he could not 'see what good is to be got from an endeavour to convey abstract ideas by means of arbitrary arrangements of lines and colours', and recommended that the futurists 'stop visualising abstract metaphysics which their master, M. Bergson, can express far more lucidly and intelligently, than any of his conscious or unconscious pictorial disciples'.[65] By 1912 formalism had become quite securely established as the appropriate terminology for criticism of modernist art.

Given the passion with which Pound was writing about painting in 1906–7, his interest in the contemporary art exhibited in London developed

---

[62] Roger Fry, 'Art: The Futurists', *Nation*, 10 (1912), 945–6 (p. 945). Severini's *The Dance of the Pan Pan at the Monico* (1911) is now lost, but was one of a number of paintings from the exhibition reproduced in the *Sketch*, 20 March 1912: see Coffin Hanson, p. 64.

[63] P.G.K., 'The Italian Futurists: Nightmare Exhibition at the Sackville Gallery', *Pall Mall Gazette*, 1 March 1912, p. 5.

[64] C. H. Collins Baker, 'Futurist Academics', *Saturday Review*, 113 (1912), 300–1 (p. 301).

[65] Frank Rutter, 'Round the Galleries: The Futurist Painters', *Sunday Times*, 10 March 1912, 19. Although the catalogue made no mention of Bergson, the emphasis on dynamism, 'interior force' and the repudiation of space would have strongly recalled Bergson in 1912. The following year, Severini referred explicitly to Bergson in his introduction to the catalogue of his solo exhibition at the Marlborough Gallery: see Gino Severini, 'Introduction', in *The Futurist Painter Severini Exhibits His Latest Works* (London: Marlborough Gallery, 1913), pp. 3–7 (p. 3).

somewhat more slowly than one might expect. Although he first met Lewis in 1909 and Epstein probably in 1912, neither feature prominently in letters until the very end of 1913: as late as 28 February 1914 Pound remarked of Lewis in a letter home, 'I dont know that I have written of him but he is more or less one of the gang here at least he is the most "advanced" of the painters and very clever and thoroughly enigmatic.'[66] He had known more conservative members of the art scene for some time, however: the *Observer* art critic P. G. Konody, Walter Sickert and the sculptor Derwent Wood, as well as Binyon.[67] Pound's letters also contain scattered references to visits to art galleries; when William Carlos Williams visited in March 1910, Pound wrote that he had 'crammed him with Turner & other such', and in September 1911 he mentioned that he had 'raked out a couple of pictures in the Wallace gallery', referring to the Wallace Collection off Oxford Street, a predominantly eighteenth-century collection.[68] During these years he had not lost his tendency to explain literary points by copious reference to the visual arts, but even as late as November 1913 his canon of allusions was restricted to Blake, Dürer, Rembrandt, Turner, Velázquez and Whistler, a list that conspicuously omits not only contemporary art, but also sculpture and the art of the Italian Renaissance, with which Pound would later be so closely identified.[69] In this light, his emergence as a leading propagandist for contemporary art in February 1914 seems remarkably sudden. How were his relatively conventional interests in painting and his visual analogies for an ideal language transformed into an active commitment to modernist painting and sculpture?

It is possible to trace the growth of Pound's knowledge about modern art in some detail from his letters. Pound missed *Manet and the Post-Impressionists*, which ran during the winter of his eight-month visit to the United States, spent mainly in New York. He therefore also missed the 1910–11 debates in the press that gradually educated the London public: it was not until February 1913 that the United States was introduced to new developments in painting and sculpture in a comparably spectacular fashion through the Armory Show. In New York, it was the architecture,

[66] Carpenter, p. 244; Evelyn Silber, *The Sculpture of Epstein* (Oxford: Phaidon, 1986), p. 27; Letter to Homer Loomis Pound, [28 February 1914], EPP, Beinecke, 60.2673.

[67] Letter to Homer Loomis Pound, [17 March 1909], EPP, Beinecke, 59.2659, Letter to Isabel Weston Pound, 21 January 1910, Letter to Isabel Weston Pound, 19 February [1910], EPP, Beinecke, 59.2664.

[68] Letter to Isabel Weston Pound, 12 March 1910, EPP, Beinecke, 59.2664, Letter to Isabel Weston Pound, [17 September 1911], EPP, Beinecke, 59.2667.

[69] See, for example, *SR*, pp. 157, 162, 'I Gather the Limbs of Osiris, IV: A Beginning', *New Age*, 10 (1911), 178–80 (p. 178), 'The Wisdom of Poetry', p. 498, 'Patria Mia, VIII', *New Age*, 11 (1912), pp. 611–12, 'The Serious Artist, IV', *New Freewoman*, 1 (1913), 213–14 (p. 214).

rather than the painting and sculpture, that impressed Pound, 'I am getting
quite interested in New York architecture – and in the "possibilities" of the
country', he wrote to Margaret Cravens in November 1910, 'our new cam-
panile – the Manhattan Life building [the Metropolitan Life Building] –
is very beautiful & it and madison sq. are only a block or so the other
way.' He visited the Metropolitan, which, he thought, 'has acquired some
decent pictures – 2 Goyas & four Rembrandts that fill me with content,
2 Turners that Turn & 2 that almost do' (*L/MC*, 55). Towards the end
of his stay, however, Pound read an article by Marius de Zayas, a prominent member of Alfred Stieglitz's circle, that appears to have provided an
inspirational introduction to modern French art: he wrote to his mother,
'Read "The New Art in Paris" in the February Forum. There's an answer
to a number of things. That ought to prove my instinct for where I can
breathe. It's mostly news to me, but of the right sort.'[70] The article gave a
vivid account of artistic innovation in Paris, focussing mainly on cubism,
but relating the developments in painting to music and literature too.
Attending a performance of free verse poetry, de Zayas remarked, 'these
poets believe themselves incomprehensible, and they do not try to make
themselves understood: they are ultra-sensitive, and they make us feel'. He
concluded with a eulogy to Paris, and an implicit repudiation of New York
as complacent and provincial: 'In no other artistic centre of the world is
there a greater liberality in making concessions to the thinking genius',
he wrote, 'nor are so many projects admitted to discussion, nor so many
attempts and systems shown, without scandalizing the public, who do not
listen to the outcry of scholastic conventionalisms.'[71] What a compelling
paragraph this must have seemed to Pound, under pressure from his parents to return home, but feeling increasingly confident about his vocation
abroad.

The significance of de Zayas's article can be gauged from the fact that
three days after returning to London Pound left for Paris: on arrival he
wrote to his mother that he would 'be here for 3 weeks inspecting the state
of Art'.[72] In fact, he stayed for considerably more than three weeks, working
on troubadour songs with Walter Rummel, as well as visiting galleries and
having his portrait painted by a friend of Margaret Cravens, the American
painter, Eugene Paul Ullman. His reports home demonstrate that he was

---

[70] Letter to Isabel Weston Pound, [n.d.], EPP, Beinecke, 59.2666. Since this letter was written from
the Barnard Club, New York, it must have been composed between 10 January, when Pound was
elected to the club, and 22 February 1911 when he left the United States.
[71] Marius de Zayas, 'The New Art in Paris', *Forum*, 45 (1911), 180–8 (pp. 185, 187).
[72] Letter to Isabel Weston Pound, 2 March 1911, DDP, Beinecke, 1.8.

energetic in his inspection of art, but there is little sign of an aesthetic conversion. He told his mother, 'I've seen a number of Cezanne pictures in a private gallery', 'Have met Walter's [Rummel's] brother who paints and plays the cello, and diverts me more or less', and, in another letter, 'I am to inspect the studio of a brand new painter sometime this week.'[73] To his father he wrote, 'the picture shows are various. The Salon Independent has some very interesting pictures in it & two masterpieces by Dezire. Castellucho & le Doux also have good things. & Matisse one canvas is well painted. Freaks there are in abundance. The old salon has two or three good groups, – & the "artists Francais" nothing at all.'[74] The downbeat tone of this letter belies the fact that the Salon des Indépendants afforded Pound an excellent opportunity to appraise the works he had read about in de Zayas's article and come to Paris to see. Its Salle 41 contained the first formal group exhibition of the cubists, including works by Robert Delaunay, Albert Gleizes, Marie Laurencin, Fernand Léger and Jean Metzinger, though not Picasso nor Braque.[75] This letter thus constitutes an important marker of Pound's knowledge and taste in 1911, since it testifies to his explicit rejection of the art he knew was being vaunted by the most progressive English and American critics. It records a limited attraction to Matisse, but it reserves its most emphatic approval for the pre-modernist works of Henri Déziré, Claudio Castelucho Diana, and Charles Picart-le Doux – artists hardly at the vanguard of Paris's artistic revolution.

The next stage of Pound's trip, for which he met up with William Carlos Williams's brother, Edgar, in Italy, proved more memorable than this abortive attempt to learn about modern art. During their visit to the church of San Zeno in Verona, Williams, an architecture student, pointed out a carved column signed by the workman, and made the remark that Pound would treasure as a key insight into the relationship between art and capitalism: 'How the hell do you expect us to get any buildings when we have to order our columns by the gross?'[76] For Pound, it was still the art of the past, not the present, that interrogated modern culture most effectively.

Pound returned to London in August 1911. The following summer he attended the *Loan Collection of Works by James McNeill Whistler* at the Tate

[73] Letter to Isabel Weston Pound, [March 1911], Letter to Isabel Weston Pound, 26 March 1911, EPP, Beinecke, 59.2666. In their edition of Pound's letters to Cravens, Omar Pound and Robert Spoo imply that the painter is Ullman (*L/MC*, 32).

[74] Letter to Homer Loomis Pound, [March 1911], EPP, Beinecke, 59.2666.

[75] Mark Antliff and Patricia Leighten, *Cubism and Culture* (London: Thames & Hudson, 2001), pp. 18–19.

[76] 'Paris Letter', *Dial*, 74 (1923), [85]-90 (p. 89). See Hugh Witemeyer, 'Ruskin and the Signed Capital in Canto 45', *Paideuma*, 4.1 (1975), 85–91.

Gallery, and the energy of his response contrasts strongly with his recent indifference towards the art in Paris. In 'Patria Mia', his new series running in the *New Age*, he remarked that it had given him 'more courage for living' than he had gained from 'any other manifestation of American energy whatsoever'.[77] He sent a poem on the exhibition as one of his first two contributions to the new Chicago-based periodical, *Poetry*, picking out as his favourite paintings Whistler's self-portrait, *The Artist in His Studio* (1865–66), and two late portraits *Brun et Or – De Race* (1896–1900) (fig. 2) and *Grenat et Or: Le Petit Cardinal* (1900–1).[78] His accompanying letter emphasised that, for Pound, Whistler was still the most important model for all American artists, writers as well as painters: 'I count him our only great artist', he wrote, 'and even this informal salute, drastic as it is, may not be out of place at the threshold of what I hope is an endeavor to carry into our American poetry the same sort of life and intensity which he infused into modern painting' (*L*, 10). While Pound's excitement at Whistler's achievements clearly had much to do with their shared nationality, it nevertheless highlights his comparative reluctance to engage with modern European art.

There is no evidence that Pound attended the *Second Post-Impressionist Exhibition* during the winter of 1912, though it is surprising that he did not, given his social connections of the period. In particular, his regular attendance at Hulme's Tuesday night salon brought him into proximity with the most innovative young artists in London, including contributors to the exhibition's English section. Epstein, Lewis and the English futurist, Christopher Nevinson, all attended Hulme's salon, as did the 'neo-realist' artists of the Camden Town Group, Robert Bevan, Harold Gilman, Charles Ginner, Spencer Gore and, at least once, Walter Sickert.[79] In fact, the poet W. H. Davies described Hulme's salon as 'mostly for artists, and not so much for literary people', and John Gould Fletcher recalled that by this point Hulme 'was far more interested in modern art and philosophy than poetry'.[80]

It was during 1913 that Pound became markedly more interested in contemporary art. An undoubtedly significant yet somewhat enigmatic influence was his relationship with Dorothy Shakespear. Although Shakespear

---

[77] 'Patria Mia: VIII', *New Age*, 11 (1912), 611–12 (p. 612).

[78] 'To Whistler, American: On the loan exhibit of his paintings at the Tate Gallery', *Poetry*, 1 (1912), p. 7.

[79] Alun R. Jones, *The Life and Opinions of T. E. Hulme* (London: Gollancz, 1960), p. 98.

[80] W. H. Davies, *Later Days* (London: Cape, 1925), pp. 157–8; John Gould Fletcher, *Life is My Song: The Autobiography of John Gould Fletcher* (New York: Farrar & Rinehart, 1937), p. 75.

2 James McNeill Whistler, *Brun et Or – De Race* (1896–1900)

herself characterised her painting style before the influence of vorticism as 'Victorian', reproductions from 1912 suggest that she was moving away from her relatively conventional style of landscape painting towards an identifiably modern idiom somewhat earlier.[81] She was also studying East Asian art: Pound reported that she was 'painting chinese pictures' during December 1912, and in February 1913 she began studying Japanese prints in the British Museum's Print Room, as Pound had recently (*L/DS*, 190, 177).[82] Her letters to Pound during a holiday in Rome during April and May 1913 indicate that she was consciously working to transform her style: she comments on 5 April, 'this morning the sun was out – & hot – & we sketched. I find it so difficult to paint any new way – & the old way bores me [. . .]. I suppose two or three fit to be seen is all one can do in a month?' (*L/DS*, 197). Shakespear's keen interest in Roman architecture and Renaissance art is also vividly conveyed in these letters, and when Pound stayed in Venice in May, her letters provided a guided tour of her favourite works: 'You might go to the Accademia while you are in Venice & give my respects to the Bellini Madonna, and another one or two of his: also (I *think*) a Mantegna Madonna with a background of cherubim. Then there is the Tiziano [Titian] of the Presentation in the Temple – at the Palazzo Ducale – (free on Sundays!) and a blue & gold ceiling, somewhere in the Palazzo' (*L/DS*, 222–3). Pound's letters, by contrast, consisted almost entirely of descriptions of the poetry he was reading and writing, with the occasional anecdote about their acquaintances. He did, however, send Shakespear a postcard of the church of Santa Maria dei Miracoli as 'a reminder of the precise meaning of the term "Quattro cento"', commenting 'I've got the bases of the columns in larger reproduction' (*L/DS*, 226).

In July Pound visited the Allied Artists' Association exhibition at the Albert Hall, which included paintings by Lewis, Nevinson, Gilman and also Kandinsky, whose three works, *Landschaft mit zwei Pappeln* (1912), *Improvisation 29* (1912) and a further unidentified *Improvisation* were praised

[81] Dorothy Shakespear Pound, *Etruscan Gate: A Notebook with Drawings and Watercolours*, ed. Moelwyn Merchant (Exeter: Rougemont Press, 1971), p. 11; Richard Cork, *A Bitter Truth: Avant-Garde Art and the Great War* (New Haven, CT: Yale University Press, 1994), p. 35. In his 'Biographical Note' to the catalogue of *The Introspective Eye: Dorothy Shakespear's Modernist Vision* (Clinton, NY: Hamilton College, 1996), Omar Pound writes that 'aged 16–17 she was copying Holbeins, Japanese prints and making studies of church architectural details and trying her hand at Chinese calligraphy', and that 'during the early years of her relationship with Pound, the watercolour landscapes and drawings produced on visits to Malvern, Worcestershire, 'show muddied edges and somewhat indeterminate blocks of color overlapping'. For reproductions of early works, see *Dorothy Shakespear* (Nacogdoches, TX: Stephen F. Austin Gallery, 1997).
[82] Qian, *The Modernist Response to Chinese Art*, p. 16.

by Roger Fry as 'by far the best pictures' in the exhibition.[83] The sculpture on exhibition was also important. Constantin Brancusi was exhibiting in Britain for the first time, showing his *Sleeping Muse I* (1910) and two other sculptures, probably *Mademoiselle Pogany I* (1912) and the black cement version of *Prometheus* (1911). Epstein showed *Female Figure in Flenite* (1913) and *Doves: First Version* (1913).[84] But Pound's visit to the exhibition is best known for his first meeting with Henri Gaudier-Brzeska, who was exhibiting his *Wrestler* (1912), 'a figure with bunchy muscles done in clay painted green', as well as *Firebird* (1912), *The Madonna of 'The Miracle'* (1912), and busts of Horace Brodzky, Haldane Macfall and Alfred Wolmark (*GB*, 45–6). All these works had been modelled in clay, although by this time Gaudier, influenced by Epstein, had also begun to carve stone.[85]

In August, Pound was reading John Cournos's drafts for a book on American painting, which he told Shakespear 'was starting in a fairly interesting manner' (*L/DS*, 238). Although the book did not appear, Cournos's discussions of Arthur B. Davies, John Twachtman, John Singer Sargent, and three painters of the Ash Can School, Robert Henri, George Luks and George Bellows, were published as articles over the next two years. The references to Pater, Whistler and Binyon, and the high estimation of paintings that do 'not depend on their subject matter, but upon their intrinsic merit as painting' place the work in a familiar formalist context.[86]

During November Pound visited both the *Spanish Old Masters* exhibition at the Grafton Galleries, and Frank Rutter's *Post-Impressionist and Futurist Exhibition* at the Doré. *Spanish Old Masters* aimed to 'represent the whole course of Spanish painting from the days of the primitives down to

[83] Gruetzner Robins, p. 133; Hans K. Roethel and Jean K. Benjamin, *Kandinsky: Catalogue Raisonné of the Oil Paintings*, vol. 1 (London: Sotheby Publications, 1982), pp. 427, 431; Roger Fry, 'The Allied Artists', *Nation*, 13 (1913), 676–7 (p. 677). See also 'The London Salon: Effects of Artistic Freedom', *Times*, 7 July 1913, p. 11, col. d.

[84] Gruetzner Robins, p. 136; Friedrich Teja Bach, Margit Rowell, Ann Temkin, *Constantin Brancusi, 1876–1957* (Philadelphia, PA: Philadelphia Museum of Art, 1995), pp. 105, 120, 108; Silber, *The Sculpture of Epstein*, pp. 133–4.

[85] Evelyn Silber, *Gaudier-Brzeska: Life and Art* (London: Thames and Hudson, 1996), pp. 40, 252–5, 261, 247–8. See also Roger Cole, *Burning to Speak: The Life and Art of Henri Gaudier Brzeska* (Oxford: Phaidon, 1978), Richard Cork, *Vorticism and Abstract Art in the First Machine Age* and *Henri Gaudier-Brzeska and Ezra Pound: A Friendship* (London: d'Offay, 1982), and Richard Humphries, 'Demon Pantechnicon Driver: Pound in the London Vortex, 1908–1920', in *Pound's Artists*, pp. 33–80. For further information on Pound's and Gaudier's friendship see Horace Brodzky's *Henri Gaudier-Brzeska: 1891–1915* (London: Faber and Faber, 1933), pp. 165–6, John Cournos, *Autobiography* (New York: Putnam's Sons, 1935), p. 70, and H. S. Ede, *A Life of Gaudier-Brzeska* (London: Heinemann, 1930), pp. 178–80.

[86] John Cournos, 'Arthur B. Davies', *Forum*, 51, (1914), 770–2, 'John H. Twachtman', *Forum*, 52, (1914), 245–8, 'John S. Sargent', *Forum*, 54 (1915), 232–6 and 'Three Painters of the New York School', *International Studio*, 56 (1915), 239–46.

those of Goya', and included works by El Greco, Goya, Murillo, Sánchez Coello and Velázquez.[87] It was enthusiastically reviewed, not least by Pound, who described it in a letter to his mother as 'the best loan exhibit I have yet seen'. In the same letter, he remarked, with somewhat less fervour, 'the post-Impressionist show is also interesting'.[88] Anna Gruetzner Robins has pointed out how Rutter's exhibition 'challenged Fry's definition of Post-Impressionism when he appointed Pissarro as the unrecognised father of Post-Impressionism', and it also accorded greater significance to Bonnard, Vuillard and the German expressionists. Works by thirty-eight European artists were shown, including Brancusi, Delaunay, Gauguin, Matisse, Picasso, Segonzac, Severini and Van Gogh. In addition, 'almost every group of British modernists was included. Only the Bloomsbury group – Bell, Fry and Grant – was not represented.'[89] But Pound commented on only one contributor to this exhibition: 'Epstein is a great sculptor', he wrote to his mother, 'I wish he would wash.'[90]

Although Pound makes no mention of it, reviews of Rutter's exhibition paid considerable attention to Wyndham Lewis's large canvas *Kermesse* (1912), painted for Frida Strindberg's cabaret club, The Cave of the Golden Calf. Cournos, writing in the *New Freewoman*, found it 'conscientious', but 'laboured and uninspired'; Ramiro de Maetzu, in a lengthy article in the *New Age*, described how his attempts to understand the painting necessitated three visits to the exhibition. *The Times*, however, compared its 'impressive design' favourably to the 'systematic' futurism of Severini, and Clive Bell described it as conveying 'something of the austere and impressive unity of great architecture'.[91] Bell's praise, though qualified, is all the more notable in light of the fact that Lewis, with Frederick Etchells, Cuthbert Hamilton and Edward Wadsworth, had left Fry's Omega Workshops in October, and was now cultivating a strategic association with Marinetti and

---

[87] 'Spanish Old Masters: Exhibition at the Grafton Gallery', *Times*, 3 October 1913, p. 10, col. b.

[88] Letter to Isabel Weston Pound, [November 1913], EPP, Beinecke, 60.2672.

[89] Gruetzner Robins, pp. 117, 137.

[90] Epstein was exhibiting *Doves: Second Version* (1913) and, according to the catalogue, '*Baby's Head* (1907)' [*Romilly John*?]. See [Catalogue to the] *Post-Impressionist and Futurist Exhibition* (London: Doré Galleries, 1913), Silber, *The Sculpture of Epstein*, pp. 29, 120, 134, and Gruetzner Robins, p. 136.

[91] John Cournos, 'The Battle of the Cubes', *New Freewoman*, 1 (1913), 214–15 (p. 214); Ramiro de Maetzu, 'Expressionism', *New Age*, 13 (1913), 122–3 (p. 123); 'Post-Impressionist Pictures: Exhibitions at the Doré Gallery', *Times*, 16 October 1913, p. 12, col. c; Clive Bell, 'The New Post-Impressionist Show', *Nation*, 14 (1913), 172–3 (p. 172). Pound records a visit to The Cave of the Golden Calf in a letter to Dorothy Shakespear on 11 October 1913, *L/DS*, 270. For richly detailed discussions of *Kermesse* in its cabaret context, see Richard Cork, *Art Beyond the Gallery in Early 20th Century England* (New Haven, CT: Yale University Press, 1985), pp. 61–115 and Lisa Tickner, *Modern Life & Modern Subjects: British Art in the Early Twentieth Century* (New Haven, CT: Yale University Press, 2000), pp. 79–115.

the Italian futurists. With Etchells, Hamilton, Nevinson and Wadsworth, Lewis organised a dinner for Marinetti at the Florence Restaurant on 18 November.[92]

In December, Pound spent time with Charles Demuth, who was visiting London, and attended Epstein's controversial exhibition at the Twenty-One Gallery.[93] He also bought two marble carvings by Gaudier: *Samson and Delilah (The Embracers)* (1913) and *Torso 3* (1913).[94]

The fact that this record can be built up from Pound's letters demonstrates not only that he was exposed to a variety of artistic influences in 1913, but that he was actively responding to them and recording his interest. Over the course of the year, he attended the major exhibitions in London and by the second half of 1913, he was paying particular attention to contemporary sculpture, an art which had previously held little appeal for him. However, the belatedness of Pound's response to contemporary art is worth registering, not least because, before Pound demonstrated any interest in it, his critics were already associating him with its post-impressionism. The following section investigates how those associations were made, and their influence on the presentation and reception of Pound's new poetic project: imagism.

INDIVIDUALIST IMAGISM: THE *EGOIST* VS. THE *NEW AGE*

Imagism, Daniel Tiffany reminds us, is not visual. The 'Image' which it proposes to present is 'equivocally, but intentionally, *nonvisual*, insofar as it resists, contests, and mediates the experience of visuality, but also in its preoccupation with the invisible'.[95] Neither, according to Lawrence Rainey, did it have a commonality with contemporary avant-gardes in the visual arts like Italian futurism: 'though Imagism is commonly treated as the first avant-garde in Anglo-American literature, it was really something quite different – the first anti-avant-garde'.[96] Both points appear to be borne out by Pound's own statements at the time of imagism's launch. In

---

[92] Cork, *Vorticism and Abstract Art in the First Machine Age*, 1: 100. I have found no record of Pound's attendance, although he wrote to Shakespear from Sussex that he would be 'coming up on Monday' 17 November (*L/DS*, 276).

[93] *L/WCW*, 23; Letter to John Quinn, 26 May 1916, in *EPVA*, 236.

[94] For information on Pound's purchases see Silber, *Gaudier-Brzeska*, p. 128, *L/DS*, 286–7, 289, *L/WCW*, 22. Pound also owned *Boy with a Coney* (1914), *Head of Ezra Pound* (1914), *Green Stone Charm* (1914) – and, later, *Cat* (1913) and *Water Carrier* (1914), which he had bought from the Omega Workshops for John Quinn in 1916. Dorothy Shakespear owned *Small Fawn in Brown Stone* (1914).

[95] Daniel Tiffany, *Radio Corpse: Imagism and the Cryptaesthetic of Ezra Pound* (Cambridge, MA: Harvard University Press, 1995), p. 21

[96] Rainey, *Institutions of Modernism*, p. 30.

his prefatory note to 'The Complete Poetical Works of T. E. Hulme', the appendix to *Ripostes* (1912) which contains the first public announcement of imagism, Pound distinguished the poetry of Hulme's 'School of Images', and, implicitly, that of its imagist descendants, from the pictorial verse of both 'the Impressionists', who wrote, he said, of '"Pink pigs blossoming upon the hillside"', and of the 'Post-Impressionists who beseech their ladies to let down their slate-blue hair over their raspberry-coloured flanks' (*R*, 59). In the 'Imagisme' essay he co-authored with Flint, he asserted that the imagists 'have nothing in common' with the 'Post Impressionists and the Futurists [. . .] they had not published a manifesto. They were not a revolutionary school; their only endeavor was to write in accordance with the best tradition, as they found it in the best writers of all time.'[97]

Despite these pronouncements, imagism was immediately associated with the visual art avant-garde. On 12 December 1912, Harold Hannyngton Child reviewed 'Some Recent Verse' in the *Times Literary Supplement*. 'Among all the beauty, fine workmanship, and lyric movement' of the books under review, only two were singled out as 'in any way original': Evelyn Underhill's *Immanence* and Pound's *Ripostes* – 'and Miss Underhill has no originality of form'. Pound's poetry, however, according to Hannyngton Child, recalled the disintegration of form in Matisse's series of busts, *Jeanette, I–IV* (1910–12):

At the Post-Impressionist exhibition some spectators may be seen dancing with fury, others quaking with laughter, others indiscriminately worshipping, and a few using their brains coolly. Mr. Ezra Pound's book will have the same effect, no doubt, on its readers. Now and then it is hard not to join the first group. Perhaps, on reading [Pound's poem] 'from a thing by Schumann' it is safer to pass by, as one might pass by a bust in its third stage by Matisse, with the polite reflection that we do not understand its aim and therefore cannot see the beauty of it.[98]

In the United States, imagism's appearance coincided with the Armory Show, and once again reviewers saw similarities between Pound's poetry and the works that had excited most censure, this time, the cubist paintings and Marcel Duchamp's *Nude Descending a Staircase, No. 2* (1912). On 18 April 1913, the *Chicago Daily Tribune* parodied Pound's poem, 'Salutation', published in *Poetry* earlier that month, in its satirical column 'A Line-O'-Type Or Two':

---

[97] F. S. Flint [and Ezra Pound], 'Imagisme', *Poetry*, 1 (1913), 198–200 (p. 198).
[98] Harold Hannyngton Child, 'Some Recent Verse', *Times Literary Supplement*, 12 December 1912, p. 568.

'"Salutation" – to the New Poetry':

> O degenerates in the art of writing,
>   and fallen ones,
> I have seen Cubists splattering their paints,
> I have seen them make hideous splotches,
> I have seen their riots of color
>   and found nothing in them.
> You are far worse than they are,
> And they are much worse than nothing;
> And the nude descends the staircase,
>   and does not even own clothing.[99]

Clearly, there are a number of factors motivating these negative comparisons. At the simplest level, Child and the *Tribune*'s parodist are making opportune reference to the most newsworthy cultural events of the day, and the reference might be seen as to some extent invited by Pound's choice of name for his movement and his over-anxious distinctions from impressionism, post-impressionism and futurism. Both parodies evidently see contemporary art's repudiation of naturalism as an appropriate analogy for imagism's rejection of regular verse forms. The association of contemporary art and free verse was far from unusual, and the comparison could serve a variety of ends. For Child and the *Tribune* parodist, the comparison is comic, but we saw earlier that for de Zayas, in 'The New Art in Paris', it had suggested an underlying unity to contemporary experiment across the arts. However, it could also be interpreted more ominously. For the *New York Times*, the fact that an assault on convention could be tracked across several artistic forms was testimony to the reality and gravity of its threat: its editorial comment on the Armory Show on 16 March 1913 warned, 'It should be borne in mind that this movement is surely a part of the general movement, discernible all over the world, to disrupt and degrade, if not to destroy, not only art, but literature and society, too. [. . .] The cubists and futurists are own cousins to the anarchists in politics, the poets who defy syntax and decency, and all would-be destroyers who with the pretense of trying to regenerate the world are really trying to block the wheels of progress in every direction.'[100]

It is all too easy to dismiss this response to artistic innovation with hindsight: the association of free verse poetry and modernist art with

[99] S.P.W., '"Salutation" – to the New Poetry', *Chicago Daily Tribune*, 18 April 1913, p. 8. For a comprehensive account of the Armory Show, and a catalogue of the exhibition, see Milton W. Brown, *The Story of the Armory Show* (New York: Hirshhorn, [1963]).
[100] 'Cubists of All Sorts', *New York Times*, 16 March 1913, pt. iv, p. 6.

anarchism might appear to be no more than the alarmist product of a conservative editorial. But there were historical and biographical grounds for the *Times*' association, as recent research on the relation between anarchism and late nineteenth- and early twentieth-century painting has shown.[101] In the case of imagism, moreover, the connection between the disruption of artistic conventions and the disruption of 'society' was actively fostered by the context of its English publication in Dora Marsden's feminist and anarchist journal, the *New Freewoman* (renamed the *Egoist* in January 1914). The ideology that imagism was understood to be communicating, and the reason it contributed to imagism's association with contemporary visual art, becomes clearer when one examines the response to imagism, the *New Freewoman*, and to Pound by A. R. Orage's *New Age*, Pound's other main organ of dissemination during the imagist period.

The *New Age* effectively launched Pound's career as a critic. It followed its publication of his 'I Gather the Limbs of Osiris' with four more substantial series during 1912 and 1913, 'Patria Mia', 'Through Alien Eyes', 'America: Chances and Remedies', and 'The Approach to Paris'. Pound was not publishing his poetry in the *New Age*, however, and his imagist poems, published first in the United States in *Poetry*'s April 1913 number, appeared in England in the *New Freewoman* in August 1913. During the second half of 1913 and throughout 1914 Pound also contributed most of his prose to the *New Freewoman*, including his first published art criticism. He returned to the *New Age* with his 'Affirmations' series in January 1915.

The journals had certain similarities: both were vehemently anti-liberal and anti-rationalist, and both included Bergson and Nietzsche in their intellectual pantheon. But whereas the *New Age* espoused 'Guild Socialism', the *New Freewoman* was inflected towards individualist anarchism, particularly as expressed in the nineteenth-century egoist philosophy of Max Stirner, whose work Marsden had encountered in 1911, and which the *New Age* derided as 'the philosophy of the possessive case'.[102] Following Michael Levenson's influential discussion in *A Genealogy of Modernism*, a number of critics have examined the relationship between imagism and Marsden's Stirnean individualism; Robert von Hallberg makes the most positive connection between the two, arguing that Marsden wanted 'a literary flank to her movement, and Imagism was to be just that, lending cultural breadth

---

[101] Antliff, *Inventing Bergson*, John G. Hutton, *Neo-Impressionism and the Search for Solid Ground: Art, Science and Anarchism in Fin-de-Siècle France* (Baton Rouge, LA: Louisiana State University Press, 1994), Patricia Leighten, *Re-Ordering the Universe: Picasso and Anarchism, 1897–1914* (Princeton, NJ: Princeton University Press, 1987).

[102] A.E.R., 'Views and Reviews', *New Age*, 10 (1912), 592–3 (p. 593).

to her brand of feminism, and claiming for it too the timeliness and fruit-fulness of a philosophy in close touch with the arts'.[103] Marsden's protégée Rebecca West brokered Pound's contribution to the journal. Early in 1913 West suggested expanding the journal's literary component, 'a literary side would be a bribe to the more frivolous minded in London', she wrote to Marsden, 'and I don't see why a movement towards freedom of expression in literature should not be associated with and inspired by your gospel'. That summer she met Pound through Violet Hunt, and invited him to contribute.[104]

When the *New Freewoman*, subtitled 'An Individualist Review', had risen from the ashes of its predecessor, the more explicitly feminist *Freewoman*, in June 1913, Marsden's editorials had almost immediately begun to move into philosophical and broadly cultural territory. Discussions of celibacy, eugenics and the Pankhursts were replaced with articles on 'Intellect and Culture', 'Thinking and Thought', and 'Concerning the Beautiful'. In these editorials, Marsden developed the critique of abstract political concepts that had fuelled her opposition to the suffragist movement into an account of contemporary culture as a whole. In 'Thinking and Thought', Marsden, like Bergson, argued that 'thinking' inevitably falsifies the primary state of 'Being', which can only be apprehended through 'experienced emotion'. This necessarily required a 'purging' of language. Following Stirner, who maintained that 'language, or "the word" tyrannizes hardest over us, because it brings up against us a whole army of *fixed ideas*', Marsden declared that 'analysis of the process of naming' is 'more urgently needed than anything thinkable in the intellectual life of to-day'.[105]

It was in the context of this discussion that Pound's imagist poetry was presented to the *New Freewoman*'s readership. West's introduction, which characterised imagism as a reaction against poetry's degradation into 'the idle hussy hung with ornament kept by Lord Tennyson, handed on to Stephen Phillips and now supported at Devonshire Street by the Geor-gian School', together with the three imagist rules quoted from *Poetry*, effectively framed imagism as a logical correlative of Marsden's logophobic

[103] Levenson, pp. 63–79; Robert von Hallberg, 'Libertarian Imagism', *Modernism/Modernity*, 2 (1995), 63–79, p. 67. See also Bruce Clarke, *Dora Marsden and Early Modernism: Gender, Individualism, Science* (Ann Arbor, MI: University of Michigan Press, 1996), Kadlec, pp. 54–74, and Andrew Thacker, 'Dora Marsden and *The Egoist*: "Our War Is With Words"', *English Literature in Transition, 1880–1920*, 36 (1993), 179–96.

[104] Rebecca West, Letter to Dora Marsden, n.d. [ca. February 1913], qtd in Clarke, pp. 96, 106.

[105] See Marsden's editorials for 1 July, 15 August and 1 September 1913; [Dora Marsden], 'Thinking and Thought', *New Freewoman*, 1 (1913), [81]-83 (p. 82); Max Stirner, *The Ego and His Own* (1845), trans. Steven T. Byington (New York: Tucker, 1907), p. 462.

campaign.[106] The poetry itself, though unlike any verse previously published in the *Freewoman* and the *New Freewoman*, could be read as contributing to the same argument: 'Salutation the Second', for example, connects stripped-down language ('Here they stand without quaint devices/ Here they are with nothing archaic about them'; 'Go, little naked and impudent songs') to the invigoration of culture, perceived as coagulating in outmoded institutions ('Go! rejuvenate things!/ Rejuvenate even "The Spectator"'), and guarded by purveyors of rhetoric ('Watch the reporters spit,/ Watch the anger of the professors').[107]

The extent to which Pound was consciously invested in Marsden's individualist programme is illustrated by his well-known article 'The Serious Artist'. In one of his early letters to Marsden, Pound had responded to her request for his 'philosophical credentials' with the statement that 'I suppose I'm individualist, I suppose I believe in the arts as the most effective propaganda for a sort of individual liberty that can be developed without public inconvenience [. . .]. I don't suppose a literary page will queer the editorial columns.' 'The Serious Artist', written at Marsden's instigation, as Bruce Clarke has shown, makes the case for art's significance to an individualist philosophy, and read in context it is remarkable for its conformity to the journal's ideals.[108] Drawing on lines of thinking inspired by Hudson Maxim and first explored in 'The Wisdom of Poetry' the previous year, but in evident dialogue with Marsden's recent editorials, too, Pound argues that 'the arts, literature, poesy, are a science, just as chemistry is a science', and their object is to 'give us our data of psychology, of man as to his interiors, as to the ration of his thought to his emotions'. Throughout the essay, Pound insists that this data's significance is in its precise measure of one's individuality: 'from the arts we learn that man is whimsical, that one man differs from another'. This leads him to make a crucial ethical correlation between good art, integrity and precision: 'by good art I mean art that bears true witness, I mean that art that is most precise', he writes, 'You can be wholly precise in representing a vagueness [. . .]. If you cannot understand this with regard to poetry, consider the matter in terms of painting.'[109]

That last sentence is telling. While it is natural that Pound would turn to painting here to clarify the metaphor of the vague or precise outline he has

---

[106] Rebecca West, 'Imagisme', *New Freewoman*, 1 (1913), 86–7 (p. 86).
[107] 'Salutation the Second', in 'The Contemporania of Ezra Pound', *New Freewoman*, 1 (1913), 87–8 (p. 88).
[108] Letter to Dora Marsden, n.d. [ca. summer 1913], qtd in Clarke, p. 107; Clarke, pp. 110–11.
[109] 'The Serious Artist, I [-II]', *New Freewoman*, 1 (1913), 161–3 (pp. 161, 163, 161, 162).

drawn from design, neither the design metaphor nor the painting analogy are accidental or arbitrary. The turn to a visual correlative is determined by the nominalist stance that underlies the 'The Serious Artist', that underlies Marsden's cultural project, and, via Maxim, Gourmont and Hulme, underlies imagism. Marsden's crusade, like imagism's, is against rhetoric, against words that persuade. Her proposals for the purging of language, like imagism's, rest on a fantasy of a natural language, one that can adequately present the 'thing' in all its vibrancy and immediacy. But even the most precise language can only ever approach this project imperfectly, because it necessarily consists of arbitrary names. Pound, however, implicitly figures the visual arts as able to effect a more adequate conjunction, not because they represent things pictorially – after all, the 'things' to be represented are 'the ration of his thought to his emotions', for which a visual language would be as arbitrary as a verbal one – but rather because the visual is conceived as prior to the verbal.

Pound repeats this move a number of times in 'The Serious Artist'. Although the essay is for the most part specific to poetry, visual analogies are repeatedly deployed with a marked confidence in their explanatory power. The *Victory of Samothrace* and the Taj Mahal prove, he writes, that 'humanity is a species of animals capable of a variation that will produce the desire for a Taj or a Victory'. The self-evident nature of beauty is explained by the feeling of being 'bucked up' when one comes across a 'fine line in a statue', or a 'swift moving thought in Plato' – and Pound's choice of 'thought' there as an equivalent to 'line', rather than 'phrase' or 'sentence' is testimony to his anti-verbalism.[110] Trying to define 'great art', Pound turns to the visual arts first, saying, 'in painting, I mean something or other vaguely associated in my mind with work labelled Durer, Rembrandt, and Velasquez, etc., and with the painters whom I scarcely know, possibly of T'ang and Sung – though I dare say I've got the wrong labels – and with some Egyptian designs that should probably be thought of as sculpture'. Only then does he turn to his own medium, remarking 'in poetry I mean something associated in my mind with the names of a dozen or more writers', whom he does not list.[111]

Marsden responded to Pound's essay in her lead article of 1 November 1913, 'The Art of the Future'. Although she frames her argument in opposition to Pound, commenting on the 'coyness' artists exhibit when 'asked to define their business', her prescription for art is fundamentally the same as

[110] 'The Serious Artist, I-[II]', p. 162.
[111] 'The Serious Artist, IV', *New Freewoman*, 1 (1913), 213–14 (p. 214).

his. Like Pound, she measures art against science, and suggests art should adopt the 'experimental method' of science, to establish precise 'knowledge of the "thing"', in place of 'futile guesses'. The art she anticipates this will produce bears a strong resemblance to imagism: 'Poetry is the expression of the soul-motion: perfect knowledge free both of redundance and hesitancy: it is brief because it is reduced to the exact equivalent: it has reached the completeness of knowledge when its dimensions can be expressed in a formula. It *is* the formula.' [112]

Although Marsden's and Stirner's philosophies were not the direct source of imagist individuality, particularity and nominalism, a certain amount of shared intellectual heritage accounts for these significant correlations between their projects. Hulme's Bergsonism provided imagism with the nominalism Marsden drew from Stirner, and the origin of the image itself in French symbolism connected it to individualist anarchists such as Laurent Tailhade and Gourmont, the latter described by Pound's fellow imagist and *New Freewoman* contributor Richard Aldington as 'a great Individualist, one of the last and boldest defenders of individual liberty against the increasing tyrannies of democracy and socialism'. [113]

But the *New Freewoman*'s ideological framing of imagism did not stop with Marsden's editorials. The art criticism of the *New Freewoman* and its successor, the *Egoist*, also had an impact on imagism. The journal's main art critic, Huntly Carter, was the first in the journal to establish the arts as a manifestation of individualist anarchism, through his alignment of contemporary visual art with the journal's politics. He thus prepared the ground for Marsden's reading of imagism and created the conditions through which imagism came to be associated with innovations in the visual arts.

Carter arrived at the *Freewoman* just before its demise, having previously contributed art criticism to the *New Age*. After a period on the European continent during 1911, he had become a vocal advocate of contemporary art in the *New Age*, just at the point of Pound's first contributions. The Salon des Indépendants that Pound had found full of 'freaks' was for Carter 'the manifestation of a movement tremendously big, tremendously vital'. He was responsible for reproducing Picasso's *La Mandoline et le Pernod* (1911) in the journal when examples of cubism had barely been seen in England, and he promoted the work of the Fauvists Anne Estelle Rice and

---

[112] 'The Art of the Future', *New Freewoman*, 1 (1913), 181–3 (pp. 181, 183).

[113] Richard Aldington, 'Introduction', in *Selections from Remy de Gourmont* (London: Chatto and Windus, 1932), pp. [1]-34 (p. 19).

J. D. Fergusson, leaders of the 'Rhythm' group.[114] His art criticism was explicitly Bergsonian, and his columns introduced *New Age* readers to a Parisian cultural matrix that was 'actively expressing the new idea', which he described as

the belief that the individual must be completely himself and be allowed at all times to be completely himself, yet must express that corporate life of which he is but a part; which accordingly demands conscious intuition, clarity of suggestion, simple and direct expression, and withal a tremendous analysis, but not the analysis of academical logic.

For Carter, this matrix included 'the poets headed by Tristan Derème, the Yellow Syndicalists by Sorel, the literary critics by Remy de Gourmont, [and] above all the post-Impressionists', the milieu that forms the focus of Mark Antliff's revisionist account of the pre-war avant-garde, *Inventing Bergson*. As Antliff describes, Carter, with John Middleton Murry, was a key disseminator of the vitalist and individualist theories surrounding cubism in Paris, a version of Bergsonism which had in turn been adapted from that of the neo-symbolists Hulme had discussed in the *New Age* a few months earlier.[115]

This was not a popular philosophy in the socialist *New Age*, as the reactions of both regular contributors and readers demonstrated. From 23 November 1911, when the Picasso was reproduced, to 7 March, by which time further reproductions had appeared, the letters pages were taken up with the 'Picarterbin' controversy (Pic[asso] + Carter + [Her]bin), in which 'M. B. Oxon' (Lewis Alexander Wallace), Ebenezer Wake Cook, Frederick H. Evans, Harold B. Harrison and Walter Sickert, to name just a few, ridiculed Picasso's and Herbin's work and expressed their despair about the course of modern painting. Carter's last article for the *New Age* appeared on 27 June 1912, and on 12 September he made his debut in the *Freewoman*.

Carter's aesthetic philosophy was far more appropriate to the *Freewoman* than the *New Age*. In his first article, 'The Circle of Intelligence', he established his individualist credentials and distanced himself from the *New Age*, proclaiming that his call for 'a circle of intelligent individuals working

---

[114] Huntly Carter, 'The Independants and the New Intuition in Paris', *New Age*, 9 (1911), 82–3 (p. 82); 'The Plato-Picasso Idea', *New Age*, 10 (1911), p. 88; Huntly Carter, 'Letters from Abroad: The Post-Expressionists', *New Age*, 9 (1911), 617–18.

[115] Huntly Carter, 'The "Blue Bird" and Bergson in Paris', *New Age*, 9 (1911), 43–5 (p. 44). As one would expect from his terminology, Carter found Binyon's *The Flight of the Dragon* 'an admirable little book' due to its designation of rhythm as a key element of all art: see Carter, *The New Spirit in Drama and Art*, pp. 4–5; Antliff, *Inventing Bergson*, pp. 67–105; 18–30.

separately, yet together, to realise the extreme value of a whole of which each of their values is a necessary part [. . .] has nothing to do with the Guild idea of any kind. Beneath the Guild idea is a subtle and, in some cases, poisonous tyranny.'[116] Carter's avowed individualism and vitalism brought his criticism into close concert with Marsden's editorials. Almost a year before imagism emerged as the *New Freewoman*'s potential literary wing, Carter was establishing contemporary art's ideological affinity with the *Freewoman*. His 'The Dances of the "Stars"', published on 26 September 1912, considered Dalcrozian dancing, Matisse's *La Joie de vivre* (1905–6), and an unnamed 'amazing Picasso' as aspects of 'the circle of intelligence', a means of 'break[ing] down as far as possible the mechanical barriers which man has set up between himself and vital and spiritual forms of expression'.[117] In his first article for the journal's relaunch as the *New Freewoman*, he set out his theory of art at length, arguing that 'Art and The Soul are one [. . .] Art is life-centred not man-centred.'[118] Carter's Bergsonism led him, like Marsden and Pound, to a distrust of words, especially of words used to define art, resulting in his condemnation not only of the ethical critiques of art against which Pound and Fry were also positioning themselves, but, ironically, almost all art criticism. Reviewing Muriel Ciolkowska's *Rodin*, for example, he criticises her praise of Rodin's admirers who encouraged him to write about his art: 'was there ever such a conspiracy to destroy the visionary in a man by leading him to suppose that the key to his genius does not lie in its development and may be known only by tracing this development through his works of art, but is to be sought in theories and opinions?'[119]

Idiosyncratic as Carter's criticism is, it constitutes an important and unexamined context for imagism's appearance in the *New Freewoman*, and for the first forays into art criticism Pound was to publish there in 1914. Carter's vitalist, individualist readings of contemporary art provided a bridge between Marsden's philosophy and the arts that rendered imagism legible to *New Freewoman* readers. For both Pound and Carter, art provides particular insights into the nature of man, though Pound's description of its discoveries as 'data' and Carter's as 'spiritual potentialities' are indicative of their differences, too.[120] When Pound defines art in 'The Serious Artist'

---

[116] Huntly Carter, 'The Circle of Intelligence: The Resurrectionists', *Freewoman*, 2 (1912), 325–6 (p. 325).
[117] Huntly Carter, 'The Dances of the "Stars"', *Freewoman*, 2 (1912), [361]–362 (p. 362).
[118] Huntly Carter, 'The Golden Age', *New Freewoman*, 1 (1913), 16–17.
[119] Huntly Carter, 'The House of Vision', *New Freewoman*, 1 (1913), 197–9 (p. 199). See Muriel Ciolkowska, *Rodin* (London: Methuen, 1912), p. 3.
[120] 'The Serious Artist, I [-II]', p. [161]; Carter, 'The Golden Age', p. 16.

as 'a sort of energy', he echoes Carter's description of art as a 'universal vibrative force known to science as Energy'.[121] Carter's conception of 'a circle of intelligent individuals working separately, yet together' corresponds to Pound's marketing of imagism, and would become even more significant in his framing of vorticism.[122] Both writers share a distrust of writing about art, and while Carter's is more thoroughgoing than Pound's, when Pound baldly states in his first work of art criticism that 'art is to be admired rather than explained', his misgivings have a strong precedent in the *New Freewoman* in Carter's persistent attacks on art criticism.[123]

This is not to say that Carter would have welcomed a comparison between his criticism and Pound's. While Carter's work established an important interpretative context for imagist poetry, the differences between their aesthetics should not be minimised. Carter's essentially Romantic conception of the creative process had no place for the technical experiments which, for Pound, were essential to the achievement of good style. Carter mercilessly satirised those who spent 'laborious days in the British Museum practising "style" as a muddied Oaf practises football', deriding an easily recognisable poet who 'acquires all languages, learns several million lines of poetry, translates the whole of the ancients including Schiller and Goethe, addresses tedious odes to long-suffering deities, experiments in every conceivable verse-form, makes the acquaintance of, and quotes every known versifier since the Flood'. For Carter, stylists are the antithesis of the artists admired by the *New Freewoman*, they are 'artificial', 'the natural outcome of the passing Age of Systems just as Guild Socialism, aiming to bring workers together in mechanical relations, is the apotheosis of the Machine Age'.[124] He made this point even more explicitly in 1915, when he wrote an article for the *Little Review* complaining about imagism's dominance in the *Egoist*: 'Now Imagism is not egoism. I do not think the Imagists themselves are egoists. To me they appear to be socialists by instinct and individualists by profession.' In other words, the imagists, for all their rhetoric, would be more at home in what had become Carter's *bête noir*, the anti-individualist *New Age*.[125]

---

[121] 'The Serious Artist, III: Emotion and Poesy', *New Freewoman*, 1 (1913), 194–5 (p. 194); Carter, 'The Golden Age', p. 17.

[122] Carter, 'The Circle of Intelligence: The Resurrectionists', p. 325.

[123] 'The New Sculpture', *Egoist*, 1 (1914), 67–8 (p. 68).

[124] Huntly Carter, 'My Hypothesis', *New Freewoman*, 1 (1913), 255–6 (p. 255). Pound replied to Carter in the next issue in the guise of 'Henery Hawkins': 'Mr. Hawkins on Mr. Carter [letter]', *Egoist*, 1 (1914), 19.

[125] Huntly Carter, 'Poetry versus Imagism', *Little Review*, 2.6 (1915), 27–37 (p. 30). See Carter's diatribes against the *New Age* in 'The Stone Citizen', *New Freewoman*, 1 (1913), 134–6 and 'Blaspheming Creation', *New Freewoman*, 1 (1913), 238–9.

Yet the *New Age* saw imagism as antithetical to its ideology, too. Ann Ardis's recent work on the periodical has demonstrated that the *New Age*, conventionally taken to be a modernist organ, in fact subjected its modernist contributions to severe criticism: 'over and over again in the pages of the *New Age*, modernists themselves are critiqued with gusto', she writes, 'in feature articles, regular columns, letters to the editor, and the dialogue essays with which the periodical so often pursues its case about the need for "brilliant common sense"'.[126] Ardis provides extensive evidence of the satire directed at the modernists and notes that it focussed especially on Pound, a fact that is particularly striking given that Pound's vocal appreciation of the *New Age*, and especially of Orage's editorship, has provided much of the rationale for taking the journal's modernist sympathies for granted.

The most remarkable quotation Ardis brings forward in this context is from the editorial 'Readers and Writers' column for 13 November 1913. It defends the publication of Beatrice Hastings's parodies of Pound's 'The Approach to Paris', his review of French poetry that had begun in the *New Age* on 4 September:

Nobody, I suppose, thinks it odd that Mr. Belloc should write in THE NEW AGE in criticism of the National Guilds System, and nobody will think it odd if the editorial exponents of that system reply either currently or at the conclusion of the series. Why, then, should it be thought strange to publish Mr. Pound's articles and to subject them to criticism while they were still before our readers? But Mr. Pound, it will be said, was not attacking THE NEW AGE, he was only defending certain tendencies in French poetry. This view assumes too readily the eclecticism of THE NEW AGE which is much more apparent than real. We have, as discerning readers know, as serious and well-considered a "propaganda" in literature as in economics or politics. Why should it be supposed that the economic writers are jealous to maintain their views and to discredit their perversions or antitheses; and the critics of literature be indifferent? It will be found, if we all live long enough, that every part of THE NEW AGE hangs together, and that the literature we despise is associated with the economics we hate as the literature we love is associated with the form of society we would assist in creating. Mr. Pound – I say it with all respect – is the enemy of THE NEW AGE.[127]

This is a very strong statement against a regular *New Age* contributor, a figure who was also part of the *New Age* social circle. It is particularly arresting because, until the 'The Approach to Paris' series, very little notice had been

[126] Ardis, p. 144. Ardis quotes 'R.H.C.', 'Readers and Writers', *New Age*, 13 (1913), 393–5 (p. 395).
[127] 'R.H.C.', 'Readers and Writers', *New Age*, 14 (1913), 50–2 (p. 51).

taken of Pound, who restricted his contributions to his commissioned series, and rarely intervened in debates in the letters pages.[128]

However, closer inspection shows how Pound's criticism had positioned him as 'the enemy of THE NEW AGE'. One of the journal's major campaigns was for what it called a 'common-sense' criticism, which it saw as specifically English. Several regular columns were devoted to reviews, satires and opinions of contemporary critical writing, including J. C. Squire's 'The Practical Journalist' and 'Steps to Parnassus: Some Essentials of Criticism', the anonymously authored 'Present Day Criticism', Alfred E. Randall's 'Views and Reviews', and the 'Readers and Writers' column written by Orage, Beatrice Hastings and others.[129] Pound's 'Approach to Paris' series, like Carter's tributes to Bergson and Parisian art, is immediately suspect in its intense admiration for French, rather than English, culture, and Pound's statement in his first instalment that Parisian poets think 'with good cause that Paris is always at least twenty years ahead of all other "worlds of letters"' is highly provocative.[130] Indeed, the editorial group pre-emptively undermines the whole premise of Pound's series by reminding readers of the journal's stance the week before it begins: 'The notion that Paris is a sort of literary Mecca, a journey to which "saves" an author's style, is one of the superstitions of lower middle-class Englishmen (these include Americans)', 'R.H.C.' writes. 'The best preparation for writing great English is living in England and reading, writing, and, above all, talking, English.'[131]

Two weeks after 'The Approach to Paris' began, Beatrice Hastings, writing as 'T.K.L.', began weekly parodies of Pound's series. In her final parody, 'All except Anything', she summed up her objections. 'I have shown you', she has Pound say,

Remy de Gourmont, Imagiste; Vildrac, Humaniste; Tailharde [*sic*], Helleniste; Romains, Unanimiste, and others each one in his own unique way bent upon clarifying poetic diction, making a plain statement and scheduling his times for posterity. But to Jammes I allot a special niche upon the new Parnassus, for Jammes is more uniquely unique than – I had nearly said – than any other French poet, but we must conserve our plaudits – any of the above-mentioned unique poets; he

---

128 Between 30 November 1911, when the first instalment of 'I Gather the Limbs of Osiris' appeared, and 4 September 1913, when 'The Approach to Paris' began, Pound published only four non-commissioned items in the *New Age*: 'On the "Decline of Faith" [letter]', *New Age*, 10 (1911), 191, 'The Art of the Novel [letter]', *New Age*, 10 (1912), 311, 'The Black Crusade [letter]', *New Age*, 12 (1912), 69, 'The Black Crusade [letter]', *New Age*, 12 (1912), 116. He had also published one letter before 30 November 1911, 'A Correction', *New Age*, 6 (1910), 620.
129 'Readers and Writers', *New Age*, 13 (1913), 395–6 (p. 395).
130 'The Approach to Paris: 1', *New Age*, 13 (1913), 551–2.
131 'R.H.C.', 'Readers and Writers', *New Age*, 13 (1913), 513–14 (p. 513).

makes things more his own than I can express; he has perfected the new perfection of being a man in the street; he is your very ordinary self, your office-boy, your office, your telephone, your insurance card, and your stamp! He is the great eliminator of the abstract, the general, the universal, the essential, the transcendental – but he is the grand recorder of the Detail![132]

In this passage, the aspects of Pound's criticism Hastings is targeting come clearly into view. She satirises his pretentious labels ('Imagiste', 'Humaniste'), his emphasis on originality ('uniquely unique'), his over-writing ('perfected the new perfection'), his talking up of what seem to be everyday achievements ('he is your very ordinary self'), and his repetitions and tautologies ('the abstract, the general, the essential'). In the next issue 'R.H.C.' called the parodies 'a tour de force of amazing cleverness' which show that 'Mr. Pound's own English style is a pastiche of colloquy, slang, journalism and pedantry.'[133]

But Pound was not only failing to produce common-sense criticism. The final sentence of Hastings's parody highlights a set of values that go some way towards explaining the violence with which Pound is described as 'the enemy of THE NEW AGE'.[134] The *New Age* opposes the 'eliminator of [. . .] the general, the universal' and the 'recorder of Detail', who insists on what is 'uniquely unique', rather than what is shared, because these are the values of the individualist. Indeed, most of the poets Pound discussed were associated with the left-wing individualist Bergsonism promoted by Carter. In his instalment on Jules Romains, whose 'unanimist' exploration of the individual's intuition of a collective consciousness was one of the most influential literary responses to Bergson, Pound even remarked 'I, personally, may prefer the theory of the dominant cell, a slightly Nietzschean biology, to any collectivist theories whatsoever.'[135] But for the *New Age*, 'Individualism and "thinking for one's self" inevitably lead to chaos in artistry or handicrafts', as J. M. Kennedy had written in an earlier issue. His quotation from A. J. Penty, a key contributor to Guild Socialism, framed modern art as antithetical to the journal's ideology: 'traditional ways of working [. . .] were universally recognised, so that when the craftsman was called to design he was not, like his modern successor, compelled to create something out of nothing, but had this tradition ready to hand as the

---

[132] 'T.K.L.', 'All except Anything', *New Age*, 13 (1913), pp. 733–4.
[133] 'R.H.C.', 'Readers and Writers', *New Age*, 13 (1913), 761–3 (p. 761).
[134] 'R.H.C.', 'Readers and Writers', p. 51.
[135] On Romains's Bergsonism, see Antliff, *Inventing Bergson*, pp. 40, 57; 'The Approach to Paris, III', *New Age*, 13 (1913), 607–9 (p. 608).

vehicle of expression understood by all'.[136] Pound could hardly be described as anti-traditional, but that makes the fact that he is characterised as such in the *New Age* all the more revealing.

However, the *New Age*'s linking of Pound to individualism was not made solely on the basis of the 'Approach to Paris' series; it was his association with the *New Freewoman* that appears to have generated this reading of his criticism's submerged politics. Pound's individualism, in its loosest sense, could have been observed in his earlier articles, as could the 'pastiche of colloquy, slang, journalism and pedantry' that made up his critical style. If one wanted to attack Pound for his preference for detail over abstraction, 'I Gather the Limbs of Osiris' provided an earlier opportunity. Imagism, too, was a known quantity before September 1913, yet no direct criticism of it had appeared in the *New Age*.[137] But Pound's new involvement in the *New Freewoman* and the publication of 'The Serious Artist', which had appeared the day before the last instalment of 'The Approach to Paris', sharpened perception of the ideological investments of both his criticism and his poetry, and unleashed a wave of satire. Thus, it was not until 6 November that Edward Moore contributed a pastiche of 'Salutation', published in the *New Freewoman* nearly three months before, accusing it of superficiality and insincerity: 'To weave vain words your only aim/ Meaningless words as in a game.'[138] On 27 November 'E.A.B.' castigated 'Portrait d'une Femme', first published in *Ripostes* a year before, as 'shreds and tatters' that 'are the fruits of Unanism [*sic*], paroxysm, cliqueism and all these wonderful discoveries of Mr. Pound's Parisian year'.[139]

Just as the *New Freewoman*'s interpretation of the visual arts facilitated a positive reading of Pound's poetic and critical project, so in the *New Age* the highly charged debates about contemporary art consolidated the terms by which Pound was criticised. The French poets Pound advocated were closely associated with cubism, and while the *New Age* was by no means consistently averse to contemporary art, it was not as positive as

---

[136] J. M. Kennedy, 'Toryism and Social Reform', *New Age*, 9 (1911), 490–1 (p. 491). Kennedy quotes Arthur J. Penty, *The Restoration of the Gild System* (London: Swan Sonnenschein, 1906), p. 49.

[137] 'The Complete Poetical Works of T. E. Hulme' in *Ripostes* were satirised in the journal's 'Pastiche' column, despite the fact that they had first appeared there: see 'Pastiche. Epigrams: Manners Series: To Mr. T. E. Hulme', *New Age*, 12 (1913), p. 212. The journal also satirised poetry related to imagism, yet conspicuously did not target the imagists themselves: see 'Literary Notes', *New Age*, 12 (1913), 555–6 (p. 555) and P. Selver, 'Pastiche. A Phantasmagoria, Being the Lamentable Result of Perusing Modern French Poetry', *New Age*, 13 (1913), p. 368.

[138] Edward Moore, 'Pastiche. Salutation', *New Age*, 14 (1913), 25–6 (p. 26).

[139] 'E.A.B', 'Readers and Writers: American Notes', *New Age*, 14 (1913), 113–15 (p. 114).

some critics have suggested.[140] It was particularly distrustful of what it saw as contemporary art's emphasis on technical experiment at the expense of broader social issues: Orage's oft-reiterated belief that artists should stall the 'spread of ugliness' in England, and 'devote their lives to making beauty prevail, live for beauty, if necessary, starve for beauty' is characteristic of the journal's Ruskinian socialism.[141]

By the time the *New Age*'s attack on Pound had begun in September 1913, its art criticism had become considerably more conservative than during the period of Carter's contributions. Carter's replacement was Anthony Ludovici, who, like Orage, insistently connected aesthetic taste to social theory, deploring as 'recklessly stupid' the prevalent conception 'that a moral attitude which condones anarchy and chaos in scenery' has 'no bearing on our attitude towards life'. Consequently, Ludovici's columns are frequently preoccupied with finding some form of 'meaning' in art, as, for example, when he recommends that four paintings exhibited in Henry Bishop's one-man show at the Goupil Gallery should be cropped because 'unless a sky conveys some message [. . .] it is trite to extend it indefinitely up the canvas'. Almost all post-impressionist art, 'from the innovations of the Pointillistes to the revolting anarchy of the Futurists', is denigrated for being 'a matter of a new technique'. For Ludovici, the lamentable state of contemporary art was a consequence of 'the march of uncontrolled commerce and industry' that had erased 'the distinction between artist and business men [*sic*]': The 'stampede in search of pure novelty for novelty's sake [. . .] that the vulgar can understand' disdains the genuine novelty of 'a new quality, a new virtue, or an old one resuscitated to sudden perfection', he complains, 'it must be a mere trick of the brush or of the pen, a simple new feat of legerdemain, which every smoke-sodden suburbanite can comprehend at a glance'.[142]

Ludovici's argument shows how Pound could be positioned against the *New Age*, even while he sympathised with a number of its tenets. Pound, after all, also disapproved of 'the march of uncontrolled commerce and industry', and he also saw the artist as a potential regenerator of a degraded

---

[140] Martin, p. 185. For the connections between Bergsonian poets and painters, see Antliff, *Inventing Bergson*, pp. 16–66.

[141] [A. R. Orage], 'Unedited Opinions', *New Age*, 9 (1911), 510–11 (p. 511).

[142] Anthony M. Ludovici, 'Art: Raw Material at the Dudley Galleries', *New Age*, 13 (1913), 703–4 (p. 704); 'Art: The Carfax, the Grosvenor, and the Goupil Galleries', *New Age*, 13 (1913), p. 273; 'The New English Art Club and the Chenil Gallery: 1', *New Age*, 12 (1913), p. 260; 'The Poster-Impressionist Exhibition', *New Age*, 13 (1913), 521–2 (p. 521); 'Art: Over Production in the Graphic Arts', *New Age*, 13 (1913), 638–9 (p. 638).

society. But, at the same time, his insistence on artistic originality could be read as a repudiation of tradition and a marketing of novelties, and his focus on the individual artist's poetic technique could be read as a downgrading of the social dimension of craft. Pound's turn away from his highly wrought and erudite early poetry, with its demonstrated knowledge of poetic tradition, towards the ironic conversational gambits that formed much of his 'Contemporania' sequence, his deployment of an advertising programme superficially reminiscent of the 'commercial' futurist and post-impressionist movements, and his involvement in an individualist anarchist magazine, struck the *New Age* as a capitulation to exactly the values against which it was constructed.

VORTICIST CRITICISM

The *New Age*'s criticism of 'The Approach to Paris' was only the beginning of its very public antipathy towards Pound; during 1914 and 1915 it consistently ridiculed and lampooned his work, especially that which promoted imagism and vorticism. To the contributors and readers of the *New Age*, these movements appeared to develop the aspects of French poetry and art that they found most objectionable: originality, individualism, technical virtuosity, and commercialism.[143] Furthermore, Pound had now given the *New Age* extra grounds for animosity: his criticism was finally taking up the cause of contemporary art directly, and what is more, it was doing so in the *Egoist*, in direct opposition to the art criticism published in the *New Age*.

Although Pound's published and unpublished writings had long engaged with the visual arts, it was not until 16 February 1914 that he published his first article of art criticism. This was 'The New Sculpture', a response to T. E. Hulme's lecture to the Quest Society on 22 January 1914 on 'The New Art and Its Philosophy'.[144] The article's slightly wider context is the debate in the *New Age* that had begun with Hulme's notoriously insulting response to Ludovici's derogatory review of Epstein's exhibition at the Twenty-One Gallery. When one reads Pound's art criticism in the *Egoist* in relation to the debates in the *New Age*, it emerges as a more politically engaged discussion of art than is usually understood.

---

[143] See Paige Reynolds, '"Chaos Invading Concept": *Blast* as a Native Theory of Promotional Culture', *Twentieth Century Literature*, 46 (2000), 238–68 (pp. 254–8).

[144] Letter to Isabel Weston Pound, [23 January 1914], EPP, Beinecke, 60.2673; Hulme's lecture was first published in T. E. Hulme, *Speculations: Essays on Humanism and the Philosophy of Art*, ed. Herbert Read (London: Kegan Paul, Trench, Trubner, 1924), pp. 75–109 under the title 'Modern Art and Its Philosophy', the title also adopted by Csengeri in Hulme, *Collected Writings*, pp. 268–85.

3 Jacob Epstein, *Figure in Flenite* (1913)

The Twenty-One Gallery was exhibiting Epstein's most recent primitivist work, including *Female Figure in Flenite* (1913), *Figure in Flenite* (1913) (fig. 3), *Doves: First Version* (1913), *Doves: Second Version* (1913), and two drawings of the *Rock Drill* (1913–15).[145] To Ludovici, Epstein's work was the epitome of modern decadence: 'when the plastic arts can no longer interpret the external world in the terms of a great order or scheme of life, owing to the fact that all great schemes or orders are dead, they exalt the idiosyncrasy or individual angle of the isolated ego', he wrote. Such art can only have interest for 'cranks and people who have some reason of their own in abetting or supporting purposeless individualism à out rance'.[146] Hulme, however, saw Epstein's work as representative of a new anti-humanist *Weltanschauung* that had a profound sympathy with what he termed the 'attitude' of pre-Renaissance cultures, like Byzantium and ancient Egypt. In his reply to Ludovici, 'Mr. Epstein and the Critics', Hulme drew on his recent discovery of Alois Riegl's and Wilhelm Worringer's art history to argue that Epstein's geometric style was neither idiosyncratic, nor the product of slavish imitation of primitive models, but rather the inevitable result of expressing the same emotions as those models: 'Man remaining constant, there are certain broad ways in which certain emotions must, and will always naturally be expressed, and these we must call formulae. They constitute a constant and permanent alphabet. The thing to notice is that the use of these broad formulae has nothing to do with the possession of or lack of individuality of the artist.'[147]

Hulme's article drew substantial attention from the *New Age*'s readers, less for its argument than for its aggressive attack on Ludovici: Hulme had called him 'a little Cockney intellect' best dealt with by 'a little personal violence'. Ardis quotes the outraged letters and witty parodies at length and it is not necessary to repeat them here.[148] Ludovici's own response to Hulme was to develop his argument against artistic individualism. In his long and diffuse 'An Open Letter to My Friends' he warned that 'this anarchy in painting and sculpture is only a forecast of what the most disintegrating and most dissolvent influences of modern times are accomplishing and

---

[145] Silber, *The Sculpture of Epstein*, pp. 133–5; Richard Cork, *Vorticism and Abstract Art in the First Machine Age*, II: 467.

[146] Anthony M. Ludovici, 'Art. The Carfax, the Suffolk Street, and the Twenty-One Galleries', *New Age*, 14 (1913), 213–15 (pp. 214–15).

[147] T. E. Hulme, 'Mr. Epstein and the Critics', *New Age*, 14 (1913), 251–3 (p. 251). Hulme first encountered Riegl's and Worringer's work in Paul Ernst's 'Die Stilarten in der Kunst' (1912), in *Der Weg zur Form: Abhandlungen über die Technik vornehmlich der Tragödie und Novelle* (Munich: Müller, 1928), pp. 301–11: see Hulme, *Collected Writings*, p. 271.

[148] Hulme, 'Mr. Epstein and the Critics', p. 252; Ardis, pp. 150–1.

will ultimately try to achieve in every other department of life'. Thus far, Ludovici was rehearsing a typical *New Age* argument. But his solution to the anarchic strain in modern life turned out to be a Nietzschean adherence to 'the hierarchical principle', where a select few establish a 'sound flourishing life' through their superior ability in the 'process of selecting and rejecting correctly'. The artist has a relatively lowly position in Ludovici's vision of 'a great order or scheme of life': '[the artist] is essentially a dependent – a dependent upon the superior man who is the artist or poet legislator'.[149]

Orage initially put a certain editorial weight behind Ludovici's review. He remarked that 'Mr. T. E. Hulme [had] constructed an imposing myth' to explain Epstein's carvings, but that it was 'rigmarole, I say, rigmarole'. As the debate developed, however, Hulme appeared to be better served by the journal than Ludovici. 'Mr. Epstein and the Critics' had been supported by the reproduction of one of Epstein's *Rock Drill* studies and, from 15 January, the journal began to publish Hulme's art criticism, the 'Modern Art' and 'Contemporary Drawings' series, which explicitly undermined Ludovici's criticism. At the same time, Orage, in the guise of 'R.H.C.', began to contest Ludovici's hierarchical theory of culture in the 'Readers and Writers' column.[150]

Although Ludovici and Hulme differed in their estimation of Epstein's work, their more general perspectives on art were in fact not diametrically opposed. Under the influence of the classicist *Action Française* group, Hulme, like Ludovici, deplored self-expression without the disciplining pressure of 'a superior order common both to himself and his fellow-men', as Ludovici put it.[151] Ludovici's argument was more directly opposed to the expressivism articulated in the *New Freewoman* by Carter and, subsequently, Pound. The polemical moves of Pound's 'The New Sculpture' should be read as a component of the *New Freewoman*'s cultural theory, which, since the beginning of 1914, at just the point when the *New Freewoman* became the *Egoist*, had culminated in a series of articles supporting the artworks the *New Age* was simultaneously denigrating. On 1 January, Wyndham Lewis made his first appearance in the *Egoist* as author of 'The Cubist Room', reprinted from the catalogue to the Brighton *Exhibition of the Work of English Post Impressionists, Cubists and others*, praising Epstein as 'the only great sculptor at present working in England, and calling for the public to 'change entirely their idea of the painter's mission, and penetrate,

---

[149] Anthony M. Ludovici, 'An Open Letter to My Friends', *New Age*, 14 (1914), 278–81 (pp. 281, 280).
[150] 'R.H.C.', 'Readers and Writers', *New Age*, 14 (1914), 306–8 (p. 307); 'R.H.C.', 'Readers and Writers', *New Age*, 14 (1914), 338–40 (p. 339).
[151] Ludovici, 'An Open Letter to My Friends', p. 281.

deferentially, with him into a transposed universe, as abstract as, though different from, the musicians'. In the same issue, Richard Aldington praised Lewis's *Timon of Athens* portfolio (1913). Carter's new series, 'The Public Ownership of the Artist', argued vigorously that the artist had been 'devitalised by a social system of which he is a part and which has reduced him to slavery', and must be 're-individualise[d]'. On 2 February, readers were told of Pound's and Aldington's trip to see the ageing poet, Wilfred Scawen Blunt, for whom Gaudier-Brzeska had carved a 'reliquary of Pentelican marble' to memorialise the occasion. In the issue which saw Pound's debut as an art critic, Carter contributed an essay that related his theory of rhythm, now named 'mass rhythm', to Epstein, Arnold Schoenberg and, somewhat surprisingly, G. K. Chesterton.[152]

'The New Sculpture' is of a piece with the *Egoist*'s stance on contemporary art. Pound evidently found Hulme's and Worringer's oppositions useful in articulating his admiration for Epstein's work; he draws attention to their distinction between vital and geometric art, and he repeats Hulme's correlation between this opposition and that of humanism and anti-humanism. But he is conspicuously uninterested in Hulme's and Worringer's theory that artistic style is related to a society's attitude towards its environment. Where Hulme's major point had been that the 're-emergence of geometrical art may be the precursor of the re-emergence of the corresponding attitude towards the world, and so, of the break up of the Renaissance humanistic attitude', Pound has the artist able to choose either a humanist or anti-humanist attitude: 'one might regard the body either as a sensitized receiver of sensations, or as an instrument for carrying out the decrees of the will (or expressioning the soul, or whatever you choose to term it). These two views are opposed and produce two totally opposed theories of æsthetic.' Although he writes that he 'got himself disliked' for making this statement, his supposed attempt to 'tri[m]' his words to the wind' and bring his remarks into closer relation to Hulme's lecture only repeats his collapse of Hulme's and Worringer's teleology: 'you could believe that man was the perfect creature, or creator, or lord of the universe or what you will, and that there was no beauty to surpass the beauty of man or of man as conceived by the late Sir Lawrence Alma-Tadema; or that on the contrary you could

[152] Wyndham Lewis, 'The Cubist Room', *Egoist*, 1 (1914), 8–9 (p. 9), see also the praise of Epstein in Horace Holley's 'Epstein's Oscar Wilde Monument: An Interpretation', *Egoist*, 1 (1914), 30–31, and John Cournos's 'The Battle of the Cubes', *New Freewoman*, 1 (1913), 214–15; Richard Aldington, 'Books, Drawings, and Papers', *Egoist*, 1 (1914), 10–12; Huntly Carter, 'The Public Ownership of the Artist', *Egoist*, 1 (1914), 32–4 (p. 33–4); Richard Aldington, 'Presentation to Mr. W. S. Blunt', *Egoist*, 1 (1914), 56–7 (p. 56); Huntly Carter, 'Schönberg, Epstein, Chesterton and Mass-Rhythm', *Egoist*, 1 (1914), 75–6.

believe in something beyond man, something important enough to be fed with the blood of hecatombs'.[153]

Pound's artist, unlike Hulme's and Worringer's, is not representative of the culture's *Weltanschauung*: the artist is an individual who is profoundly *un*representative. So although Pound begins the second section of his article echoing Hulme ('The artist has been for so long a humanist!'), and even seems to be making the same argument ('The artist recognises his life in the terms of the Tahitian savage'), by the end of the article it has emerged that the artist is not at war with 'his' environment, but with the public: 'The artist', writes Pound, 'has been at peace with his oppressors for long enough. He has dabbled in democracy and he is now done with that folly.' Here the influence of the *Egoist* becomes clear: like Carter, Pound calls for an 'aristocracy of the arts': 'we artists who have been so long the despised are about to take over', he writes. And like Carter, he repudiates the notion of artistic responsibility, so dear to the heart of the *New Age* and central to Ludovici's 'hierarchical principle': 'The artist [. . .] has had enough sense to know that humanity was unbearably stupid and that he must try to disagree with it. But he has also tried to lead and persuade it; to save it from itself. [. . .] The artist has at last been aroused to the fact that the war between him and the world is a war without truce.' One consequence of this war between artist and 'the world' is that, like Carter again, Pound's art criticism refuses to interpret artworks, or even make them intelligible: 'Art is to be admired rather than explained. The jargon of these sculptors is beyond me. I do not know precisely why I admire a green, granite, female, apparently pregnant monster with one eye going around a square corner.'[154]

Pound's first published art criticism is therefore explicitly anti-democratic and individualist. Only certain individuals can produce art and appreciate art. Such individuals are not characterised by their knowledge, but by their intuitive appreciation. Consequently, art criticism can only point out good art, it cannot inspire appreciation in a non-artistic sensibility. On the other hand, as in his first literary articles in *Book News Monthly*, Pound's emphasis on intuitive appreciation removes art from the exclusive Academy and well-educated connoisseurs, and makes it available to the untrained. While this anti-democratic criticism argues that not everyone is responsive to art, responsiveness is at least not measured by class or wealth.

---

[153] Hulme, *Collected Writings*, p. 269; 'The New Sculpture', p. 67.
[154] 'The New Sculpture', p. 68. The sculpture to which Pound refers here is *Figure in Flenite* (1913) (fig. 3).

After the appearance of 'The New Sculpture', Pound continued to promote Epstein's work and he also became a vocal advocate of the artists
associated with Lewis's Rebel Art Centre, especially the future vorticists,
Gaudier-Brzeska, Wadsworth and Lewis himself. Over the course of the following year, during which he made his most important statements about
vorticist art, Pound developed a formal vocabulary that not only gave his art
criticism more authoritative weight, but also, as Ronald Bush has discussed,
informed his poetic practice.[155] Having keenly felt his lack of appropriate
vocabulary in 'The New Sculpture', his next article on contemporary art,
'Exhibition at the Goupil Gallery', introduced terms that attempted to
describe the works more precisely, although they were still marked by some
anxiety. This review contained the notoriously unsuccessful description of
Gaudier's animal sculptures as having 'a "snuggly," comfortable feeling', but
it also managed slightly more successful, if somewhat obscure, descriptions,
such as 'the planes of Mr. Epstein's work seem to sink away from their
outline with a curious determination and swiftness', and '[Wadsworth's]
"Radiation" [. . .] is the "pictorial equivalent" of a foundry as perceived –
and there is no need to ridicule these terms before having considered them –
as perceived by the retina of the intelligence'.[156]

By the beginning of the following year, when the 'Affirmations' series was
published in the *New Age*, Pound had settled on a more stable set of terms,
drawing on what he called the 'musical conception of form, that is to say the
understanding that you can use form as a musician uses sound, that you can
select motives of form from the forms before you, that you can recombine
and recolour them and "organise" them into new form'.[157] By pinpointing a
musical origin for the terms, he emphasised his vocabulary's lineage through
Whistler's 'arrangements', Binyon's explication of the importance of rhythm
in Chinese aesthetics, and Carter's art criticism in the *Egoist*. Pound now
defined painting as 'an arrangement of colour patches on a canvas', he
had derived the terms 'masses' and 'planes' from Gaudier's review of the
1914 Allied Artists' Association exhibition and from his 'Vortex. Gaudier
Brzeska' manifesto in *Blast*, and he developed the concept of 'pattern-units,
or units of design' first in relation to Wyndham Lewis and subsequently to
describe imagism.[158]

[155] Ronald Bush, *The Genesis of Ezra Pound's* Cantos, rev. edn (Princeton, NJ: Princeton University
Press, 1989), pp. 37–45.
[156] 'Exhibition at the Goupil Gallery', *Egoist*, 1 (1914), p. 109.
[157] 'Affirmations, II: Vorticism', *New Age*, 16 (1915), 277–8 (p. 278).
[158] Henri Gaudier-Brzeska, 'Allied Artists' Association Ltd.: Holland Park Hall', *Egoist*, 1 (1914), 227–9
(p. 227), 'Vortex. Gaudier Brzeska', *Blast*, 1 (1914), 155–8 (p. 155); 'Wyndham Lewis', *Egoist*, 1 (1914),
233–4 (p. 233); 'Affirmations, IV: As for Imagisme', *New Age*, 16 (1915), 349–50 (p. 349).

Pound's terminology is not categorically different from that used by other proponents of the new art. In his 'Modern Art' and 'Contemporary Drawings' series, Hulme discussed the same group of artists and his discussion of the 'new constructive geometrical art' in terms of 'a certain simplification of planes', a 'sense of form', and, most consistently, 'relation between planes' draws on a closely related vocabulary.[159] Both Hulme's and Pound's criticism is indebted to Fry's: just two paragraphs of one of Fry's reviews supply the influential phrases, 'simplification of forms', 'rhythm of life', 'lines of movement', 'sequences of mass', and 'colour oppositions'.[160] But if the terminology is not distinct, the trajectory of Pound's articles does differ from that of other reviewers. The predominant concern for Fry, Bell and Hulme was to ascertain the relation between form and emotional effect, or 'aesthetic emotion', to use Bell's phrase.[161] Pound, by contrast, is more interested in the emotions and conceptions that create aesthetic form; he is more interested, in short, in the artist than the audience. As a result, his vocabulary tends to be directed towards highlighting the artist's creativity and intelligence, so the weight of his formulations falls less on the forms and their effects, than it does on the active 'arrangement' or 'organisation' of forms. The 'organisation of form and colour is "expression"; just as a musical arrangement of notes by Mozart is expression', he writes, 'the vorticist is expressing his complex consciousness'.[162]

To the *New Age*, however, both Pound's art criticism and vorticism itself were complicating entirely commonplace ideas. Beatrice Hastings took up her pen once more to ridicule the 'Affirmations' series, cheered on by the journal's readers; not a single reader wrote in to support Pound. Her, and their, chief objection was to Pound's terminology and what they interpreted as its claims to novelty. Hastings called Pound's arguments 'fiddling with terms', and maintained that 'the state of things in Art which Mr. Pound deplores is somewhat due to just such florid, pedantic, obscurantist critics as himself [. . .]. The main reason for the helplessness of artists during the past century is the subjection of all other ideas to the idea of commercial

---

[159] T. E. Hulme, 'Modern Art, I: The Grafton Group', *New Age*, 14 (1914), 341–2 (p. 341), 'Modern Art, II: A Preface Note and Neo-Realism', *New Age*, 14 (1914), 467–9 (p. 290), 'Modern Art, IV: Mr. David Bomberg's Show', *New Age*, 15 (1914), 230–2, 'Contemporary Drawings', *New Age*, 14 (1914), p. 821.

[160] Fry, 'The Allied Artists', pp. 676–7.

[161] Bell, *Art*, p. 7. In his later art criticism Hulme explicitly repudiated the concept of a 'specific aesthetic emotion', probably in reaction against Bell. Nevertheless, his focus remained the relation between form and emotion; he simply described the emotion aroused by form as 'ordinary everyday human' [i.e. not aesthetic] emotion 'produced in a different way'. See Hulme, 'Modern Art, IV: Mr. David Bomberg's Show', p. 231.

[162] 'Affirmations, II: Vorticism', pp. 188.

prosperity.' She drew attention to the repetition and lack of specificity of Pound's vocabulary by applying it to ancient Egyptian sculpture, 'Rameses, a mass, sits upon a mass in a position possible to the human form. His skull is not twisted so as to oblige you to search for it underneath his shoulders; but most different from all Vorticist arrangements of masses, out of relation, he has a face, and a face the arranged masses of which express remarkable human intellectual force.'[163] In the letters pages, John Riddle claimed, 'If Mr. Pound has given us anything, he has given us a muddle'; 'Schiffsbauer' parodied Pound, 'the economic world is confronted with a stupendous phenomenon, called Ordinariness, which I am, for the first or last time, incarnated to proclaim over all the earth'; John Duncan sent instructions, 'Be clear, Mr, Pound. Never say exiguous for narrow; nor talk of the intellectually-inventive-creative spirit when you mean what Englishmen once called wit, quick-parts and fancy' and Constantia Stone complained, 'Sir, – There are phrases in Mr. Ezra Pound's "As for Imagisme" that I do not understand. He says: "Energy creates pattern." But is not everything created by energy, or, to phrase it more carefully, is not everything created by means of energy? Therefore, Mr. Pound's statement tells us nothing about "Pattern," unless he has a special meaning for "energy," in which case he ought to give us a definition.'[164]

What this avalanche of criticism suggests is that while Pound's terms themselves are not particularly unusual, the weight he makes them carry is. Whereas Fry's criticism, for example, deploys words like 'mass' and 'plane' descriptively and relatively neutrally, in Pound's criticism such words are so frequently repeated, and endowed with such a heavy positive valence that the subject matter buckles under their weight. As Pound develops his critical framework for vorticist art he makes these terms carry a defining force and his readers, understandably, question their validity. As Hastings's connection between Pound's criticism and art's craving for 'commercial prosperity' makes clear, a recurrent concern is that Pound's promotion of vorticist art appears too closely related to the empty rhetoric of advertising merchants.

The *New Age* was particularly suspicious of Pound's explanation of the correlation between imagist poetry and vorticist painting and sculpture. In September 1914, when the *Fortnightly Review* published Pound's 'Vorticism',

---

[163] 'Alice Morning' [Beatrice Hastings], 'Impressions of Paris, [I]', *New Age*, 16 (1915), pp. 308–9; 'Impressions of Paris, [V]', *New Age*, 16 (1915), 425–6 (p. 425).

[164] John Riddle, 'Vorticism [letter]', *New Age*, 16 (1915), p. 327, 'Schiffsbauer', 'Vorticism [letter]', *New Age*, 16 (1915), p. 350, John Duncan, 'Vorticism [letter]', *New Age*, 16 (1915), p. 415, Constantia Stone, 'Imagisme [letter]', *New Age*, 16 (1915), p. 390.

his most important statement of interdisciplinary aesthetics in this period, 'R.H.C.' ridiculed Pound's attempt to establish a connection between vorticist art and imagist poetry: 'As usual, he is very obscure and the more so for the pains he takes to disguise the real relations. I imagine myself that the only connection between the two was due to the accident of friendliness. Mr. Pound happened to like Mr. Wyndham Lewis, and there you are!'[165] In the 'Pastiche' column the following month, Lazarus Aaronson satirised Pound and Hulme in 'A Faery Tale': Hulme is depicted as a 'male-goblin' who dislikes nature and bright colours, Pound appears as a 'very foolish male-faery' who 'was so fond of colour and [. . .] had such a little soul that he could not bear subtleties of tone and shade':

After a while he came to a place of many streets and many people; but they were all sombrely dressed. Once he saw a red tie . . . and was nearly converted to Socialism by it. . . . After much walking he came upon a very wide road rolling out along a river . . . and here were wonderful colours [. . .]. And he clapped his hands and shouted with glee. He nearly forgot his hunger. Later he came to an underground railway station and there he saw brightly-painted advertisements . . . and the women were so loudly dressed: he almost forgave them their black shoes and white faces.
   So he became an utter imbecile, and a painter à la mode Kandinsky, and in his spare time he painted advertisement posters.[166]

The description of Pound seduced by an array of 'wonderful colours', rather than the single 'red tie' of socialism, portrays him as superficial in his political commitments and attracted to chaos, rather than order – a typical contemporary distinction between anarchy and socialism. Furthermore, it reads Pound's poetry through this politics. The centrepiece of 'Vorticism' is Pound's famous account of the composition of 'In a Station of the Metro', first published the previous year as the epiphanic moment that concluded Pound's contribution to the regular 'How I Began' column in *T.P.'s Weekly*. Its republication, however, involved some strategic changes. Both versions begin by recounting Pound's experience in the Paris Métro of seeing 'a beautiful face, and then, turning suddenly, another and another', and the difficulty of finding words for 'what this made me feel'. In the first version, Pound then remarked that, walking home along the rue Raynouard, 'I could get nothing but spots of colour. I remember thinking that if I had been a painter I might have started a wholly new school of painting'; he tried to write a poem instead, 'but found it useless' until, 'well over a year'

[165] 'R.H.C.', 'Readers and Writers', *New Age*, 15 (1914), p. 449.
[166] L. Aaronson, 'A Faery Tale', *New Age*, 15 (1914), p. 553.

later, he realised that he could 'make a very little poem' as one might in Japan. 'And there, or in some other very old, very quiet civilisation', he concluded, 'some one else might understand the significance.'[167]

In the second version, mention of the Japanese model is delayed for several pages, and Pound instead introduces a markedly contemporary referent. His walk home along the rue Raynouard is presented as more rewarding in this account: 'I found, suddenly, the expression. I do not mean that I found words, but there came an equation . . . not in speech, but in little splotches of colour. It was just that – a "pattern," or hardly a pattern, if by "pattern" you mean something with a "repeat" in it. But it was a word, the begin-ning, for me, of a language in colour.' The 'new school of painting' that Pound imagined founding can, in this version, be described. It would be a school 'of "non-representative" painting, a painting that would speak only by arrangements in colour', a school, in fact, based on ideas the expression-ist painter Wassily Kandinsky had set out in his recently translated *Über das Geistige in der Kunst*. Pound frames his story with a testimony to the correlation between Kandinsky's ideas and his own: 'The image is the poet's pigment; with that in mind you can go ahead and apply Kandinsky, you can transpose his chapter on the language of form and colour and apply it to the writing of verse', he begins, and he concludes, 'when I came to read Kandinsky's chapter on the language of form and colour, I found lit-tle that was new to me. I only felt that someone else understood what I understood, and had written it out very clearly.' In this version, the relation between painting and writing has become much closer – too close, in fact: 'my experience in Paris should have gone into paint [. . .]. Colour was, in that instance, the "primary pigment".'[168]

The enthusiasm of this account belies Pound's short-lived interest in Kandinsky, but it is indicative of the artist's influence on the English avant-garde in 1914.[169] Kandinsky had been regularly exhibiting at the Allied Artists' Association since 1909 and included in Fry's 'Grafton Group' show at the Alpine Club Gallery.[170] Since its first publication in 1912, *Über das Geistige in der Kunst* had attracted attention amongst the avant-garde, but

---

[167] 'How I Began', *T. P.'s Weekly*, 21 (1913), p. 707.　　　[168] 'Vorticism', pp. 465–6.

[169] 'Affirmations, II: Vorticism', p. 278: 'I think [Wyndham Lewis is] a more significant artist than Kandinsky (admitting that I have not yet seen enough of Kandinsky's work to use a verb stronger than "think")', and *L/JQ*, 63: 'No, I don't think Kandinsky the last word. He starts out with some few sane propositions, but when it comes to saying "blue = God, pink = devil", etc. etc. we do *not* follow.' See Michael Faherty, 'The Third Dimension: Ezra Pound and Wassily Kandinsky', *Paideuma*, 21.3 (1992), 63–77.

[170] Gruetzner Robins, pp. 130, 133. See also Gail Levin and Marianne Lorenz, *Theme and Improvisation: Kandinsky and the American Avant-Garde, 1912–1950* (New York: Little, Brown, 1992), pp. 10–63.

it was Michael Sadler's 1914 translation of the treatise as *The Art of Spiritual Harmony* that confirmed Kandinsky's reputation as 'the most extreme man not only of Münich but of the entire modern art movement'.[171] Kandinsky represented contemporary art's most complete break with representation, and his delineation of the spiritual properties of modern art provided a welcome alternative for those, like Carter and Pound amongst many others, who found a purely formalist interpretation reductive. In the *Egoist*, Carter recommended the book as 'containing the most daring and revolutionary among present-day aesthetic theories of spiritual import', and compared it favourably to Bell's *Art*, which he thought wrongly 'represents Art as a provocative agent external to man and not as a power seated in the human soul'.[172] In this light, Pound's claim that he 'found little that was new to me' in Kandinsky's book is less immodest than it sounds: Kandinsky's theory of 'innere Notwendigkeit', translated by Sadler as 'inner need', could be read as a more systematic version of the vitalist, Platonic and so-called 'cosmic' theories of art in circulation.[173] Reviewers, including Edward Wadsworth in *Blast*, found it straightforward to assimilate and contextualise the work.[174]

A further advantage of Kandinsky's theory of 'inner need' over Bell's 'significant form' was that it seemed to apply not only to the turn towards abstraction in painting, but the attempt to move beyond the limitations of other media as well. 'Music, poetry, painting, architecture are all able in their different way to reach the essential soul, and the coming era will see them brought together, mutually striving to the great attainment', wrote Sadler in his review of *Über das Geistige in der Kunst* in *Rhythm* in 1912.[175] The visual sense is accorded a significant place in this process: for Kandinsky, 'Shades of colour, like those of sound, are of a much finer texture and awake in the soul emotions too fine to be expressed in words. Certainly each tone will find some probable expression in words, but it will always be incomplete, and that part which the word fails to express will not be unimportant but rather the very kernel of its existence. For this reason words are, and will always remain, only hints, mere suggestions of

---

[171] Wassily Kandinsky, *The Art of Spiritual Harmony*, trans. M. T. H. Sadler (London: Constable, 1914), pp. 85–6; Arthur Jerome Eddy, *Cubists and Post-Impressionism* (Chicago: McClurg, 1914), p. 115.
[172] Huntly Carter, 'New Books on Art', *Egoist*, 1 (1914), 235–6 (p. 236).
[173] Kandinsky, *The Art of Spiritual Harmony*, p. 52.
[174] Edward Wadsworth, 'Inner Necessity', *Blast*, 1 (1914), 119–25.
[175] M. T. H. Sadler, 'After Gauguin', *Rhythm*, 4 (1912), 23–9 (p. 25). Even Fry remarked 'I wish he [Bell] had extended his theory, and taken literature (in so far as it is an art) into fuller consideration [. . .]. Song, again, would appear to be in exactly the same position as painting as ordinarily understood' ('A New Theory of Art', p. 938).

colours.'[176] For Pound, too, the emotions he experienced coming out of the Paris Métro are first apprehended as 'spots' or 'splotches' of colour, an instinctive visual language that precedes words, which acts as a mediating stage between the experience and the poem. But while the spots and splotches may call to mind impressionism or neo-impressionism or even the Byzantine-influenced British post-impressionists, Pound is emphatic that imagism is not a response to any school of painting. The point of his anecdote is that imagist poetry aims to achieve the intensity and immediacy of seeing.

Kandinsky's anarchist associations also made his writings an appropriate gloss on imagism. Although Pound may have not known of Kandinsky's anarchist leanings, and neither the *Egoist* nor the *New Age* remark upon them, Rose-Carol Washton Long has argued that the theory of inner need, long understood theosophically, also 'reflects a central anarchist tenet that an underlying law of nature or truth lies hidden beneath the artificial structures imposed on mankind by established, authoritarian systems'.[177] In 'On the Question of Form' (1912) in the *Blaue Reiter Almanac*, Kandinsky specifically remarks that 'Many call the present state of painting "anarchy." [. . .] It is thought, incorrectly, to mean unplanned upheaval and disorder. But anarchy is regularity and order created not by an external and ultimately powerless force, but by *the feeling for the good*.'[178] It is precisely the expressivist aspects of Kandinsky's theory, so fundamental to the interdisciplinary work it does in 'Vorticism', in which its anarchist potential lies.

Thus far, I have argued that imagism came to be associated with individualist anarchism largely through its connection with Marsden's journal, its use of free verse and predilection for French poetry, and also its emphasis on its own 'absor[ption] in matters of writerly technique', that is, the aspect of its project that recent critical opinion has interpreted as evidence of its lack of politics.[179] These associations, I have suggested, fostered connections between imagism and contemporary art, which was widely, if loosely, regarded as anarchist for its own focus on technique, its disintegration of the subject, its perceived origin in France, and the well-known anarchist sympathies of some of its protagonists. But where the ideology that made

---

[176] Wassily Kandinsky, *Über das Geistige in der Kunst: Insbesondere in der Malerei* (München: Piper, 1912), p. 74, English translation Kandinsky, *The Art of Spiritual Harmony*, pp. 82–3.

[177] Rose-Carol Washton Long, 'Occultism, Anarchism, and Abstraction: Kandinsky's Art of the Future', *Art Journal*, 46.1 (1987), 38–45 (p. 41).

[178] Wassily Kandinsky, 'Über die Formfrage', in *Der Blaue Reiter* (München: Piper, 1912), pp. 74–100 (p. 81), English translation *The Blaue Reiter Almanac*, ed. Wassily Kandinsky and Franz Marc, trans. Henning Falkenstein (London: Thames and Hudson, 1965), p. 157.

[179] Rainey, *Institutions of Modernism*, p. 30.

imagism an 'enemy of THE NEW AGE' was accrued primarily by association, Pound appears to have conceived of vorticism, unlike imagism,
as explicitly politicised. This is demonstrated by Pound's important essay,
'Wyndham Lewis', which appeared in the *Egoist* on 15 June 1914. This essay,
written before Pound had fully established his vorticist terminology, provides one of his most eloquent and least formulaic accounts of a vorticist
work, but it also struggles to work out the implications for Pound's own
poetry, and his cultural programme more generally.

   Pound's praise centres on Lewis's recently published *Timon of Athens*
portfolio (see fig. 4).

If a man have gathered the force of his generation or of his clan, if he has in his
"Timon" expressed the sullen fury of intelligence baffled, shut in by the entrenched
forces of stupidity, if he have made "Timon" a type emotion and delivered it in
lines and masses and planes, it is proper that we should respect him in a way that
we do not respect men blaring out truisms or doing an endless embroidery of
sentiment.
   In Mr. Lewis' work one finds not a commentator but a protagonist. He is a man
at war. He has, in a superlative degree, a sense of responsibility and of certitude.

There is an intriguing, and perhaps partly deliberate, blurring here between
Lewis and the subject of his designs, Timon of Athens. The 'sullen fury
of intelligence baffled' refers both to Timon and to Lewis – and indeed to
'our age, our generation, the youth-spirit, or what you will, that moves in
the men who are now between their twenty-fifth and thirty-fifth years'. For
Pound, the success of Lewis's designs highlights the difficulty he and other
writers have had in expressing the same collective frustration. In a long,
but very pertinent passage, he explores the possibilities for an equivalent
achievement in literature:

Our life has not the pageantry of Waterloo to give us a send off for the beginning of
a new "Chartreuse de Parme." This is no cause for complaint. From the beginning
of the world there has been the traditional struggle, the struggle of Voltaire, of
Stendhal and of Flaubert, the struggle of driving the shaft of intelligence into the
dull mass of mankind.
   I daresay one's own art seems always the hardest. One feels that Mr. Lewis has
expressed this struggle. One feels that in literature it is almost impossible to express
it for our generation. One has such trivial symbols arrayed against one, there is
only "The Times" and all that it implies, and the "Century Magazine" and its likes
and all that they imply, and the host of other periodicals and the states of mind
represented in them. It is so hard to arrange one's mass and opposition. Labour and
anarchy can find their opponents in "capital" and "government." But the mind
aching for something that it can honour under the name of "civilisation," the
mind, seeing that state afar off but clearly, can only flap about pettishly striking at

4 Wyndham Lewis, 'Composition', in *Timon of Athens* (London: Cube Press, 1913)

the host of trivial substitutes presented to it. One's very contentions are all in the nature of hurricanes in the traditional teapot.

The really vigorous mind might erect "The Times," which is of no importance, into a symbol of the state of mind which "The Times" represents, which is a loathsome state of mind, a malebolge of obtuseness.

And having done so, some aesthete left over from the nineties would rebuke one for one's lack of aloofness.

I have heard people accuse Mr. Lewis of lack of aloofness, yet Mr. Lewis has been for a decade one of the most silent men in London.[180]

Lewis's work has demonstrated to Pound that his cultural programme needs to be sharpened against a coherent opposition, as he has seen the fringe politics of the *Egoist* and the *New Age* sharpened by their continual encounter with their powerful antagonists, '"capital" and "government"'. The aloofness associated with the technical procedures of imagism is cast off here: vorticism, for Pound, shows the way towards an engaged art, and at this point, as David Kadlec has discussed, Pound conceives of that art in relation to the anarchist, anti-statist ideology of syndicalism. Two weeks later he would remark, 'As a syndicalist, somewhat atrabilious, I disbelieve vigorously in any recognition of political institutions, of the Fabian Society, John Galsworthy, and so on.'[181] If designating Galsworthy a 'political institution' makes a joke, it is a serious joke, marking Pound's recognition that writers can institutionalise politics as effectively as any officially political organisation.

By the time 'Wyndham Lewis' appeared, Pound was already in the process of 'erect[ing] "The Times" [. . .] into a symbol of the state of mind which "The Times" represents', by printing columns of quotations from *The Times* (mainly from the *Literary Supplement*) in the *Egoist* in imitation of the 'Current Cant' column in the *New Age*.[182] *The Times* also provided the impetus for 'Salutation the Third', the opening work in Pound's poetic contribution to *Blast*:

> Let us deride the smugness of "The Times":
> GUFFAW!
>   So much the gagged reviewers,
> It will pay them when their worms are wriggling in their vitals;
> These were they who objected to newness,

[180] 'Wyndham Lewis', *Egoist*, 1 (1914), pp. 233–4.
[181] 'Suffragettes', *Egoist*, 1 (1914), 254–5 (p. 254); David Kadlec, 'Pound, Blast and Syndicalism', *ELH*, 60 (1993), 1015–31.
[182] See 'Revolutionary Maxims', 'Revelations [I]', 'Revelations [II]', 'Northcliffe's Nice Paper Again', 'God in London. A.D. 1914', 'Some Rejected Mottoes', *Egoist*, 1 (1914), 217–18, 234–5, 256–7, 278, 286, 318.

HERE are their TOMB-STONES.
They supported the gag and the ring:
A little black BOX contains them.
SO shall you be also,
You slut-bellied obstructionist,
You sworn foe to free speech and good letters,
You fungus, you continuous gangrene.[183]

While this is clearly not a major work in Pound's oeuvre, in the context of Pound's essay on Lewis it does come into view as a more serious attempt to respond to the challenge of vorticist art than is first suggested by the *Blast*-inspired patina. Contrary to received opinion, the vorticist element of this poem is less its energy, its 'polemic intensity', than the location of that energy: the structure of the work around a struggle between the artist and the self-proclaimed institutions of civilisation, in this case, *The Times*.[184] In fact, 'Salutation the Third' is a more systematic engagement with vorticism than 'Dogmatic Statement Concerning the Game of Chess', usually understood as Pound's most vorticist poem.[185] Although that poem, too, takes a battle as its subject matter, it is primarily a technical exercise, a description of vorticist painting, rather than an assimilation of its achievement. 'Salutation the Third', on the other hand, shows, in a very rough draft, how the example of Lewis's painting was turning Pound's poetry away from the analyses of language and perception that had preoccupied the early imagist works, towards contemporary satire. Here we are presented with a glimpse forward to the terrain of *The Cantos*, which would take the 'struggle of driving the shaft of intelligence into the dull mass of mankind' as its aim and its topic.[186]

By the end of 1914, Pound had developed the critical terminology he had anticipated in his very first works of literary criticism. Despite the fact that he retrospectively described this process as 'cutting away from one art the muddles due to discussing it in terms of another', the formalist vocabulary he developed for literature was hardly specific to that media.[187] The terms he used to describe imagism in January 1915's 'Affirmations' series ('pattern-unit', 'arrangement of forms', 'vortex' and 'composition or an

---

[183] 'Salutation the Third', *Blast*, 1 (1914), p. 45.
[184] Dasenbrock, *The Literary Vorticism of Ezra Pound and Wyndham Lewis*, p. 88.
[185] 'Dogmatic Statement on the Game and Play of Chess (Theme for a Series of Pictures)', *Blast*, 2 (1915), p. 19. See W. C. Wees, *Vorticism and the English Avant-Garde* (Toronto, ON: University of Toronto Press, 1972), p. 205, and Cork, *Vorticism and Abstract Art in the First Machine Age*, 1: 292–4.
[186] 'Wyndham Lewis', p. 233.
[187] 'Totalitarian Scholarship and the New Paideuma', *Germany and You*, 7 (1937), 95–6, 123–4 (p. 95). Pound, indeed, compromises his own account by going on to remark that it was Whistler, the figure who did most to popularise the use of musical terminology in relation to works of visual art, whose 'critique had forerun us'.

"organisation"') were demonstrably wrought from his encounter with contemporary visual art and the art criticism through which it was interpreted and, further, they encode a belief in the priority of the visual sense and the insufficiency of words.[188] They also encode a politics. Although Pound was no political radical at this stage and his letters, for example, show no interest in contemporary politics, Pound's criticism drew on a set of associations that signalled to his readers an allegiance to anarchist individualism. The very expressivism and formalism that has led critics to characterise his work as apolitical was integral in associating it with individualist principles. Moreover, by the middle of 1914, Pound was beginning to explore the possibilities of a more explicitly engaged art, inspired by Lewis's contemporaneous paintings that expressed 'the negativity of the relationship between the individual and the public sphere in modernity', as David Peters Corbett has remarked.[189] The first examples of Pound's poetry that tried to respond to the oppositional potential of vorticist art, such as the *Blast* poems, had the virtue of breaking apart the aesthetic contentment and containment of the early imagist poems, but they foundered, as has been pointed out many times before, in a series of reductive stylistic gestures. However, over the next years Pound would continue to be challenged by the oppositional potential of vorticist art, and the next chapter explores how the first drafts of *The Cantos* can be read as a response to that challenge.

---

[188] 'Affirmations, IV: As for Imagisme', pp. 349–50.
[189] David Peters Corbett, *The Modernity of English Art, 1914–30* (Manchester: Manchester University Press, 1997), p. 34.

CHAPTER 3

A visual poetics? From the first cantos to Mauberley

VORTICISM AS REALISM

It has long been argued that vorticism played an important role in Pound's early thinking about *The Cantos*. In *The Pound Era*, Hugh Kenner characterised *The Cantos* as 'a poem on vortices and their fate: shapings of characteristic energies'; Ronald Bush's still authoritative account of the poem's genesis attributed Pound's discovery of the organising principles of the poem to his coining of phrases to describe vorticist art, 'units of design', 'pattern-units', 'radicals in design', and 'forms in combination'; Reed Way Dasenbrock posited vorticist sculpture as the model for the 'temporal and cultural montage' that forms a 'crucial organizing principle' for *The Cantos*. Christine Froula's pioneering work on the poem's drafts confirmed these judgments: her discovery of 'explicit references to the Vorticist painting and sculpture of Henri Gaudier-Brzeska and Wyndham Lewis' in the manuscripts firmly linked the development of Pound's poetics to 'the emergence of abstract form in the visual arts'.[1] As the terms of these statements demonstrate, particular attention has been given to the formal lessons offered by vorticist art, a focus suggested by Pound's own famous, though soon deleted, lines at the end of the first published canto:

> Barred lights, great flares, new form, Picasso or Lewis.
> If for a year man write to paint, and not to music –
> O Casella![2]

A necessary supplement to such formalist analyses is an account that considers vorticism as one of the sources for *The Cantos'* subject matter and method. Pound's comparison in his 1914 essay, 'Wyndham Lewis', between

---

[1] Kenner, *The Pound Era*, p. 247; Bush, p. 45; Dasenbrock, *The Literary Vorticism of Ezra Pound and Wyndham Lewis*, p. 100; Christine Froula, *To Write Paradise: Style and Error in Ezra Pound's Cantos* (New Haven, CT: Yale University Press, 1984), p. 6.
[2] 'Three Cantos, I', *Poetry*, 10 (1917), 113–21, (p. 121).

Lewis's *Timon* series and a major source for the first cantos, Stendhal's
La Chartreuse de Parme, indicates that 'writ[ing] to paint' might not be
restricted to an emulation of 'abstract form', but rather include an examination of 'the relationship between the individual and the public sphere in
modernity', what Pound called 'the traditional struggle'.[3] Charles Altieri's
discussion of the 'ethical' lessons Pound learnt from vorticism is an important step towards an account, but whereas Altieri is primarily interested in
'the structure of various imaginative attitudes', this chapter aims to provide
an account of the relation between those attitudes and the material social
factors with which his argument is explicitly unconcerned.[4]

Pound began sustained work on *The Cantos* in the summer of 1915, as
the Great War entered its second year. Germany had introduced the use
of poison gas, the Allies had been defeated at Gallipoli, and the *Lusitania*
had been sunk with the loss of 1,201 lives, including those of 128 American
citizens.[5] By late 1915, the war had had a profound effect on non-combatants
as well: the majority of people in Britain had lost a family member or a
friend, and Pound was no exception: Henri Gaudier-Brzeska was killed
at Neuville St Vaast on 5 June. In the second and final number of *Blast*,
which appeared in July 1915, Pound characterised the previous number as
a critique of the pre-war political situation:

Throughout the length and breadth of England and through three continents
BLAST has been REVILED by all save the intelligent.

WHY?

Because BLAST alone has dared to show modernity its face in an honest glass.
    While all other periodicals were whispering PEACE in one tone or another:
while they were all saying "hush" (for one "interest" or another), "BLAST" alone
dared to present the actual discords of modern "civilisation," DISCORDS now
only too apparent in the open conflict between teutonic atavism and unsatisfactory
Democracy.[6]

This passage shows how far Pound's conception of the social relevance of
art has shifted from that expressed in 'The Serious Artist' and the documents of imagism in 1913. Previously 'good art' had been that which 'gives
us our data of psychology'.[7] Its impact was restricted to the level of individual knowledge and evaluated ahistorically. In the second volume of *Blast*,
however, Pound develops the framing of vorticism as an art engaged with

[3] Peters Corbett, *The Modernity of English Art, 1914–30*, p. 36; 'Wyndham Lewis', p. 234.
[4] Altieri, *Painterly Abstraction in Modernist American Poetry*, pp. 284, 9.
[5] Hew Strachan, *The First World War* (London: Simon & Schuster, 2003), p. 216.
[6] 'Chronicles', pp. 85–6.   [7] 'The Serious Artist, I–[II]', pp. 162, 163.

its immediate context that he had begun in 'Wyndham Lewis' the previous year, exhibiting a new sense of the historical specificity of 'modernity' and 'modern civilisation', and a new interest in art's diagnostic relationship to them.

The stridency of Pound's defence of *Blast* was in part a response to the particular cast of criticisms against vorticism during the war. In a telling revision of pre-war opinion that read post-impressionism as anarchic and French, experimental visual art was now routinely equated with a notion of Prussian mechanicality.[8] In its review of the London Group's exhibition at the Goupil Gallery in March, headed 'Junkerism in Art', *The Times* censured the 'rigid' and 'ascetic' character of Lewis's, Wadsworth's and Roberts's work 'which prevents them from taking an interest in anything actual or concrete whatever':

their pictures are not pictures so much as theories illustrated in paint. In fact, in our desire to relate them to something in the actual world, we can only call them Prussian in their spirit. These painters seem to execute a kind of goose-step, where other painters are content to walk more or less naturally. Perhaps if the Junkers could be induced to take to art, instead of disturbing the peace of Europe, they would paint so and enjoy it.[9]

The *Connoisseur*, similarly, described vorticism as 'belong[ing] to the movement which, by substituting the worship of force for the appreciation of truth, beauty, and morality, has brought about the phenomenon of modern Germany'.[10] Even in the *Egoist*, John Cournos denounced *Blast*'s 'curiously abstract representations of modern warfare' and commented that 'the true exponents of modern art were the men on the German General Staff, holding periodical meetings at Potsdam [. . .]. Their "vortex" first sucked in millions of German young men, then it was sent spinning like a huge top through Belgium and France, where in its first momentum it "dispersed" millions of other young men.'[11] Lewis responded to such attacks throughout the second issue of *Blast*. He commented explicitly on the *Times* review, claiming 'I do not mind being called a Prussian in the least', although 'I am not one' and 'aesthetically, I am not one either'. His defence was that the components of the vorticist style, 'our rigid-head-dresses and disciplined movements', were not a projection of either a temperament or a

[8] See Peters Corbett, *The Modernity of English Art*, pp. 43–5, and Sue Malvern, *Modern Art, Britain and the Great War: Witnessing, Testimony and Remembrance* (New Haven, CT: Yale University Press, 2004), pp. 5–6.
[9] 'Junkerism in Art', *Times*, 10 March 1915, p. 8, col. c.
[10] '[Review of] "Henri Gaudier-Brzeska" by Ezra Pound', *Connoisseur*, 45 (1916), 115–16.
[11] John Cournos, 'The Death of Futurism', *Egoist*, 4 (1917), 6–7 (p. 6).

politics, but 'aesthetic phenomena', developed in response to other aesthetic phenomena: 'As an antidote to the slop of Cambridge Post-Aestheticism (Post-Impressionism is an insult to Manet and Cézanne) or the Gypsy Botticellis of Mill Street, may not such "rigidity" be welcomed?' Prussian art he connected to conservatism: 'the Junker, obviously, if he painted, would do florid and disreputable canvases of nymphs and dryads, or very sentimental "portraits of the Junker's mother"'.[12]

Pound had discovered early in the war how the animosity directed at vorticism could affect his own career, and this also shaped his representation of *Blast*'s reception. In October 1914 George Prothero, the editor of the prestigious *Quarterly Review*, which Pound had been cultivating since June 1912, had rejected his proposals for further contributions, on the basis of his affiliation with *Blast*.[13] This disappointment lies behind 'Et faim sallir le loup des boys', one of the eight poems Pound contributed to the second *Blast*, in which he figures himself as an anti-establishment crusader, shipwrecked by 'insidious modern waves, civilization, civilized hidden snares':

> Cowardly editors threaten: "If I dare"
> Say this or that, or speak my open mind,
> Say that I hate may [*sic*] hates,
>   Say that I love my friends,
> Say I believe in Lewis, spit out the later Rodin,
> Say that Epstein can carve in stone,
> The Brzeska can use the chisel,
> Or Wadsworth paint;
>   Then they will have my guts;
> They will cut down my wage, force me to sing their cant,
> Uphold the press, and be before all a model of literary decorum.
> Merde![14]

Although the situation with the *Quarterly* provided the immediate inspiration for this poem, Pound's castigation of the press as full of 'cant', and of its editors for sacrificing truth in favour of 'literary decorum', was part of the broader campaign against the press he had begun the previous year in 'Wyndham Lewis'. Here as there contemporary art is opposed to the periodicals as a model of probity. Pound's conception of this opposition had taken on a new urgency by the middle of 1915, however. As the war progressed, Pound began to see Anglo-American periodical culture as

---

[12] Wyndham Lewis, 'The London Group', *Blast*, 2 (1915), 77–9 (p. 78). See also 'The God of Sport and Blood' and 'The Exploitation of Blood', *Blast*, 2 (1915), 9–10, 24: 'the Kaiser, long before he entered into war with Great Britain, had declared merciless war on Cubism and Expressionism' (p. 9).

[13] G. W. Prothero, Letter to Ezra Pound, 22 October 1914, EPP, Beinecke, 42.1809; *L/DS*, 125.

[14] 'Et faim sallir le loup des boys', *Blast*, 2 (1915), p. 22.

contributing directly to the 'discords of modern "civilisation"', and in four articles for the *New Age* in the second half of 1915, he developed his critique of periodicals into an analysis of English complacency, American 'inertia', and German *Kultur*.[15]

The first, 'The Pleasing Art of Poetry', appeared on 8 July, inveighing against 'the defunct standards of "the Better Magazines," which same "better magazines" have done their utmost to keep America out of touch with the contemporary world, and have striven with all their inertia to "keep things" anchored to 1876'.[16] In the pair of articles entitled 'American Chaos', published two months later, Pound argues the effect of this intellectual isolation is a lack of understanding between the United States and Britain, which has in turn made the United States disinclined to enter the war as a British ally.[17] In his final article on the topic, 'This Super-Neutrality', he extends his argument that 'the impression of national character or national honesty is a *literary* impression' from Britain and the United States to its more usual target, Germany, arguing that tyranny is 'insidiously present in "Kultur," i.e. German State-education, press campaigns, subsidised professors, etc.' as well as in its militarism.[18]

Pound's attacks on *Kultur* during the war years were in keeping with its denunciation in the Allied press and propaganda, but his animosity was sharpened by his long-standing hostility towards German scholarship and philology. In a further article from late 1915, 'The Net American Loss', intended for American publication but unpublished in his lifetime, Pound imagined an extreme version of Prussian culture in which 'all the Prussian empire and its philology [was] turned into one vast reference-magazine, one vast catalogue of minute facts filed in quadruple-cross-reference', a type of 'state-culture', he emphasised, that had no attraction for 'the men of free minds, the men of swift and subtle-moving intelligence'.[19] The opposition here is not only one of oppression to freedom, but of the state to the individual, and Pound made this point in 'American Chaos', too: 'Germany believes in the state and individuals be damned, and "the Allies" believe that the individual has certain inalienable rights which it is the duty of the State to preserve to him.'[20] Yet this patriotic sentiment stands in contradiction to the rest of Pound's argument which implies that the literary cultures of Britain, the United States, and Germany are all oppressive to

---

[15] 'Chronicles', p. 86.
[16] '"The Pleasing Art of Poetry"', *New Age*, 17 (1915), 229–31 (p. 229).
[17] 'American Chaos. I', *New Age*, 17 (1915), p. 449; 'American Chaos. II', *New Age*, 17 (1915), p. 471.
[18] 'The Super-Neutrality', *New Age*, 17 (1915), p. 595.
[19] 'The Net American Loss' (1915), *Paideuma*, 18.1&2 (1989), 206–11 (p. 209).
[20] 'American Chaos, II', p. 471.

the individual. Only in *Blast* did Pound allow himself to make this explicit, when he characterised the war as a 'conflict between teutonic atavism and unsatisfactory Democracy'.[21]

The antidote to both German tyranny and English and American inertia is, according to Pound, literary 'realism'. Literature must disseminate intelligent reflection and do so with clarity and integrity. The first instalment of 'American Chaos' had begun by remarking that 'we are faced with an insoluble ignorance, we are so faced because, since the death of Laurence Sterne or thereabouts, there has been neither in England nor America any sufficient sense of the value of realism in literature, or the value of writing words that conform precisely with fact, of free speech without evasions and circumlocutions'.[22] In a review of Joyce's *A Portrait of the Artist as a Young Man* in February 1917, Pound repeated the point in relation to German literature: 'it is very important that there should be clear, unexaggerated, realistic literature. It is very important that there should be good prose. The hell of contemporary Europe is caused by the lack of representative government in Germany, *and* by the non-existence of decent prose in the German language. Clear thought and sanity depend on clear prose.'[23]

Ronald Bush has described in detail the importance of Pound's conception of realism to the early stages of *The Cantos*' composition. Pound's several explorations of the topic between 1913 and 1918 posit Sterne, Stendhal, Turgenev, Flaubert, James and Joyce as the major figures of the prose realist tradition, and important models for what he famously termed 'the prose tradition in verse', whose main contemporary exponent was Ford.[24] He described its approach as 'constatation of fact. It presents. It does not comment. It is irrefutable because it does not present a personal predilection for any particular fraction of the truth [. . .]. It is not criticism of life, I mean it does not deal in opinion. It washes its hands of theories. It does not attempt to justify anybody's ways to anybody or anything else [. . .]. It is open to all facts and to all impressions [. . .]. The presentative method is equity.'[25]

Pound also found this 'presentative method' in the work of certain visual artists. In an essay on Edgar Lee Masters published in May 1915, Pound explains his 'preference [. . .] for realism, for a straight statement of life'

---

[21] 'Chronicles', p. 86.   [22] 'American Chaos. I', *New Age*, 17 (1915), p. 449.
[23] 'James Joyce: At Last the Novel Appears', *Egoist*, 4 (1917), 21–2 (p. 22).
[24] Bush, p. 144. The chapter in which Bush discusses Pound's realism, 'Toward a New Narrative Voice', provides an invaluable analysis of Pound's engagement with these models (pp. 142–82). Forrest Read's earlier 'Pound, Joyce and Flaubert: The Odysseans', in *New Approaches to Ezra Pound*, ed. Eva Hesse (London: Faber and Faber, 1969), pp. 125–43 concerns the prose tradition more indirectly, but is particularly informative on Pound's use of Flaubert.
[25] 'The Approach to Paris, V', *New Age*, 13 (1913), 662–4 (p. 662).

by remarking that 'the lasting enjoyment of a work of art is that it leaves you confronted with life, with the objective fact. Rembrandt's old Jews are there. Dürer's old father is there. It is not a matter of opinion.'[26] Epstein, too, had been earlier described as having 'taken count of all the facts. He is in the best sense realist', and in 'Wyndham Lewis', Pound compared Lewis's project to his favoured realists, Voltaire, Stendhal and Flaubert.[27] In the second issue of *Blast*, Lewis himself had characterised the vorticists as realists, distinct from the 'neo-realism' of the Camden Town Group, which he called 'naturalism': 'Mr. Wadsworth, in his painting of BLACKPOOL is purely "realistic." That is the REALITY, the essential truth, of a noisy, garish sea-side. A painting of Blackpool by a Camden Town Artist would be a corner of the beach much as seen by the Camera.'[28]

A conception of realism that looks to Sterne as a major progenitor and includes artists elsewhere praised for their 'musical conception of form' is clearly an unorthodox one, and Pound's use of the term in 1915 is highly strategic. His definitions of it emphasising 'facts', 'truth', 'equity' and a 'presentative method' that is not mimetic, enable him to retain his individualist emphasis on the integrity of the artist's expression, in contrast to the rhetoric and mendacity he attributes to both German *Kultur* and the aspects of English and American civilisation represented by their periodicals. For Pound, both the 'evasions and circumlocutions' of English and American journalistic prose and the 'mush of the German sentence, the straddling of the verb out to the end' are contributing factors to the war situation.[29] By the time Pound was working on *The Cantos*, he had in mind a clear distinction between two types of writing, state-sponsored rhetoric that contributed to international antagonism, and the individual artist's realism that could diagnose its causes and contribute to peace.[30] The challenge was to write a poem that was consistent with those beliefs.

THE FIRST CANTOS: ANTI-TEXTUALITY AND
THE VISIONARY INSTINCT

The first versions of *The Cantos* emerge directly out of this complex of ideas: the poem was to be realist, with all that term implied for Pound.

---

[26] 'Affirmations: Edgar Lee Masters', *Reedy's Mirror*, 13 (1915), 10–12 (pp. 10, 12).
[27] 'Exhibition at the Goupil Gallery', p. 109, 'Wyndham Lewis', p. 234.
[28] Lewis, 'The London Group', p. 78.
[29] 'American Chaos. I', p. 449; 'James Joyce: At Last the Novel Appears', p. 22.
[30] This series of associations is cognate to those recently delineated by Vincent Sherry in his *The Great War and the Language of Modernism* (Oxford: Oxford University Press, 2003), which argues that London-based modernists, including Pound, 'reenact the disestablishment of a rationalistic attitude and practice in language, in the verbal culture of a war for which Liberal apologies and rationales provided the daily material of London journalism' (p. 14).

Unpublished drafts give ample evidence of the poem's realist aims: a clutch of notes at the bottom of one page includes the lines 'circle from self. vortex of Romoe, spider web, realism in lit. diagnosis, and patters, reason for realism'; the familiar names of Pound's realist canon are littered across the pages: 'Crabbe, Sterne' is scrawled on one page, 'Fabrice [Fabrizio] del Dongo', the protagonist of Stendhal's *La Chartreuse de Parme*, on another.[31] A 1915 draft begins by positing Stendhal as Pound's major precursor in depicting 'the modern world': 'Here is your modern world, and I'm no Stendhal', he writes in a characteristically defensive mode, only to spend the next lines invoking Stendhal's 'spirited ignorant boy', Fabrizio, and the 'first eleven chapters' of *La Chartreuse de Parme*. These lines are followed by Pound's attempt at his own realist narrative: he introduces his Fabrizio-substitute, a 'bullet headed fellow', educated in Germany and trapped there by the beginning of the war, who, despite having been 'pro-german', enlists with the British army as soon as he escapes to England.[32]

This story not only provides Pound with a method of introducing contemporary history through the eyes of a character as usefully impressionable as Stendhal's Fabrizio; it allows him to place the arguments he had advanced in his *New Age* articles directly into the fabric of the poem. Pound's protagonist tells us that he 'drank up kultur' in Germany, enrolling for doctoral study at Jena. But in Poland he had seen how *Kultur* was used oppressively. The first draft's observation that 'Millions [were] spent on Kultur, and no effect/ The Poles still use their cafes/ and the Prussians/ use quite a separate set' becomes a more damning indictment in the second draft of the passage:

> Posen resists kultur, millions like water
>   poured out to make them German,
> Poles have their cafes, germans still have theirs,
> The place a fortress, people will talk polish,
> Children beaten in school, but will talk polish,
> The place a fortress.[33]

The Cantos begins, then, with an explicitly patriotic argument, denigrating Germany, *Kultur*, and, most importantly, the tyrannous political use of culture Pound saw *Kultur* as representing.

---

[31] 'Ur-Cantos: Autograph ms. and typescript', EPP, Beinecke, 69.3099.

[32] 'Ur-Cantos: Autograph ms. and typescript'. This draft is a precursor of the ninety-eight line passage referred to by Froula as 'the earliest version of the Fourth Canto, MS UrI [. . .] composed as Pound worked on "Three Cantos". This is the poem to which Pound most likely alluded in his first mention of the cantos to his father on December 18 1915: "I don't want to muddle my mind now in the Vth Canto by typing the first three cantos"' (*To Write Paradise*, p. 15).

[33] 'Ur-Cantos: Autograph ms. and typescript'; 'Ur-Cantos [II]: Typescript', EPP, Beinecke, 69.3100.

But Pound is not content to make this argument through narrative statement alone: he is aware that this has inevitable ramifications for his style, which must transfer the qualities of realist prose to the poetic terrain. Despite the fact that Pound had been theorising this 'prose tradition of poetry' since 1913, the drafts demonstrate that writing in this mode was by no means a straightforward task and that Pound felt himself to be constantly in danger of falling into precisely the style he was writing against, the style he associated with German *Kultur*. The first version of the bullet-headed fellow's narrative is followed by a page that dramatises this difficulty. Beginning by addressing either himself or an imagined belligerent reader, Pound asks 'What am I at?', and replies:

> You silly fool
> How often must I stop the narrative to say
> That this is life. These things are life,
> Of which neither you nor I make head or tail.:
> A maxim, pain, and half a sentence or two.
> "Its low to try to coerce another person.,
>
> Low to desire controll.
>   All we can do 's to set forth our own good
> within some other's reach.
>   not force it on him.
> We have few rights, the right of self protection.
> "Art's but integrity.[34]

The 'presentative method' of the Poundian realist narrative requires that coherence and completeness must be sacrificed for truth and lack of coercion, but Pound's philological training continually tempts him into aiming for a 'thoroughness' entirely inappropriate for a narrative structured against *Kultur*. The text continues:

> Dig up some text's of greek philosophy,
> etc. etc. etc. etcetera. etc.
> 3 dramatists, much praised. The bellowing Theban.
> Make a complete kultur
>   (be damned with "thoroughness"
> loose all the spirit,
>   talk of all better men as
> "superficial". . a modus, an apparatus criticus.
> Never the flaw, the pulse, the surge,
>   the uprorious, and outrageous,

---

[34] 'Ur-Cantos: Autograph ms. and typescript'.

> The uncontrolled, indecorous, actual living."
>   Your scholarshipt be drowned. build pyramids
> and bury yourselved beneath 'em.[35]

It is worth stressing Pound's association here of art with life, with 'the uncontrolled, indecorous, actual living', as opposed to 'dig[ging] up some text's of greek philosophy', because it is so foreign to most readers' experience of the published *Cantos*, which give every impression of setting great store by scholarship. After all, Pound thought the section of the *Odyssey* he translated in Canto I 'shouts aloud that it is older than the rest' (*L*, 274). But the earliest drafts of the poem could not be less ambivalent in their aversion to scholarship: 'Your scholarshipt be drowned. build pyramids/ and bury yourselved beneath 'em.'

As he has done before when distinguishing his own method from that of philology, Pound turns away in these early drafts from the problematic textual realm, associated as it is here with mediating, rhetorical scholarship, and instead frames his ambitions in terms which cultivate the immediacy of the visual. He complains that it is 'beyond my grapple' to 'set out my fancy, make the horses jingle / make the life move' with a 'disembowled Catullus', and in despair exclaims 'Paint it Raffael / bring back the ancient beauty. / I fail I fail, nothing but half filled note books.'[36] This approach is experimental and by no means pursued consistently, but the trajectory of these early drafts is nevertheless away from the use of texts and towards immediate experience, and this entails a serious debate about the possibility of disguising writing as seeing. In this, the early cantos look to the visual arts as a potential stylistic model.

This turn to the visual has a strong literary precedent for Pound in the work of Robert Browning. We have seen that in 1907 Pound declared that the 'kin art' of Browning's poetry was 'that of the brush', and that he modelled 'In Praise of the Masters', his dramatic monologue in the voice of Rembrandt, on Browning's poems in the same form. Even at that early stage, Pound associated Rembrandt and Browning with a realist vision, having Rembrandt inveigh against 'beauty' and emphasise, 'i paint what i see sir.'[37] When Pound draws on Browning in *The Cantos*, however, it is no longer the dramatic monologues that form his model, but the poem Pound called his 'great work': *Sordello*.[38] The many critical discussions of Pound's use of *Sordello* have analysed his appropriation of Browning's

[35] 'Ur-Cantos: Autograph ms. and typescript'.
[36] 'Ur-Cantos: Autograph ms. and typescript'.   [37] 'In Praise of the Masters', [pp. 1, 3].
[38] Letter to Homer Loomis Pound, 18 December 1915, EPP, Beinecke, 60.2669.

conversational diction, idiosyncratic vocabulary, juxtapositional strategies, and, since the publication of Jacob Korg's important 1972 article, his adoption of Browning's 'romantic' historicism, reframed in more recent work by James Longenbach and Mary Ellis Gibson in terms of Fredric Jameson's category of 'existential historicism'.[39] But here too Browning provides lessons in a visual poetics, though of a different sort from those Pound learned from 'Pictor Ignotus' and 'Fra Lippo Lippi'. The existential historicist experiences the past as having a 'vital urgency' for the present, a 'spiritual enthusiasm [. . .] for the traces that life has left behind it', and, most relevantly for this study, a 'visionary instinct for all the forms of living praxis preserved and still instinct within the monuments of the past'.[40]

The 'visionary instinct' on which *The Cantos* drafts base their claim to authenticity is most conspicuously worked out through the foregrounding of Browning's own use of visual metaphors in *Sordello*. In book three, Browning describes a tripartite hierarchy of poets: 'the worst of us' who can 'say they have so seen', 'the better' who can say 'what it was they saw', and 'the best', the 'Makers-see' who can 'impart the gift of seeing to the rest', an ideal Pound had expressed in his 'Vorticism' essay the previous year.[41] The beginning of the poem dramatises the latter concept by introducing a narrator, who, as Daniel Stempel has influentially argued, presents the poem as scenes from a diorama.[42] In the first of the 'Three Cantos' published in *Poetry* in 1917, debating how to present the 'thought' of the 'modern world', Pound suggests taking on Browning's 'whole bag of tricks', including 'your trick, the showman's booth', which he considers turning 'into the Agora, / Or into the old theatre at Arles', either of which would enable him to 'set the lot, my visions, to confounding / The wits that have survived your damn'd *Sordello*.'[43] Browning's dioramic narrative showed Pound a device by which the 'modern world' could confront the reader with a 'straight

---

[39] Jacob Korg, 'The Music of Lost Dynasties: Browning, Pound and History', *ELH*, 39 (1972), 420–40 (pp. 429–30); James Longenbach, *Modernist Poetics of History: Pound, Eliot, and the Sense of the Past* (Princeton, NJ: Princeton University Press, 1987), pp. 13–14; Gibson, pp. 3–4. See also Christine Froula, 'Browning's *Sordello* and the Parables of Modernist Poetics', *ELH*, 52 (1985), 965–92 and Michaela Giesenkirchen, '"But Sordello, and My Sordello?": Pound and Browning's Epic', *Modernism/ Modernity*, 8 (2001), 623–42.

[40] Fredric Jameson, 'Marxism and Historicism', *NLH*, 11 (1979–80), 41–73, (p. 51).

[41] Robert Browning, 'Sordello', in *The Poetical Works of Robert Browning*, vol. II, ed. Ian Jack and Margaret Smith (Oxford: Clarendon Press, 1984), pp. 193–498 (pp. 340, 344); 'Vorticism', p. 464: 'A Russian correspondent, after having called it ['Heather'] a symbolist poem, and having been convinced that it was not symbolism, said slowly: "I see, you wish to give people new eyes, not to make them see some new particular thing."'

[42] Daniel Stempel, 'Browning's *Sordello*: The Art of the Makers-See', *PMLA*, 80 (1965), 554–61 (p. 556).

[43] 'Three Cantos, I', pp. 117–18.

statement of life', while at the same time admitting the inevitable subjectivity of the history presented in painted or imagined scenes, and solving the practical difficulty of moving between different narratives.[44] The drafts include several examples of Pound's own experiments with similar devices: they include the time-honoured contrivances of falling asleep to awake in another era, riding on a magic carpet, surrounding oneself with ghosts, summoning genies from bottles – and 'our historical method: vortices'.[45]

This phrase occurs at the top of a two-page draft, part of which was subsequently used in a discarded version of Canto 4 that has been discussed by Christine Froula, Vincent Sherry and Mary Ellis Gibson.[46] It introduces a long passage that posits Lewis's painting, Gaudier-Brzeska's sculpture, and also Gaudier's vorticist writings, as models for the poem. The whole draft reads as follows:

> Then our historical method: vortices.
>
> Sculpture sprung up, the best man killed in france
> Struck by a prussian bullet, at St Vaast,
> with just enough cut stone, left here behind him
> To show a new way to the kindred arts,
> And one man left,, and we have Brzeska's vortex
> Laying a method, quite outside his art,
> bent to a word. Paris, and Reincah had done
> good work, in school book manuals,
> given us France, or Rome, philology,
> and this young boy hits on the clearer method.
> Vortex, dispersal, the whole history.
> A maze of images, and a full volley of questions;
> What is our life, what is our knowing of it
> Say that prose is life, scooped out of time
> A bristling node, a vortex. And, am all too plain
> Too full of foot notes, too careful to tell you how
>   and why my meaning.
> Lewis, with simpler means,
> Catches the age, his Timon,
> Throws our few years onto a score of pasteboards,

[44] 'Affirmations, VII: The Non-Existence of Ireland', *New Age*, 16 (1915), 451–3 (p. 452); 'Affirmations: Edgar Lee Masters', p. 10.

[45] 'Ur-Cantos: Autograph ms. and typescript', 'Ur-Cantos [III]: Autograph ms. and transcript', EPP, Beinecke, 69.3101

[46] Froula refers to the subsequent, discarded version (also part of 'Ur-Cantos [III]: Autograph ms. and transcript') as 'MS Ur2' and notes that 'These pages originally followed a 28-page typescript draft of "Three Cantos" which Pound made in late 1916 or early 1917' (*To Write Paradise*, p. 63); Sherry, *Ezra Pound, Wyndham Lewis, and Radical Modernism*, pp. 67–9; Gibson, pp. 90–1.

> Says all our conflict, edgy, epigramatic.
> This Timon lived in Greece, and loved the people,
> And gave high feasts, and dug his rabbit burrow.
> "And Ka-hu churned in the sea,
>   churning the ocean, using the sun for a churn stick"[47]

The importance of this passage is that it describes in quite explicit terms how Gaudier's and Lewis's vorticist work presents not only a formal model for *The Cantos*, but a 'historical method', an alternative means of representing history to that of philology. Gaudier's sculpture shows 'a new way to the kindred arts' and Lewis's *Timon* portfolio 'catches the age', 'throws our few years onto a score of pasteboards.' Gaudier's written legacy is just as important: his 'Vortex' article published in the first *Blast* compressed the histories of sculptures from different cultures into a 'whole history' of sculpture in less than four pages.[48] For Pound, this was an advance on the best of the philological tradition he had inherited, the comparative philological method of Gaston Paris and Salomon Reinach.[49] Gaudier's 'Vortex' showed a 'clearer method' than theirs, and a method Pound could use, since it was 'bent to a word'. But thinking about Gaudier's and Lewis's achievements induces a crisis of confidence in Pound, who reprimands himself for being 'all too plain/ Too full of foot notes, too careful to tell you how and why my meaning.' In contrast to his own over-scholarly, self-consciously mediated descriptions, Pound commends the vorticist artists for representing history, both past and present, more simply, more vigorously, and in an effective compressed form.

In late 1916 or early 1917, when Pound typed out a fair copy of the cantos completed to date, this passage became the second half of the canto designed to follow the three *Poetry* cantos, where it operated as 'an acknowledgement of the inadequacy of the "Three Cantos" mode to Pound's intentions and a groping first step toward the poetics of the final Canto IV'.[50] The passage on Gaudier and Lewis was prefaced by a passage that began by characterising the 'Three Cantos' as 'this clattering rumble' and asked 'Bewildered reader, what is the poet's business?' As an answer it presented a virtuosic display of poetic beauty that returned to the terrain of Pound's earliest published poetry, and his admiration for the Raphaelite Latinists. The role of the poet, Pound writes, is

---

[47] 'Ur-Cantos [III]: Autograph ms. and transcript'. I have transcribed this draft without incorporating the pencil and pen corrections Pound subsequently added to the sheet, most of which were incorporated in 'MS Ur2', transcribed in Froula, *To Write Paradise*, pp. 74–5.

[48] Henri Gaudier-Brzeska, 'Vortex. Gaudier Brzeska', *Blast*, 1 (1914), 155–8.

[49] 'Affirmations, VI: Analysis of this Decade', *New Age*, 16 (1915), 409–11 (p. 410).

[50] Froula, *To Write Paradise*, p. 18.

> To fill up chaos, populate solitudes, multiply images
> Or streak the barren way to paradise
> ~~(Here was the renaissance)~~
> [To] band out fine colours, fill [up] the void with stars
> And make each star a nest of noble voices.[51]

In 1906, Pound had described this style of poetry as 'poetic utterness' and contrasted it with Browning's 'vital [. . .] prose in verse'.[52] This early fourth canto was intended to present a burst of poetry in its purest form to contrast with the previous cantos' verse modelled on Browning and realist prose.

But Lewis and Gaudier did not, finally, have a place in that fourth canto. And even in this draft, the significance of their presence has become ambiguous. In the first typescript, they were represented as providing 'a historical method', 'catch[ing] the age', expressing 'all our conflict', terms that suggested correlation with the aims of the realist prose narrative. Most of that first passage, including the latter two phrases, was transferred into the second typescript, yet there it follows a demonstration of poetic beauty, not prose realism, of paradise, not history. Pound's negotiations between poetry and prose – and they are explicitly represented as such in the drafts, 'Come prose, come verse, back off, you are not one', he comments at one point – are triangulated by his introduction of vorticist art, which is equated with both at different stages.

Vorticism's ambiguous allegiance is not resolved, and it results in the elliptical, unfulfilled and oft-quoted final passage of the first *Poetry* canto:

> How many worlds we have! If Botticelli
> Brings her ashore on that great cockle-shell –
> His Venus (Simonetta?),
> And Spring and Aufidus fill all the air
> With their clear-outlined blossoms?
> World enough. Behold, I say, she comes
> "Apparelled like the spring, Graces her subjects,"
> (That's from *Pericles*).
> Oh, we have worlds enough, and brave *décors*,
> And from these like we guess a soul for man
> And build him full of aery populations.
> Mantegna a sterner line, and the new world about us:
> Barred lights, great flares, new form, Picasso or Lewis.
> If for a year man write to paint, and not to music –
> O Casella![53]

---

[51] 'Ur-Cantos [III]: Autograph ms. and transcript'.
[52] 'M. Antonius Flamininus and John Keats', p. [445].
[53] 'Three Cantos, I', *Poetry*, 10 (1917), 113–21 (p. 121).

The last three lines were a late interpolation. In an earlier version of the canto, the lesson of painting was provided by Botticelli and Mantegna alone, with the allusion to Mantegna's 'sterner line' followed immediately by the description of the Palazzo Ducale at Mantua, home of Mantegna's patron, Lodovico Gonzaga, that subsequently began the second of the *Poetry* 'Three Cantos'. The inserted lines about contemporary painting initially read:

> Or here, this new world that's a-burst about us
> barred lights, great flares,
>   colours turned loose, as colours
> form taken down
>   for form
> Wadsworth, or Lewis
> "Casella mia"
>   where once men wrote to sounds
> We write to painting?[54]

On the typescript that formed the next stage of the drafts, Pound crossed out Edward Wadsworth's name and replaced it with 'Picasso', then crossed out 'Picasso' and replaced it with the name of the Italian futurist painter Giacomo Balla.[55] The changes record Pound's deliberate broadening of the context of his poem, setting it in relation to a European-wide revolution in art, rather than the British movement with which he was closely associated. Similarly, after the question that ended the first draft, Pound pencilled in '(for a year) 1915', the year in which he was writing, but the revisions turn this personal resolution into a more general injunction. After the publication of the *Poetry* 'Three Cantos', these lines were revised further and compressed for the American editions of *Lustra* (1917) and the *Egoist*-published *Quia Pauper Amavi* (1919).[56]

---

[54] 'Three Cantos: Autograph ms.', EPP, Beinecke, 70.1303.

[55] 'Three Cantos: Autograph ms. and typescript', EPP, Beinecke, 70.3105. Pound's choice of Balla might seem surprising given his well-known criticisms of Italian futurism, but in reviews and articles he consistently rates Balla and Severini as the most important of futurist artists, and between 1914 and 1916 his admiration is at its peak. Writing to John Quinn on 10 July 1916, Pound argued that Lewis was significantly different from cubist and futurist painters, but admitted 'I must grant that Balla (who might just as well call himself an expressionist) isn't very unlike [. . .]. Perhaps it is only the Marinetti part of futurism that one need very greatly object to' (*EPVA*, 238). Pound had praised Severini and Balla (again calling the latter an expressionist) in 'Edward Wadsworth, Vorticist. An Authorised Appreciation', *Egoist*, 1 (1914), 306–7 (p. 306), and grouped them with Picasso and Lewis as 'modern and ultra-modern' painters in 'The War and Diverse Impressions. Mr. Nevinson Thinks That the Public Is More Interested in the War than It Is in Art', *Vogue*, (1916), 74–5 (p. 75). Pound also makes passing references to Balla in 'Art Notes: At the Alpine Club Gallery', *New Age*, 22 (1918), 503–4 (p. 504), and 'Art Notes', *New Age*, 24 (1919), 310–11 (p. 310).

[56] 'Three Cantos of a Poem of Some Length', in *Lustra of Ezra Pound with Earlier Poems* (New York: Knopf, 1917), pp. 179–202 (p. 187), 'Three Cantos', *Quia Pauper Amavi* (London: Egoist, [1919]), pp. 22–3.

The various versions of these lines present a different perspective on the role of vorticism in *The Cantos* from that presented by the passage in the discarded Canto 4. Vorticism is still represented as depicting 'the new world', but the emphasis now falls on its representation of form, rather than history. Like Botticelli and Mantegna, praised for their painterly style, respectively 'clear-outlined' and with a 'sterner line', vorticism is aligned here with the image-making function of poetry, rather than the diagnostic qualities of realist prose. Yet when these lines were written, and even when they were first published in 1917, they were to be supplemented by Canto 4's portrayal of Gaudier and Lewis as not only creating a world of form, but providing an historical method. When Canto 4 was published in 1919, however, the section on Gaudier and Lewis had been excised.[57]

Vorticism's disappearance from the text of the first cantos was not the result of a single decision, but rather the consequence of a number of factors arising from the poem's development. The poem began as a portrayal of 'the modern world' in a very immediate sense, juxtaposing passages about the war, conversations with acquaintances, and questions about the role of poetry with historical incident, literary quotation, and mythic allusion. As Pound worked, he began to remove or postpone his discussions of present-day concerns, taking a longer historical view to prepare his 'palette' of themes (*L*, 180). The poem also became more impersonal; Pound excised the many passages of autobiographical interrogation, with the result that his verbalised interactions with his sources, including those with Browning and the vorticists, disappeared.[58] The growing confidence signified by these changes is also felt in Pound's increased emphasis on the poem's textuality. While in the first drafts Pound registered considerable anxiety about the ease with which the poem could slip into rhetoric and imagined a potential solution in 'writ[ing] to paint', his revisions to the drafts highlighted and theorised the poem's textual nature. In 1923 he moved his translation of the Nekyia section of the *Odyssey* from its place in the second half of the third *Poetry* canto to the opening of the poem, thus replacing the conversation with Browning about the form one might use to encapsulate the diverse elements of the 'modern world' with an example of how one could. Odysseus's calling up of the dead is the definitive analogy for the procedures of existential historicism, in which the past speaks to the present without mediation. But the source reference following the translation

---

[57] *The Fourth Canto* (London: Ovid Press, 1919).

[58] Bush notes that Pound eliminated twenty-one personal pronouns from 'Three Cantos: 1' before its publication in the American *Lustra*, and speculates that his discussions with Eliot, then developing his theory of poetic impersonality, contributed to this decision (p. 187).

('Lie quiet Divus. I mean, that is Andreas Divus,/ In officina Wecheli, 1538, out of Homer' [1: 5]) marks how this example of an unmediated vision is simultaneously an inevitably mediated textual translation.[59] Versions of this reference, this 'footnote', had accompanied the translation in the third *Poetry* canto and its subsequent revisions, but Pound gave it more weight when he placed it at the end of the first canto. There, it is the first clot of materiality that brings the reader's eye to a halt, effectively making the argument that the immediacy and clarity of vision must be tempered by an acknowledgement of its verbal mediation. Between 1915 and 1923, then, Pound's anxieties about his poem's textual nature became less pressing, and 'writ[ing] to paint', therefore, lost its programmatic urgency.

While working on the *Cantos* drafts, Pound was also editing Fenollosa's 'The Chinese Written Character as a Medium for Poetry', an essay with immediate relevance to the questions about the relationship between the verbal and the visual addressed by *The Cantos*.[60] To Fenollosa, Chinese notation appeared to be uniquely poetic because it 'is something much more than arbitrary symbols. It is based upon a vivid shorthand picture of the operations of nature', so that a sentence 'holds something of the quality of a continuous moving picture'.[61] This erroneously pictographic reading has become notorious, and although Pound subsequently became aware of the limitations of Fenollosa's interpretation, his editing of the essay in 1919 demonstrates his enthusiasm for this aspect of the argument. To the passage in which Fenollosa made explicit his belief that all ideographs were derived from a pictorial root, contrary to the arguments of 'Chinese lexicographers', Pound added his now famous footnote: 'Professor Fenollosa is well borne out by chance evidence. The vorticist sculptor Gaudier-Brzeska [. . .] was able to read the Chinese radicals and many compound signs almost at pleasure. [. . .] He was amazed at the stupidity of lexicographers who could not discern for all their learning the pictorial values which were to him perfectly obvious and apparent.'[62]

---

[59] Jameson, pp. 51–2; Bush, pp. 192–4, 255. See Mao, pp. 159–60, for a close reading that demonstrates how irresolute a move this is.

[60] Pound's first reference to the essay occurs in 'Imagisme and England: A Vindication and an Anthology', *T. P.'s Weekly*, 25 (1915), p. 185, published on 20 February 1915. See Qian, *The Modernist Response to Chinese Art*, pp. 141–54.

[61] Ernest Fenollosa and Ezra Pound, 'The Chinese Written Character as a Medium for Poetry, [II]', *Little Review*, 6.6 (1919), 57–64 (pp. 57, 58).

[62] Ernest Fenollosa and Ezra Pound, 'The Chinese Written Character as a Medium for Poetry, IV', *Little Review*, 6.8 (1919), 68–72, (p. 70). The note also contains a description of Pound's friend, the illustrator Edmund Dulac, 'giving an impromptu panegyric on the elements of Chinese art, on the units of composition, drawn from the written characters'. Pound had revised his interpretation by 1935: see the new notes (the first of which is dated 1935) added to Ernest Fenollosa, *The Chinese*

There was much in Fenollosa's essay that was already familiar to Pound. As Robert Kern succinctly remarks, 'Fenollosa's discovery of Chinese as a natural or ordinary language, a linguistic mode that is not "fossil" but *living* poetry, is less a "discovery" than a projection of Emersonian linguistic assumptions upon a highly exotic script.' Pound had encountered these linguistic assumptions in 1910 in Hudson Maxim's *The Science of Poetry and the Philosophy of Language*, and Fenollosa's essay also has much in common with Hulme's and Gourmont's discussions of poetic language.[63] Like Maxim, Fenollosa saw metaphor as 'the very substance of poetry', like Hulme, he believed that 'poetry differs from prose in the concrete colors of its diction [. . .]. It must appeal to emotions with the charm of direct impression, flashing through regions where the intellect can only grope', and like Gourmont, he privileged the eye over the ear, and the 'thought picture' over 'abstract meaning'.[64] Small wonder, then, that Pound was so receptive to Fenollosa's theory of poetry, finding repeated echoes of ideas he had already expressed, which led him to view the essay as 'not a bare philological discussion, but a study of the fundamentals of all aesthetics'.[65]

Fenollosa's essay did, however, make an important point that Pound had not encountered in his reading of Maxim, Hulme and Gourmont. Where they had tended to emphasise the noun as the focal point for a visual poetics, Fenollosa emphasised the verb. 'It might be thought that a picture is naturally the picture of a *thing*,' Fenollosa wrote, 'but examination shows that a large number of the primitive Chinese characters, even the so-called radicals, are shorthand pictures of actions or processes.' As a number of critics have noted, this suggested a way of thinking about language that could take account of the dynamism of vorticist painting and sculpture. Moreover, Fenollosa's discussion of how this 'concrete *verb* quality [. . .]' becomes far more striking and poetic when we pass from such simple,

Written Character as a Medium for Poetry, ed. by Ezra Pound (London: Nott, 1936), pp. 37, 43, and *GK*, p. 204. For an excellent account of the intellectual background to Fenollosa's essay, see Ming Xie, *Ezra Pound and the Appropriation of Chinese Poetry: Cathay, Translation, and Imagism* (New York: Garland, 1999), pp. 19–50.

[63] Robert Kern, *Orientalism, Modernism and the American Poem* (Cambridge: Cambridge University Press, 1996), p. 116. See also John T. Irwin, *American Hieroglyphics: The Symbol of the Egyptian Hieroglyphics in the American Renaissance* (New Haven, CT: Yale University Press, 1980) and Richard Sheppard, *Modernism – Dada – Postmodernism* (Evanston, IL: Northwestern University Press, 2000), pp. 110–16.

[64] Ernest Fenollosa and Ezra Pound, 'The Chinese Written Character as a Medium for Poetry, [III]', *Little Review*, 6.7 (1919), 55–60 (pp. 57–8); Fenollosa and Pound, 'The Chinese Written Character as a Medium for Poetry, [II]', p. 58.

[65] Ernest Fenollosa and Ezra Pound, 'The Chinese Written Character as a Medium for Poetry, [I]', 6.5 (1919), 62–4 (p. 62). See Pound's references to *The Spirit of Romance* and 'Vorticism' in the notes appended to pages 57 and 58 in the third instalment.

original pictures to compounds' articulated, with what must have seemed to Pound remarkable prescience, the distinction between the imagist poem and the diagnostic *Cantos*: 'in the process of compounding, two things added together do not produce a third thing but suggest some fundamental relation between them'. Fenollosa's is a theory of language and of poetry that not only evinces a greater faith in language's representational power than that which had been encoded in imagism, it portrays language as able to actually embody causal relations: 'the truth is that acts are successive, even continuous; one causes or passes into another'.[66] Language, as theorised by Fenollosa, was inherently diagnostic after all.

Pound had written of the power of verbs before; Arnaut Daniel, he wrote in *The Spirit of Romance*, 'makes his picture, neither by simile nor by metaphor, but in the language beyond metaphor, by the use of the picturesque verb with an exact meaning' (*SR*, 33). But Fenollosa's essay renewed Pound's faith in language at a time when public declarations, including those in the form of poetry, appeared to have relinquished the integrity of the individual voice in favour of the rhetoric of the state. If Pound's effort to reinvigorate poetic language by 'writ[ing] to paint' meant imitating vorticism's immediacy, compression and vigour, Fenollosa's essay reassured Pound that these were 'natural' characteristics of language, and not only the Chinese language. 'The normal and typical sentence in English as well as in Chinese', according to Fenollosa, could express the 'universal form of action in nature', that is, of a subject acting on an object. This 'natural order' was not preserved, however, in 'Latin, German or Japanese', an argument Pound echoed when he attributed Germany's 'hell' to its 'straddling of the verb out to the end'.[67]

MODERN ART IN THE COMMON CULTURE

Although the contemporary art of the vorticists, cubists and futurists became a less compelling model for *The Cantos* during the course of its revision, the visual arts nevertheless play an important role in the version of the poem published from 1925, the date of its first publication in book form.[68] From passing references, such as those to 'eyes of Picasso' in Canto 2,

---

[66] Fenollosa and Pound, 'The Chinese Written Character as a Medium for Poetry, [II]', pp. 58–9.
[67] Fenollosa and Pound 'The Chinese Written Character as a Medium for Poetry [II]', pp. 60–1 (a printing error in the *Little Review* breaks 'the normal and typical sentence in English as well as in Chinese' across two pages). See also Pound's 'Imagisme and England', p. 185, which stresses the connection Fenollosa made between English and Chinese; 'James Joyce: at Last the Novel Appears', (p. 22).
[68] *A Draft of XVI. Cantos* (Paris: Three Mountains Press, 1925).

'lake waves Canaletto'd' in Canto 110, and Degas, Manet, Rembrandt, Velázquez and Whistler in the Pisan Cantos, to more extended descriptions in Cantos 8 to 11 (the Malatesta Cantos), Canto 45 (the 'Usura Canto'), and Canto 49 (the 'Seven Lakes Canto'), the visual work of art is both part of the world described, and, as Michael André Bernstein has said, quoting Canto 46, '"part of/ The Evidence" [. . .] a kind of painted or sculpted word that can be heard to utter an unmediated, transparent truth about the fiscal conditions prevalent at the time of its creation.'[69] Yet this use of art as 'evidence' in the revised *Cantos* is distinct from its use in the drafts, where it appeared primarily as a methodological and stylistic model. The transformation of the role of the visual arts is emblematic of the poem's movement away from a textual openness ('Low to desire controll. / All we can do 's to set forth our own good / within some other's reach') towards increasing didacticism. The two references to the art of Andrea Mantegna in *Poetry*'s 'Three Cantos' of 1917 are illustrative of this shift.

When Pound invokes the 'clear-outlined blossoms' of Botticelli and the 'sterner line' of Mantegna at the end of the first *Poetry* canto, he is making a comparison with the modernist art of Lewis, Wadsworth, Balla and Picasso, advancing a polemical genealogy for the modernist art he admires. The aim is to show that contemporary art is as worthy of veneration as that produced by revered Quattrocento artists, and its method is to draw a comparison between the formal achievements of named individuals. The choice of Botticelli and Mantegna seems to have been suggested by contemporary influences; neither painter figures prominently in Pound's writings prior to the references in the draft cantos. In 1913 Laurence Binyon had published *The Art of Botticelli*, the first and longest chapter of which had explored 'Botticelli's Significance for Modern Art'.[70] Given the questions he was exploring in his journalism and his poetry at this time, Pound could not have failed to have found interest in Binyon's presentation of Botticelli as the prime example of a Quattrocento painter who resisted the 'rhetorical' modes of the emerging high Renaissance, in favour of 'harking backward' to the spiritual values of earlier work, recommended in terms Pound would later echo: 'we cannot throw away our heritage [. . .], we must make it new and our own'.[71] Mantegna also came to Pound's attention at this time. Although Pound had long admired the church of San Zeno, it is notable that

[69] Bernstein, 'Image, Word, Sign', p. 351.
[70] David Peters Corbett, '"Make it New": Laurence Binyon, Pound and Vorticism', *Paideuma*, 26 (1997), 183–94.
[71] Laurence Binyon, *The Art of Botticelli: An Essay in Pictorial Criticism* (London: Macmillan, 1913), pp. 8, 17.

he had not remarked on Mantegna's renowned altarpiece there.[72] However, Mantegna had a privileged place in the vorticist aesthetic via Wyndham Lewis, who particularly admired his engravings. He referred approvingly to Mantegna's 'tense and angular' art in the second issue of *Blast*, later commenting that 'in Mantegna you get a mechanical ideal expressed with great beauty and with consummate power. That is why vorticist literature (which is of course mainly my handiwork) returns so often to the name of the great Renaissance engraver.'[73] Both artists thus first came to Pound's attention as progenitors of the contemporary art he admired, rather than as representative of Quattrocento art.

However, in contrast to the reference to Mantegna at the end of the first *Poetry* canto, the submerged reference that opens the second *Poetry* canto concerns itself not with the individual artist's formal achievement, but rather the wider culture's role in creating and conserving art:

> Leave Casella.
> Send out your thought upon the Mantuan palace –
> Drear waste, great halls,
> Silk tatters still in the frame, Gonzaga's splendor
> Alight with phantoms! What have we of them,
> Or much or little?[74]

These lines were later revised to refer directly to Mantegna's frescoes in the Palazzo Ducale's Camera degli Sposi (1474), and placed at the end of Canto 3: 'Drear waste, the pigment flakes from the stone, / Or plaster flakes, Mantegna painted the wall' (3: 12). In both versions, the author of the palace's splendour is not only the artist, but his patron Lodovico Gonzaga, and the culture he created in Mantua that enabled the art to be produced. Thus the art itself operates as evidence of cultural vitality. Yet the speaker is remembering that vitality, not looking at it: the tatters of silk and the flaking of the pigment from the stone are evidence of the cultural disintegration that Pound believed began in the Cinquecento, the period following Lodovico's rule.[75] In this context, Pound's reference to

---

[72] Pound first referred to the church of San Zeno in 1910 in *SR*, 13.

[73] Wyndham Lewis, 'A Review of Contemporary Art', *Blast*, 2 (1915), 38–47 (p. 48); Wyndham Lewis, 'The Skeleton in the Cupboard Speaks', in *Wyndham Lewis The Artist: From 'Blast' to Burlington House* (London: Laidlaw & Laidlaw, 1939), 67–94 (p. 80).

[74] 'Three Cantos, II', *Poetry*, 10 (1917), 180–8 (p. 180).

[75] See Paul Kristeller, *Andrea Mantegna*, trans. S. Arthur Strong (London: Longmans, Green, 1901), pp. 240–1. Pound may also have had in mind Mantegna frescoes that were deteriorating rather closer to home. He would have been aware of Roger Fry's involvement in the restoration of *The Triumphs of Caesar* frescoes at Hampton Court (c. 1486–92), bought by Charles I from the Gonzaga collection, especially since Edward Wadsworth had assisted Fry in 1912. See Andrew Martindale, *The Triumphs*

Mantegna's 'sterner line', which had in previous drafts actually been part of the description of the Palazzo Ducale, takes on a moral force. While the morality of 'clear demarcation', and the immorality of the line that 'grows thick' would become familiar markers of *The Cantos*' ethics, such didacticism was absent from its early stages (45: 229). In the 'Three Cantos', the visual arts' role as a model is still registered, but Pound has also begun to use art as "part of/ The Evidence". After 1917, visual art appeared primarily in this guise, for which contemporary art was less appropriate.

This shift in the representation of art might be glossed as a move from a Whistlerian to a Ruskinian perspective. In his use of the early Renaissance as a vantage point from which to critique the conditions of modernity, Pound is working in the tradition of the nineteenth-century critics of industrialism like Browning, Thomas Carlyle, William Morris and Ruskin. For Ruskin, Quattrocento art was of greater spiritual and artistic significance than that of the more widely esteemed High Renaissance because 'its imperfection is in some sort essential to all that we know of life', and 'to banish imperfection is to destroy expression, to check exertion, to paralyze vitality'; Browning made the same opposition in *Men and Women* when he favourably contrasted the vigour of Fra Lippo Lippi with the technical perfection of Andrea del Sarto.[76] In the drafts, Pound had transferred these values to the contemporary stage and linked them to a patriotic argument, praising the energy and immediacy of Lewis and Gaudier over his own over-scholarly style, which he associated in turn with *Kultur*. But modern art could not perform the critical function that Quattrocento art had for Ruskin and Browning. Its perspective on modernity was inevitably compromised by its status as a product of the conditions against which it tried to protest. As Hugh Kenner observed, 'Mantegna painted Duke Gonzaga and his family in fresco on the wall above the fireplace of the Camera degli Sposi in the palace in Mantua, and there is no way to detach and sell a

of Caesar by Andrea Mantegna in the Collection of Her Majesty the Queen at Hampton Court (London: Miller, 1979), pp. 17, 117–18, 127; Barbara Wadsworth, *Edward Wadsworth: A Painter's Life* (Wilton: Russell, 1989), pp. 32–3.

76 John Ruskin, *The Stones of Venice,* vol. II, in *The Works of John Ruskin,* ed. E. T. Cook and Alexander Wedderburn, 39 vols (London: Allen, 1903–1912), X: 203–4; Robert Browning, 'Fra Lippo Lippi' and 'Andrea del Sarto (Called "The Faultless Painter")', in *The Poetical Works of Robert Browning,* vol. V, ed. Ian Jack and Robert Inglesfield (Oxford: Clarendon Press, 1995), pp. 35–53, 263–74. See Hilary Fraser, *The Victorians and Renaissance Italy* (Oxford: Blackwell, 1992), pp. 91–133, and also J. B. Bullen, *The Myth of the Renaissance in Nineteenth-Century Writing* (Oxford: Clarendon Press, 1994), Peter Allen Dale, *The Victorian Critic and the Idea of History: Carlyle, Arnold, Pater* (Cambridge, MA: Harvard University Press, 1977), Wallace K. Ferguson, *The Renaissance in Historical Thought: Five Centuries of Interpretation* (Boston: Houghton Mifflin, 1948), pp. 195–252, 290–328, John Hale, *England and the Italian Renaissance: The Growth of Interest in its History and Art,* rev. edn (London: Fontana, 1996).

fresco. For a certain portable Wyndham Lewis portrait £2000 was recently being asked. Lewis received for it perhaps 1/20 of that. Three of its inter-mediate purchasers have been dealers, and one of these dealers brought it from another dealer.'[77] While Lewis's works ably satirised their own con-text, as cultural 'evidence' they were nevertheless testimony to the modern commercialization of the institution of art.

Although Pound's turn to the early Renaissance had a strong liter-ary precedent and was consolidated by his own academic background in medieval literature, his knowledge of the visual art of the period was by no means well established, as is often assumed. He had spent considerable time in Italy, read Browning and some Ruskin, but before 1915 his comments about the period's paintings had been restricted to conventional remarks about the Old Masters, and his correspondence with Dorothy Shakespear in 1913 suggests that her knowledge of Renaissance painting was consider-ably greater than his (*L/DS*, 222–3).[78] He was, however, more compelled by early Renaissance sculpture and architecture, although his comments do not suggest a wide range of reference. He sent Shakespear a card of Santa Maria dei Miracoli in Venice in 1913, also buying a reproduction of the bases of the columns for himself (*L/DS*, 226), and in later years he associated the twelfth-century church of San Zeno with the spirit of the Quattrocento.[79] His wartime interest in the Renaissance appears to have been initiated less by an active engagement with its art and architecture, than by the portrayal of the period by nineteenth-century historiographers. From early 1915 Pound began to write noticeably more frequently about the Renaissance, and in his 'Affirmations' series for the *New Age* and a three-part series on American culture for *Poetry* entitled 'The Renaissance', its relevance becomes clear.

The sixth instalment of the 'Affirmations' series, 'Analysis of this Decade', draws an extended comparison between the intellectual life of the 1910s and that of the Renaissance. Pound argues, as Hulme had before, that 'it is only recently that men have begun to combat the Renaissance [. . .], we have begun deliberately to try to free ourselves from the Renaissance shackles'. However, unlike Hulme, and the Guild Socialists of the *New Age*, Pound

---

[77] Kenner, *The Pound Era*, p. 315.
[78] See Peter Nicholls, 'Ruskin's Grotesque and the Modernism of Ezra Pound and Wyndham Lewis': 'Pound, we conclude, must have read Ruskin, but we are hard pressed to find many specific references in his writings. [. . .] why does Pound never engage directly with Ruskin's writings on Venice, given his own intense interest in the city? And why [. . .] does he never discuss Ruskin's economic theories?' (p. 168).
[79] Carpenter, p. 141. See Peter Robinson, 'Ezra Pound and Italian Art', in *Pound's Artists*, pp. 121–76 (pp. 137–43).

does not see the rejection of the Renaissance as a return to the values of an earlier civilisation, 'we are scarcely returning to a pious Catholicism or to a limited mediævalism', he writes. Instead, he frames the second decade of the twentieth century as having 'a new focus', and just as 'a certain number of fairly simple and now obvious ideas moved the Renaissance', 'a certain number of simple and obvious ideas, running together and interacting, are making a new, and to many a most obnoxious, art'. The generators of these ideas are revealed as Ford, Lewis, Gaudier-Brzeska, Wadsworth, Fenollosa, and Pound himself.[80]

The comparison with the Renaissance is not only deployed as an audacious advertisement for vorticist art; Pound's aim is far more ambitious. In the first paragraph Pound emphasises that he is interested in a particular version of the Renaissance, that presented by Jacob Burckhardt and Pasquale Villari, who 'considered the whole age, the composite life of the age, in contradistinction to those who have sentimentalised over its aesthetics'. For Pound, the significance of the Burckhardtian tradition is twofold: it depicted the Renaissance as containing the seeds of 'modern civilisation', and it read the Renaissance as the product of the deliberate circulation of ideas by 'a few very different men, with each one a very definite propaganda'. 'The Renaissance was in part the result of a programme', Pound writes, 'we believe in the value of a programme in contradistinction to, but not in contradiction of, the individual impulse.' 'The modern sense of the value of the "creative, constructive individual" [. . .] is just as definite a doctrine as the Renaissance attitude De Dignitate, Humanism.' The programme Pound attributes to these Renaissance individuals and the vorticists alike is 'a search for a certain precision', the 'revival of a sense of realism', which in the Renaissance enabled the discussion of 'tyranny, democracy, etc'.[81]

These terms mark out 'Affirmations, VI: Analysis of this Decade' as a precursor of the four articles on literary realism and the war Pound wrote later that year, and clarify vorticism's relation to that argument. Vorticism is not only able to 'present the actual discords of modern "civilisation"', as Pound wrote in *Blast*, its 'creative, constructive individual[s]' have the potential to transform political and social life through the lessons of their art, as Pound believed his early Renaissance heroes did.[82] Lorenzo Valla, for example, 'had a great passion for exactness, and he valued the Roman vortex', so that 'the revival of Roman Law, while not his private act, was

[80] 'Affirmations, VI: Analysis of this Decade', pp. 410–11.
[81] 'Affirmations, VI: Analysis of this Decade', pp. 409, 411, 410. See Robert Casillo, 'The Italian Renaissance: Pound's Problematic Debt to Burckhardt', *Mosaic*, 22.4 (1989), 13–29.
[82] 'Chronicles', p. 86.

made possible or accelerated by him'. Pico della Mirandola's 'propaganda' was based on the claim 'that science and knowledge generally were not, or, at least, should not, or need not be, grounded solely and exclusively on the knowledge of the Greeks and Romans'.[83] In 'The Renaissance' articles for *Poetry*, Pound makes the same argument, repeating that 'we have not realized to what an extent a renaissance is a thing made – a thing made by conscious propaganda', and recommending 'the biographies of Erasmus and Lorenzo Valla' for 'consolation'. In these latter articles, his focus is not a vorticist Renaissance but an American Renaissance, but this too, he argues, must be created by energetic individuals: 'We have looked to the wrong powers. We have not sufficiently looked to ourselves.'[84]

Pound's interest in the Renaissance in these articles is patently not nostalgic. It is not as a golden period of artisan production that he looks back to the Quattrocento; indeed, he makes a point in 'Affirmations' of praising the modern 'enjoyment of machinery' as 'just as natural and just as significant a phase of this age as was the Renaissance "enjoyment of nature for its own sake"'.[85] Instead, the Renaissance begins its incursion into Pound's writing as an inspiring example of how individual writers could affect world events through literary style, a model programme for his own milieu. When Mantegna and Botticelli made their way into *The Cantos* later that year, it was accordingly the precision of their painterly line that Pound isolated as vorticism's inheritance. If vorticism could attain equivalent clarity it might create the intellectual tools for a debate about 'tyranny, democracy, etc', obviating the need for war. But to have that effect, it would have to disseminate its values effectively. Although only a year earlier Pound had presented the artist as at 'war' with a 'humanity' described as 'unbearably stupid', by the time he wrote 'The Renaissance' articles he was arguing that 'the arts are noble only as they meet the inner need of the poor. Bach is given to all men, Homer is given to all men: you need only the faculty of music or of patience to read or to hear. Painting and sculpture are given to all men in a particular place, to all who have money for travel.'[86] The war had given vorticism's aesthetic programme an object and an urgency.

Pound's separation of literature and music from painting and sculpture in this quotation hints at a potential difficulty in this otherwise optimistic statement of aesthetic egalitarianism. Painting and sculpture are confined to 'a particular place', they require 'money for travel'. As Pound's emphasis

---

[83] 'Affirmations, VI: Analysis of this Decade', p. 410.
[84] 'The Renaissance, II', *Poetry*, 5 (1915), 283–7 (p. 285).
[85] 'Affirmations, VI: Analysis of this Decade', p. 411.
[86] 'The New Sculpture', p. 68; 'The Renaissance, II', p. 284.

on the importance of the circulation of ideas and popularisation of the arts grew over the following years, the distinguishing feature of the plastic arts, their materiality, became a problematic issue, to the point that by the end of the decade Pound was stridently denouncing painting and sculpture as a 'luxury-trade'.[87] But his recognition of the essential difference of the plastic arts was not merely theoretical. The summer of 1915 marked the beginning of an intense period of practical engagement with contemporary painting and, especially, sculpture, and Pound's disillusionment with these arts considered in the abstract was at least as much affected by his personal experience of the procedures of the contemporary art world as it was by an intellectual analysis of the place of art in modernity.

With Pound's realisation that 'a renaissance is a thing made – a thing made by conscious propaganda', came the requirement to launch that propaganda, and in this period Pound becomes substantially more practically involved in the infrastructure of modernism, transferring his attention increasingly from the individual artwork to the field of cultural production.[88] He had already begun his propagandist programme on behalf of vorticism with his September 1914 'Vorticism' article in the *Fortnightly Review*, which brought the movement to a broader and more diverse readership than *Blast* and the *Egoist*, and the 'Affirmations' series in the *New Age* allowed him to provide a still more extended account of vorticism. Pound's long-cherished ambition to found a 'College of Arts' had been advertised in an article in the *Egoist* and a prospectus distributed in November 1914. It promised 'an intellectual status no lower than that attained by the courts of the Italian Renaissance', and its core staff were vorticists: Pound, Gaudier, Lewis, Wadsworth, and the photographer Alvin Langdon Coburn (with Pound, the inventor of 'vortography'), alongside John Cournos, Arnold Dolmetsch, and Katherine Ruth Heyman, among others.[89] But the articles and the college were largely personal projects, and it was Wyndham Lewis, not Pound, who had been orchestrating the most public demonstrations of vorticism's group identity: *Blast* and the 1915 *Vorticist Exhibition* at the Doré Gallery. However, when Lewis became ill shortly after the outbreak of war and enlisted in March 1916, Pound took over his role as vorticism's chief activist, and one event in particular transformed his involvement: the death of Gaudier-Brzeska on 5 June 1915. As a direct consequence of Gaudier's

---

[87] 'B. H. Dias' [Ezra Pound], 'Art and Luxury', *New Age*, 26 (1920), 238–9 (p. 238).

[88] 'The Renaissance, II', p. 285.

[89] *L/MC*, 55, 'Patria Mia, VII', *New Age*, 11 (1912), 587–8 (p. 588); 'Preliminary Announcement of the College of Arts', *Egoist*, 1 (1914), 413–14; *Preliminary Announcement of the College of Arts* (London: Complete Press, 1914).

death, Pound composed his influential *Gaudier-Brzeska: A Memoir*, took
a central role in organising an exhibition of vorticist works in New York,
and became an unpaid dealer in vorticist art.

When Pound heard on 'about the 28th' of June that Gaudier-Brzeska
had been killed, he began to make plans to memorialise his art. Pound's
first letter after Gaudier's death to the American collector, John Quinn,
suggested several possibilities: 'We hope to bring out a well illustrated
memoir to Brzeska', 'the next number [of *Blast*] may contain nothing but
Brzeska', and 'I suppose a loan exhibit of Brzeska might be arranged for
the Metropolitan Gallery in New York.' Almost immediately, he realised
that these activities also provided opportunities to disseminate the vorticist
programme; in a postscript written up the side of the letter, Pound modified
his last proposal, 'If the *metropolitan* has sense enough to arrange a Brzeska
show. They might go the whole hog & do a Vorticist show' (*L/JQ*, 29–
30). While there was no 'next number' of *Blast*, Pound's *Gaudier-Brzeska:
A Memoir* was published on 14 April 1916 (the American issue appeared
in June), the *Exhibition of the Vorticists* took place at the Penguin Club
in New York in January 1917, though Gaudier was not represented, and
the *Memorial Exhibition of the Work of Henri Gaudier-Brzeska*, organised
by Robert Bevan and Stanislawa de Karlowska, was held at the Leicester
Galleries in London during May and June 1918.[90]

Gaudier-Brzeska: A Memoir was conceived as the accompaniment to the
proposed exhibition of Gaudier's work at the Metropolitan Museum of Art.
Once it had become clear that there would not be another *Blast* in the near
future, Pound approached the publisher John Lane on 10 August 1915 with
his proposal for the memoir. Although Pound thought that Lane himself
'with sure instinct, devines [*sic*] that there is no money to be got out of me',
the manager was 'impressed with news of N.Y. show, and of sales of work'.
Pound asked Quinn to contact Lane's American office and 'get the New
York house, Lane & co. or whatever it is to write over to J. L[ane]. saying
that they want the book'; on 8 September he reported that he had received
the contract from Lane (*L/JQ*, 31, 44). He constructed the book over the

---

[90] Paul O'Keeffe, *Gaudier-Brzeska: An Absolute Case of Genius* (London: Allen Lane, 2004), pp. 297–8.
Although Pound wrote a preface to the catalogue of the *Memorial Exhibition of the Work of Henri
Gaudier-Brzeska*, he had little involvement in the exhibition itself, and he and Quinn associated it
with Sophie Brzeska in their letters: Quinn quotes her writing, 'I wish to hold a show of all Henry's
work', and tells Pound that 'she can keep all the things [i.e. the sculptures he has bought or plans to
buy] there for the memorial exhibition, provided it will be held within the next six months' (John
Quinn, Letter to Ezra Pound, 15 March 1916, EPP, Beinecke, 43.1814); Pound refers to 'her [Sophie
Brzeska's] memorial show' in his letter to Quinn of 8 April 1916 (*L/JQ*, 70).

autumn, and was offering to send Quinn the galley proofs 'in a few days' on 19 January 1916 (*L/JQ*, 59).[91]

Gaudier-Brzeska might be read as Pound's own vorticist exhibition in textual form: the book is made up of Gaudier's letters and published writings, articles about Gaudier, Pound's previously published essays on Gaudier and vorticism more generally, and a catalogue that Pound described apprehensively as 'partial' and 'not [. . .] even a moderately full catalogue' (*GB*, 159, 163). These disparate elements exhibited together are accompanied by Pound's commentary that is by turns a biographical and psychological portrait of the artist, a polemical reading of Gaudier's career, a combative defence of vorticism, and a general restatement of Pound's own aesthetics. In a recent essay, Christine Froula placed *Gaudier-Brzeska* in the elegiac tradition, 'in which the mourner, who speaks for a community, struggles arduously toward renewed hope for the future'. This generic context yields the insight that 'far from merely constellating a community of mourners around Gaudier's art, Pound actually seeks to conjure a new community by framing that art as an eloquent speech act, of moment for the individuals called to this community and for its future. The Gaudier of *Gaudier-Brzeska* thus functions much as does the pastoral elegy's vegetation deity, through whose death the community confronts loss and mortality, and whose symbolic rebirth restores hope for its future.'[92]

Froula's presentation of *Gaudier-Brzeska* as an effort to 'conjure a new community' is consistent with Pound's propagandist resolutions laid out at the beginning of the year, and the book clearly advances the case for vorticism as the definitive modern aesthetic. In this, Pound was implicitly arguing against the obituaries and essays published after Gaudier's death which expressed reservations about the significance of Gaudier's vorticist work, and of vorticism itself: Roger Fry, in the *Burlington Magazine*, had argued that Gaudier's vorticist work was not 'in line with [his] special gifts and artistic temperament. Brzeska himself recognized this in his later conversations with me, and states in one of his letters that he intends to return to organic forms.'[93] Similarly, John Middleton Murry, in the

---

[91] 'Gaudier [Brzeska]: Autograph ms., typescript, and printed proof', EPP, Beinecke, 104.4351–2: this typescript contains three indications of dates: in the 'Præfatio', Pound refers to Henry James's adoption of British citizenship in July 1915 as 'a few weeks ago'; he signed the 'Præfatio' 'August 1915'; and in the second section of chapter ten, 'Friendship with Wolmark', wrote 'Wolmark has done two portraits of him, one of which is now (Oct. 1915) in the "International".' The latter two dates were deleted before publication.

[92] Christine Froula, 'Gaudier-Brzeska: Abstract Form, Modern War, Vorticist Elegy', in *Ezra Pound and Referentiality*, ed. Hélène Aji (Paris: Presses de l'Université de Paris-Sorbonne, 2003), pp. 119–31 (pp. 120, 121–2).

[93] Roger Fry, 'Gaudier-Brzeska', *Burlington Magazine*, 29 (1916), 209–10 (p. 210).

Westminster Gazette, had concluded that 'Vorticism was only a passing phase in his development', and even *The Times*'s announcement of Gaudier's death had questioned 'whether his great gifts found a full scope for their exercise in this abstract art'.[94] Pound had replied furiously to Murry that Gaudier's 'Vortex' in the first issue of *Blast* 'was not in any sense the mood of a moment', and 'nor had he up to two days before his death, when he last wrote to me, made any sign of recantation'.[95]

Despite his protestations that he was 'not over-anxious to enter upon long quibbles either about his work or the group-name he chose to work under', Pound's commentary was manifestly intended to stress the intellectual and social coherence of the vorticist group (*GB*, 5). The editing of Gaudier's letters for the memoir was motivated by the same aim. Pound left out sections that related directly to Gaudier's sculpture, yet found room to include trivial remarks that highlighted his relationship with the other vorticists (*GB*, 68, 82). In the final chapters of the memoir, Pound returns to familiar elements of the idiosyncratic genealogy through which he had first theorised vorticism, the writings of Laurence Binyon and Whistler, even though, as he admits, 'I know that most of [Whistler's] dicta apply more immediately to vorticist painting than to Brzeska's sculpture' (*GB*, 145). Despite its somewhat thrown-together appearance, *Gaudier-Brzeska* is a carefully constructed piece of vorticist propaganda.

However, the book's function as an advertisement for vorticism is in tension with the most important role it had to play on publication in 1916, that is as 'a memorandum to keep [Gaudier's] work from getting lost or mislaid'.[96] In this guise, the memoir was to attest to the authenticity of Gaudier's works, give some assessment of their relative worth, state their current ownership, and also act as an expedient for potential buyers, in the first instance, John Quinn, who by this means was provided with good quality photographs as well as verbal descriptions from which to choose his purchases.[97] As a catalogue for the connoisseur and the collector, an objective approach was required, and the first chapter accordingly emphasises its critical disinterestedness: 'If this entails a certain formal and almost dreary documentation at the very outset, I must ask the reader's

[94] J.M.M., 'Henri Gaudier-Brzeska. In Memoriam', *Westminster Gazette*, 22 July 1915, p. 2; 'French Sculptor Killed in Action: M. Henri Gaudier Brzeska', *Times*, 7 July 1915, p. 13, col. e.

[95] 'The Vorticists [letter]', *Westminster Gazette*, 30 July 1915, p. 3. See Sarah Shalgosky, Rod Brookes and Jane Beckett, 'Henri Gaudier: Art History and the "Savage Messiah"', in *Henri Gaudier-Brzeska, Sculptor, 1891–1915*, ed. Jeremy Lewison (Cambridge: Kettle's Yard, 1983), pp. 21–8 and Silber, *Gaudier-Brzeska*, pp. 51–64.

[96] 'Gaudier [Brzeska]: Note for reprint: typescript', EPP, Beinecke, 104.4358.

[97] John Quinn, Letter to Ezra Pound, 26 August 1915, EPP, Beinecke, 43.1813, *L/JQ*, 22, 44.

indulgence', Pound writes, 'I am trying to leave as clear a record as possible of Gaudier's art and thought' (*GB*, 6). But as the work proceeds, Pound becomes increasingly unable or unwilling to maintain the necessary empirical method. 'In reading over what I have written I find it full of conceit, or at least full of pronouns in the first person', he laments, 'and yet what do we, any of us, know of our friends and acquaintance save that on such and such a day we saw them, and that they did or said this, that or the other, to which words and acts we give witness' (*GB*, 45). Ultimately, he finds that he can only conclude the book with a statement of personal belief: 'ROUGHLY: What have they done for me these vorticist artists?' (*GB*, 155).

If writing *Gaudier-Brzeska* put Pound in the uncomfortable position of affirming the procedures of the art market, his involvement in the *Exhibition of the Vorticists* at the Penguin Gallery in New York, and his purchase of vorticist works for Quinn, mark his active participation in those procedures. Pound and Quinn had met briefly through John Butler Yeats in 1910, but their correspondence famously began in 1915 after Pound had included an allusion to Quinn's 'buying autograph MSS. of William Morris' alongside a reference to the 'faked Rembrandts and faked Vandykes' he remembered carrying out from the fire at John Wanamaker's estate in 1907 as examples of a philistine 'plutocracy and [. . .] the remains of an aristocracy who ought to know by this time that keeping up the arts means keeping up living artists'.[98] In his first letter to Pound, Quinn informed him that he had 'sold all of my Meredith, Morris, Swinburne, Lang, Gissing, Hearn, Henley, Watson, Rossetti and other manuscripts for just what they cost me' and, far from 'buying only dead things', he had built up a major collection of modernist art, much of it by living artists. The list he gave Pound mentioned work by Cézanne, Epstein, Auguste Chabaud, Arthur B. Davies, André Derain, Duchamp, Raymond Duchamp-Villon, Raoul Dufy, Gauguin, Augustus John, Walt Kuhn, Ernest Lawson, Matisse, Picasso, Maurice Prendergast, Georges Rouault, André Dunoyer de Segonzac and Van Gogh. In addition, he wrote, he had 'done as much, if not more than you have done, to cure people of buying "faked Rembrandts and faked Vandykes"', by reforming the Tariff Act of 1909, in order to allow 'only <u>original</u> works to come in duty free'. Finally, Quinn wrote that he had 'read your article about Gaudier Brzeska with great interest' and asked where he 'could get any good work by him'.[99] Pound immediately began to negotiate sales with

---

[98] For further details of the 1910 meeting, see *L/JQ*, 1, 20 and B. L. Reid, *The Man from New York: John Quinn and his Friends* (New York: Oxford University Press, 1968), p. 86; 'Affirmations, III: Jacob Epstein', p. 312.

[99] John Quinn, Letter to Ezra Pound, 25 February 1915, EPP, Beinecke, 43.1813.

Gaudier, Sophie Brzeska and Fry, whose Omega Workshops held a small number of Gaudier's works.[100]

Following Gaudier's death, the purchase of his works became more urgent and more complicated. Pound was required to ascertain who legally owned the sculptor's work before Quinn could buy it, which involved negotiating between Gaudier's family and Brzeska, with legal tuition from Quinn (*L/JQ*, 68). Agreeing the sale took several months, obtaining the works took even longer, and Quinn did not receive all the sculptures he wanted until 1920.[101] Although he generously agreed to Brzeska's endless stipulations and rising prices, Quinn had to remind Pound repeatedly that they were conducting a business transaction. Frustrated at the high price he had paid for Gaudier's drawings, Quinn told Pound on 15 March 1916 'she has out-maneuvered you, my Boy, she out-generaled you. She sold us both. I bought the damn drawings merely because I thought I was going to have a representative selection of his sculpture, practically all of it outside of what would go into the South Kensington and the Luxembourg [. . .]. But damn sentimentality: Cold business now, an assignment, transfer and delivery before paying further cash.'[102]

Pound obtained works by Jessica Dismorr, Frederick Etchells, Lewis, Helen Saunders, William Roberts and Wadsworth, as well as Gaudier, for Quinn.[103] In these transactions he effectively became the vorticists' dealer, though with the vital difference that he received no direct financial recompense. His ambiguous role evidently caused him some disquiet and Quinn was required to reassure him. 'No, my dear Pound', wrote Quinn, 'don't you think for a moment that I for one instant have thought of your "joining the ranks of people wanting money".'[104] Nevertheless, through Quinn's

[100] Judith Collins, *The Omega Workshops* (London: Secker & Warburg, 1983), pp. 70–5.
[101] Judith Zilczer, *The Noble Buyer: John Quinn, Patron of the Avant-Garde* (Washington, DC: Smithsonian Institution Press, 1978), pp. 40, 66.
[102] John Quinn, Letter to Ezra Pound, 15 March 1916.
[103] *The John Quinn Collection: Paintings & Sculpture of the Moderns* (New York: American Art Association, 1927), Reid, pp. 251, 254.
[104] John Quinn, Letter to Ezra Pound, 14 February 1916, EPP, Beinecke, 43.1814. Pound did however receive considerable recompense through Quinn's beneficial influence on his literary career. During the same period in which the vorticist exhibition was being planned and Brzeska's works purchased, Pound was seeking editorship of a literary magazine. In 1915 he was anticipating the editorship of the *Academy*, but when that opportunity disappeared, he considered taking over a number of other periodicals, or beginning his own. Quinn looked out potential periodicals, suggested names of American contributors, editors and subscribers, and when Pound decided to concentrate on developing the *Egoist*, contributed financial backing, which he continued to provide when Pound switched his allegiance to the *Little Review*: see *L/JQ*, 9, and Pound's letters to Quinn from 1915 to 1918. Quinn also negotiated with American publishing houses to secure the publication of *Lustra*, *'Noh' or Accomplishment* and *Pavannes and Divisions* (*L/JQ*, 92).

tuition, Pound developed a noticeably more business-oriented approach and, crucially, he began to recognise the investment, as well as the aesthetic, value of art: 'I agree with you that I want what you call "monumental single works"', wrote Quinn, quoting Pound's letter back to him. 'Indeed I <u>do</u> have to "guard against loading up with too much small stuff". Artists and friends of mine are always urging me to buy "promising work". Some day I shall have to have a big clean-out of "promising work".'[105] As the quoted phrases show, Pound, always responsive to 'promising work' himself, was nevertheless willing to appraise works in terms of their market worth for Quinn.

Although the idea for the *Exhibition of the Vorticists* had been Pound's, Quinn paid for the exhibition and undertook the bulk of its organisation. Pound's tasks were restricted to obtaining the works themselves and organising their insurance and shipping.[106] The transportation was complicated by wartime conditions, and the artists' anxieties regarding the safety of their works. Lewis initially refused to allow his work to be sent in one shipment, fearing torpedoes. Sophie Brzeska wanted Gaudier's plaster works cast because 'plaster wont stand shipment', though Quinn replied that 'it can be sent perfectly safe and well' if 'carefully wrapped and carefully packed, each plaster cast in its own case, then that case [. . .] encased in a larger one'. Frederick Etchells, on the other hand, 'was praying for the boat to go down as he professed to think sales impossible and insurance very desirable'.[107] Despite Pound's and Quinn's protracted efforts at persuasion, in March 1916 Brzeska finally decided not to send Gaudier's sculptures, and in April the works by the other artists were packed and shipped.[108] They arrived on the *Minnesota* at the end of June 1916, and on 1 July Quinn wrote to Pound announcing that 'the show is going to open at Montross' [gallery] Monday week, which will be July 10th'.[109] The Montross Gallery, however, suddenly withdrew its support, and the exhibition did not open until 10 January 1917, at Walt Kuhn's Penguin Club. It contained forty-six works by Lewis, including the major works *Kermesse* (1912), *Portrait of an English Woman* (1915) and *Workshop* (1915), nine by Etchells, eight by Wadsworth, and four each by Dismorr, Roberts and Saunders. 'The things look very well. Everything is hung, the drawings as well as the paintings and they look very fine indeed', wrote Quinn to Pound. Nevertheless, he

---

[105] John Quinn, Letter to Ezra Pound, 11 February 1916, EPP, Beinecke, 43.1814.
[106] See Reid, pp. 292–3, *L/JQ*, 59, 64, 69–70, 82–3.
[107] Reid, p. 253; *L/JQ*, 59; John Quinn, Letter to Ezra Pound, 15 March 1916; *L/JQ*, 82.
[108] Reid, p. 253; Ezra Pound, Letter to John Quinn, 18 March 1916, EPP, Beinecke, 43.1814.
[109] John Quinn, Letter to Ezra Pound, 1 July 1916, EPP, Beinecke, 43.1814.

anticipated that 'the exhibition will be roasted'. In fact, the exhibition was barely noticed in the press, despite the fact that Quinn had sent out notices.[110] To Lewis, Quinn suggested that the lack of interest was partly due to animosity towards Pound, 'for some of these damn fools seem to be down on him'.[111] According to Judith Zilczer, Quinn was the only buyer.[112] The experience of organising the exhibition had a profound impact on Pound's attitude towards the visual arts.

ART AS LUXURY: 'ART NOTES' AND *HUGH SELWYN MAUBERLEY*

Pound's work on behalf of Quinn and the Gaudier estate demonstrated the extent to which the worth of a painting, drawing, woodcut or sculpture was bound up with its 'presence in time and space, its unique existence at the place where it happens to be', making its worth dependent on its own originality and authenticity.[113] To Pound, the fact that it is possible to 'own' a work of plastic art in a way that one cannot own a poem or a musical composition, even if one owns their manuscripts, made the plastic arts inevitably the preserve of the individual, wealthy collector. Even if the collector was Quinn, and his money was providing much-needed support for the artist, this elitism built into the plastic arts was an indictment of modern culture. Pound's recognition of this is reflected in his recommendation of vorticist art as a series of lessons in the 'perception of forms', its value exceeding the individual work. The same insight drives his periodic remarks about architecture in this period; Epstein, Pound writes, should be 'in some place where his work would be so prominent that people, and even British architects, would be forced to think about form'.[114] By 1918, Pound saw a hard distinction between literature and the visual arts, remarking in an essay on magazine publication that 'literature is not a commodity, that literature emphatically does not lie on a counter where it can be snatched up at once by a straw-hatted young man in a hurry'.[115] The implied opposition here, between literature and the kind of art which could and did 'lie on a counter', was to be consolidated over the following years.

---

[110] John Quinn, Letter to Ezra Pound, 12 January 1917, EPP, Beinecke, 43.1815.
[111] John Quinn, Letter to Wyndham Lewis, 15 March 1917, EPP, Beinecke, 43.1816.
[112] Zilczer, p. 40. Reid writes that Quinn was 'almost the only buyer' (p. 254).
[113] Walter Benjamin, 'The Work of Art in the Age of Mechanical Reproduction', in *Illuminations*, ed. Hannah Arendt, trans. Harry Zohn (London: Fontana, 1973), pp. 219–53 (pp. 222–3). For an illuminating discussion of differences between media, see Richard Wollheim, 'Minimal Art', in *On Art and the Mind* (Cambridge, MA: Harvard University Press, 1974), pp. 101–11.
[114] 'Affirmations, II: Vorticism', p. 278; Affirmations, III: Jacob Epstein', p. 312.
[115] 'Raoul Root' [Ezra Pound], 'America's Critic', *Little Review*, 4.9 (1918), 10–12 (p. 11).

In this light, the experiments with vorticist photography conducted by Pound and Alvin Langdon Coburn in 1916 and 1917 represent a significant missed opportunity. 'Vortography' was invented by Pound and Coburn in October 1916, in order to '[free] the camera from reality and let one take Picassos direct from nature' (*L/JQ*, 88). By fastening three mirrors into a triangle they produced an instrument – now lost – they named the 'vortescope', through which they took photographs of crystals, bits of wood and Pound himself.[116] For Coburn, creating the vortographs 'was the most thrilling experience he had ever had in all the realms of photography', and he claimed that 'it would do in photography, in the hands of the sympathetic worker, what Cezanne, Matisse, and others had done in painting, or Scriabine, Stravinsky, and others in music'.[117]

Pound was conspicuously less enthusiastic, arguing in his catalogue notes to an exhibition of Coburn's vortographs and paintings that vortography's best use would be to assist the progress of modern art 'as the anatomical studies of the Renaissance' assisted academic painting in the fifteenth century. Vortography may help the artist to work out 'certain definite problems in the aesthetics of form', he thought, which might establish 'a mathematical harmony of form, angles, proportions, etc., arranged as we have had a mathematical "harmony" arranged for us in music'.[118] Both Coburn and Pound confined their remarks to the formal properties of the vortograph: neither explored the potential of vortography as a mass medium, a means of bringing abstract design to a wider audience. Yet Pound was experimenting with vortography at precisely the same time as he was arguing for the 'free circulation of thought' in his journalism. In *Poetry* he set out a programme which involved removing the tariff on the importation of foreign books, revising the copyright law, learning more languages, translating more foreign literature, and thinking more seriously about 'the differentiation of individuals'.[119] In his important 'Provincialism the Enemy' series for the *New Age*, he told readers that 'the ultimate goal of scholarship is popularisation. (Groans from the scholar, the æsthete, the connoisseur!) [. . .] Popularisation in its decent and respectable sense means simply that the

---

[116] See Alvin Langdon Coburn, *Alvin Langdon Coburn, Photographer: An Autobiography*, ed. Helmut and Alison Gernsheim (New York: Dover, 1978), p. 102, and Mike Weaver, *Alvin Langdon Coburn, Symbolist Photographer: Beyond the Craft* (New York: Aperture, 1986), p. 9. On Pound and vortography, see Melita Schaum, 'The Grammar of the Visual: Alvin Langdon Coburn, Ezra Pound, and the Eastern Aesthetic in Early Modernist Photography and Poetry', *Paideuma*, 24.2–3 (1995), 79–106, and my 'The Modern Public and Vortography', in Aji, pp. 177–89.

[117] 'The Camera Club', *British Journal of Photography*, 64 (1917), p. 87.

[118] 'The Vortographs', in *Vortographs and Paintings by Alvin Langdon Coburn* (London: Camera Club, 1917), pp. 2–5 (pp. 4–5).

[119] 'Things to Be Done', *Poetry*, 9 (1917), 312–14.

scholar's ultimate end is to put the greatest amount of the best literature (i.e. if that's his subject) within easy reach of the public.'[120] Vortography is thus a useful marker of the limitations of Pound's avant-gardism. Although occasionally responsive to the formal possibilities of the new visual media (he had noted the previous year that cinema was 'developing an art sense'), his critical work lacks a sustained evaluation of them.[121] Despite his castigation of the way the visual arts had become part of a 'luxury trade', and his uncompromisingly populist stance on the dissemination of literature, he does not explore how photography and cinema might popularise the 'perceptions of forms' he admired in vorticist art.[122]

Pound's strongest argument against the visual arts as 'luxury trade' occurred in his 'Art Notes' column in the *New Age*. This unevenly satirical column written under the pseudonym of 'B. H. Dias' had begun in November 1917 as a chronicle of the London art world. In an instalment entitled 'Art and Luxury' published on 12 February 1920 he makes a clear distinction between literature, and the arts of painting, sculpture and music: '"Art" which means for many people "painting" or "painting and sculpture" flourishes as a luxury-trade, in comparison with literature, or poetry, "the consolation of the poor," which merely "exists"', he writes. 'Music flourishes in large cities when it provides a circus for the display of osprey plumage, etc.' For Pound, 'the painter creates objects of cash-value in a way wherein a poet or musical composer cannot'; the material visual artwork leans inevitably towards the commodity, whereas the immaterial work of literature just as inevitably leans towards 'the democracy of the art of fine speech'. He briefly counters the obvious objections that blur the distinction, such as the commodification of manuscripts and first editions and the dissemination of art through reproductions as 'minor quibbles', and states that if the writer is tempted to pander to a market, it will take the form of being 'tempted to reach a large audience', but the 'painter is tempted to appeal to the taste of a few luxury lovers, or a few dealers'.[123]

Earlier instalments of the 'Art Notes' had suggested the trajectory of Pound's thought. In February 1918, his discussion of an exhibition at the Pastel Society had led him to speculate whether the lack of durability inherent in pastel works should be seen as 'a desire to catch the day's audience with as little trouble as possible, and to care nothing for to-morrow', in

[120] 'Provincialism the Enemy, III', *New Age*, 21 (1917), 288–9 (p. 289).
[121] 'Mr. James Joyce and the Modern Stage: A Play and Some Considerations', *Drama*, 6 (1916), 122–32 (p. 130).
[122] 'Affirmations, II: Vorticism', p. 278.   [123] 'Art and Luxury', p. 238.

which case 'it is simple jerry-building, and most condemnable', or whether it could be recuperated as 'a revolt against dealers and connoisseurs', in which case 'it is excellent'. While Pound reaches this discussion via the conventional debate about finish, he makes an intellectual leap in considering the idea that certain media and certain styles can be deliberately deployed to evade the art market. His focus on architecture in the second half of 1918 is an alternative, if well-trodden, path into the discussion of art that is less susceptible to commodification.[124] But these readings do not involve support for the popularisation of art through reproduction, nor a complete turn away from the visual arts. Pound uses the 'Art Notes' column to criticise the 'democratic tendency' of artists 'to reach as many casual glances as possible' by producing work 'that is at least as interesting when reproduced on an art-brown-ink postcard as when seen on canvas', and his praise of Wadsworth, Epstein, Gaudier and, above all, Lewis is undiminished.[125] Nevertheless, the fact that at the level of theory all visual art is associated with the modern world's degeneration of beauty into luxury demonstrates how unlikely Pound would be to 'write to paint' in 1918. The institutional associations of contemporary visual art have made the form too problematic to act as a model for poetry, and 'the democracy of the art of fine speech' is now preferred.[126] How that might transfer into a modern poem, however, is a question Pound was still attempting to resolve.

Hugh Selwyn Mauberley comments on this irresolute moment in *The Cantos'* composition. Pound wrote this highly self-referential poem over the winter of 1919, at the beginning of a two-and-a-half-year break from *The Cantos*, a block apparently created by anxiety about its obscurity, its inability to communicate its programme. His apprehension appears in a number of letters written during December 1919. To his father he wrote that cantos five, six and seven were 'each more incomprehensible than the one preceding it; don't know what's to be done about it', and to Quinn that he suspected the poem of 'getting too too too abstruse and obscure for human consumption, and I cant follow Yeats into the hopes of a Tuatha

---

[124] 'Art and Pastels', *New Age*, 22 (1918), 310; 'Art Notes', *New Age*, 23 (1918), 287–8, 320, 400–10, 414.
[125] 'Art Notes', *New Age*, 23 (1918), 255–6 (p. 256); 'Art Notes', *New Age*, 23 (1918), 58–9; 'Art Notes', *New Age*, 24 (1919), 263–4; 'Art Notes [letter]', *New Age*, 24 (1919), 283; 'Art Notes', *New Age*, 24 (1919), 310–11; 'Art Notes', *New Age*, 24 (1919), 342; 'Art Notes', *New Age*, 25 (1919), 364–5; 'Art Notes', *New Age*, 26 (1919), 13–14; 'Art Notes', *New Age*, 26 (1920), 205–6; 'Art Notes', *New Age*, 26 (1920), 291–2.
[126] 'Art and Luxury', p. 238.

Daanaan audience'.[127] Recent discussion of *Mauberley* has taken its cue from this relationship between the poem and *The Cantos*. Vincent Sherry, for example, concludes that *Mauberley* 'tells the tale of an integral difficulty in the work of *il miglior fabbro*: the ambitious failure of his ideogrammic method'. Douglas Mao also interprets *Mauberley* as a reflection on the obscurity of *The Cantos*, but, in contrast to Sherry, argues that *Mauberley* affirms the allure of obscurity and 'thingly opacity'.[128] Discussing Pound's allusion to Victor Plarr's *In the Dorian Mood* in the section of *Mauberley* entitled '"Siena Mi Fe'; Disfecemi Maremma"', Mao argues that 'the aesthetes' affection for the topos of the decontextualised object' exemplified by Plarr's poems (including 'To a Greek Gem' with its focus on a 'middle-finger ring whose bezel glows/ With the most lovely of intaglios') is the basis of an aesthetic attitude Pound represents as heroic in *Mauberley*, because it rebuts the demands of the age articulated by 'Mr. Nixon'.[129]

Mao's reading, insightful as it is, is problematised by the pro-realist arguments of the first cantos, and the contemporaneous essays on art and luxury. Pound is undeniably deploring the superficiality and lack of durability in the twentieth century's taste in art, 'the mould in plaster' and the 'prose kinema', which take a passive imprint of the age. But it is a leap of logic to assume that this entails unequivocal praise for the alternative, the 'alabaster/ Or the "sculpture" of rhyme' (*HSM*, 10). The rationale for that interpretation rests on the traditional reading of this line as registering Pound's admiration for the sculpture of Epstein and Gaudier, and for what Pound called the 'polish and fineness' of Théophile Gautier's *Émaux et Camées*, in which the poet is figured as a sculptor, a point Pound highlighted in the title of an earlier homage to Gautier, 'Albâtre' (1914).[130] But the limitations of Gautier's 'sculptural' verse are clearly felt in this poem, especially in comparison to the capaciousness of the form Pound was developing for *The Cantos*. Here, Gautier's quatrains are deployed to satirise their fascination with their own perfection and their resistance to the broader responsibilities

---

[127] Letter to Homer Loomis Pound, 13 December 1919, EPP, Beinecke, 60.2681; *L/JQ*, p. 181. Pound's reference is to the Celtic gods.

[128] Sherry, *Ezra Pound, Wyndham Lewis, and Radical Modernism*, p. 84; Mao, p. 164. See also Vincent Miller, 'Mauberley and His Critics', *ELH*, 57 (1990), 961–76.

[129] Victor Plarr, 'To a Greek Gem', in *In the Dorian Mood* (London: Lane, 1896), p. 17; Mao, pp. 163–4.

[130] 'The Approach to Paris, II', p. 577. Also relevant here is Pound's attachment to a phrase from Remy de Gourmont's *Lettres à l'Amazone*, 'Je sculpte une hypothèse dans le marbre de la logique éternelle': see 'Remy de Gourmont', *Fortnightly Review*, 98 (1915), [1159]–1166 (p. 1165). See also Brantley Berryman, pp. 32–40, John J. Espey, *Ezra Pound's Mauberley: A Study in Composition* (London: Faber and Faber, 1955), pp. 27–31, and Scott Hamilton, *Ezra Pound and the Symbolist Inheritance* (Princeton, NJ: Princeton University Press, 1992), pp. 10–17, 121–30. 'Albâtre', *Poetry and Drama*, 2 (1914), p. 20.

of the arts. Similarly Pound's admiration for Gaudier's and Epstein's carving is qualified by the luxury associations invoked by the particularity of 'alabaster'. As the preference for alabaster and sculpted rhyme over plaster and prose cinema is supplemented in the next section by a longer list of past treasures, 'the mousseline of Cos', 'Sappho's barbitos', Dionysus, Ariel, 'faun's flesh' and 'the saint's vision' (*HSM*, 11), a beautiful but anachronistic aesthetic is conjured up. Pound condemns the commodified art of the present day, and the examples he sets it against characterise admired earlier cultures, but not cultures that can prescribe an aesthetic attitude for a society recovering from the war.

This limited appreciation for the cultural achievements of the past sets the tone for 'Yeux Glauques', '"Siena Mi Fe'; Disfecemi Maremma"' and 'Brennbaum', which register respect for a number of late nineteenth-century artists (Ruskin, Swinburne, Dante Gabriel Rossetti, Burne-Jones, Plarr and Max Beerbohm) while conspicuously resisting any application of their aesthetics to the twentieth century. Indeed, Pound consistently modifies his expressions of approbation: Burne-Jones and Rossetti paint women whose gaze is 'vacant' and 'passive', 'bewildered' by their world (*HSM*, 14). Monsieur Verog is also 'out of step with the decade [. . .]/ Because of these reveries' (*HSM*, 15). Brennbaum's 'sky-like limpid eyes' suggest a similar detachment: his 'impeccable' visage is only occasionally crossed by the weight of collective memory (*HSM*, 16). These passive, inward-gazing artists produce art that may be beautiful, but which is of no relevance to the modern world. Sections IV and V make it clear that their art is part of a civilisation which has failed to avert the international conflict that this poem and *The Cantos* struggle to address.

Mauberley is filled with images of luxury and both 'Envoi' and 'Medallion' employ metaphors of luxurious art objects to describe their poetic technique. What these poems represent is, as Pound writes in the conclusion to his essay in the *New Age*, 'the degradation of the sense-of-beauty into the sense of luxury'.[131] Both poems hold an image of petrifying amber at their centre: in 'Envoi', the speaker imagines his lady's 'graces' living 'as roses might, in magic amber laid', beautiful and permanent, but homogeneous: 'One substance and one colour/ Braving time' (*HSM*, 21). And in 'Medallion', the female singer is seen through a 'glaze', in which her 'basketwork of braids' seems made of 'metal, or intractable amber' (*HSM*, 28). The beauty of the living thing (the roses, the singer's face) becomes an immortal

---

[131] 'Art and Luxury', p. 239.

but decadent and lifeless object.[132] In his journalism Pound condemns just this transformation of beauty into luxury because luxury objects cannot educate public taste, only the taste of the minute group of connoisseurs who can afford to buy them. In an article published a month before 'Art and Luxury', written during the same period as *Mauberley*, Pound argued against the related ideology of the museum:

> The curse is not of "a museum," but of *museums*, it is the pest and epidemic of museums. I have one at my elbow, my right elbow, a few perfect pieces of jade, an ivory "museum piece"; and at my left elbow a portfolio that I have just shared with the public [. . .]. We have ten thousand people ferreting little bits of art into drawers, into glorified what-nots; bustling about to old curiosity shops in search of "virtue," and into second-rate and even first-rate studios in search of "Art" with the capital letter, or in search of "Name" or of "something that's going up." Yet there is not enough public taste to ensure one building that is not an eyesore'.[133]

In a culture with this attitude towards beauty, art can have no effect; it is a fetish.

The painterly and sculptural analogies of *Mauberley* are therefore finally negative: they are images of beauty that have been unable to teach the poet the lessons he required. They have only encouraged him to refine the luxurious, introspective art of the intaglio, the art of Plarr and his Rhymers' Club colleagues, Lionel Johnson and Selwyn Image, of which imagism was an extension. So where Mao posits Mr Nixon's mercenary remarks as the focal point of Pound's antipathy, this reading interprets Mr. Nixon as voicing Pound's own anxieties, some of which the poem proves well-founded. Mr Nixon tells E.P. to 'give up verse, my boy, / There's nothing in it', and E.P. remembers being advised by 'a friend of Bloughram's', 'The "Nineties" tried your game / And died, there's nothing in it' (*HSM*, 17). By the end of the poem the reiterated phrase carries authorial force, coinciding as it does with the speaker's low opinion of the verse produced by both Mauberley and E.P. Mr Nixon is right that verse produced in the wake of the 1890s poets is useless, but he is wrong about the reason: it is not because it will earn no money, but because its anti-popularity (of which its lack of material worth is a marker) makes it socially and culturally redundant in the modern age. As we are told at the beginning of the poem, E.P. was a failed poet, 'no adjunct to the Muses' diadem', because he was 'unaffected by "the

---

[132] For an alternative reading, one which I think however cannot be sustained in light of Pound's journalism, see Julie Denison, '"His Fundamental Passion": *Hugh Selwyn Mauberley* and the Ekphrastic Vortex of "The Eyes"', *Paideuma*, 30.1&2 (2001), 185–201 (p. 196).

[133] 'The Curse', *Apple (of Beauty and Discord)*, 1 (1920), 22, 24 (p. 22).

march of events"' (*HSM*, 9). And at this point, stalled in the composition of *The Cantos*, Pound is unable to give an example of a poetry that is affected.

Reading *Mauberley* as a polemic against the 'the degradation of the sense-of-beauty into the sense of luxury' sits uneasily with the fact that the poem was first published by John Rodker's Ovid Press in a privately printed edition of 200 copies, decorated with vorticist ornamental capitals by Edward Wadsworth. The cheapest copy cost fifteen shillings, almost twice the price of Pound's *Umbra* (which had four-and-a-half times as many pages), published by Elkin Mathews in the same month.[134] 'The physique of *Hugh Selwyn Mauberley* raises an image of an artistic practice that would triumph over all that "The Age Demanded"', writes Jerome McGann, 'the fact that this work, this book, is itself a part of what "the age demanded" only underscores the extremity of Pound's satiric idealism.'[135] Pound's silence on the conditions of *Mauberley*'s publication makes it somewhat difficult to ascertain his motivation, especially as, on some occasions, he used private printing as a means of circulating ideas quickly and, on others, as a way to control access to his work.[136] The latter appears more plausible in this particular case, since there is evidence that Pound saw *Mauberley* as a potential hindrance to the publication of *The Cantos*: he told his father that he wanted the *Dial* 'to remain in ignorance of the fact that there are any short poems, until the cantos have had a full chance'.[137] While *The Cantos* was conceived as a realist literature that could introduce important ideas into circulation, *Mauberley* is a more private meditation that was initially directed towards a coterie audience.[138]

Pound's well-known letter to his former teacher Felix Schelling, from July 1922, expresses these surprisingly limited ambitions for *Mauberley*, and further adumbrates the distinction between its programme and that of *The Cantos*:

---

[134] 'Art and Luxury', p. 239.

[135] Jerome J. McGann, *The Textual Condition* (Princeton, NJ: Princeton University Press, 1991), p. 157.

[136] In 1924, for example, Pound suggested that Lewis 'produce ten or a dozen designs for the two cantos dealing with Hell' because 'I have failed on various occasions in attempts to RAM unrelated designs of yours into the continental maw; and shd. like a try at ramming designs related, or supposed to be related to something that had already gone in' (*L*, 191). Equally, earlier that year, he had published the first book of cantos in a deluxe edition with William Bird's Three Mountains Press, commenting 'Not for the Vulgus. There'll only be about 60 copies for sale; and about 15 more for the producers' (*L*, 187). See Miranda B. Hickman '"To Facilitate the Traffic" (Or, "Damn the Deluxe Edtns"): Ezra Pound's Turn from the Deluxe', *Paideuma*, 28.2&3 (1999 [2000]), 173–92.

[137] Letter to Homer Loomis Pound, [April 1920], EPP, Beinecke, 60.2682.

[138] When *Mauberley* was included in the American edition of *Personae* (1926) Pound suggested his readers omit it because the poem was 'so distinctly a farewell to London' (*P*, 185).

It's all rubbish to pretend that art isn't didactic. A revelation is always didactic. Only the aesthetes since 1880 have pretended the contrary, and they aren't a very sturdy lot.

Art can't offer a patent medicine. A failure to dissociate that from a profounder didacticism has led to the errors of "aesthete's" critique.

(Of course, I'm no more Mauberley than Eliot is Prufrock. Mais passons.) Mauberley is a mere surface. Again a study in form, an attempt to condense the James novel. (*L*, 180)

Art cannot cure society's ills, as the aesthetes knew, but to turn away from those ills altogether was, in Pound's opinion, a critical error. But nor was it enough any longer to simply present 'life'. Art could have, indeed, should have, a 'profounder didacticism', and in deciding this, Pound implicitly contradicts his earlier programmatic statement in *The Cantos*: 'Its low to try to coerce another person [. . .]/ All we can do's to set forth our own good/ within some other's reach'.[139] The visual arts had been associated with immediacy and with a repudiation of the textual emphasis of *Kultur* and philology, but by the time of *Mauberley*'s composition and the 1920 articles against art and museums, they have become an inadequate model for the arguments Pound wants to present. Their messages were conveyed too obliquely, and most importantly, as he began to theorise the relation of the art object to the literary work, it became more difficult for him to register admiration for contemporary art, contaminated, he thought, by a system of cultural production geared to the collector and the connoisseur.

During 1915–20, the period with which this chapter has been concerned, Pound moves from the aestheticism of imagism towards a position that has much in common with the avant-garde, in its strictest, 'historical' sense.[140] Vorticism, especially the vorticism of Wyndham Lewis, had been an important catalyst in moving Pound towards a critique of modernity, and the questions Pound asks in *Mauberley* are those of the 'advanced artists [who] search out areas of social practice that retain some vivid life in an increasingly administered and rationalized society'. But whereas the avant-gardists find such areas in their 'selective appropriation of fringe mass culture', Pound, as his reaction to vortography should have led us to expect, stops short of doing so.[141] In *Mauberley*, Pound turns to the past, not to mass culture; nostalgia occupies the space of an active engagement with

---

[139] 'Ur-Cantos: Autograph ms. and typescript'.
[140] Bürger, pp. 15–19.
[141] Thomas Crow, *Modern Art in the Common Culture* (New Haven, CT: Yale University Press), p. 35.

the renovating potential of mass cultural forms. *Hugh Selwyn Mauberley* is a lament for a lost culture, and a failed search for the means with which to renew culture. But it was at this point, just when Pound appears to have dismissed the possibility that the visual arts could play a role in cultural renovation, that he moved to Paris. There he became part of the group since lauded as having launched the most penetrating analysis of modernity: dada.

CHAPTER 4

Conceptual art and the rappel à l'ordre

UNDERCONSUMPTIONIST AESTHETICS

Hugh Selwyn Mauberley is eloquent testimony to Pound's doubt about the place of the arts in what his nascent cantos were calling 'the modern world'.[1] In the months preceding the poem's composition, Pound's journalism had delineated his preoccupation with fundamental questions concerning the artist's role in public life: his *New Age* articles between July 1917 and March 1920, though grouped into four separate series, 'Provincialism the Enemy', 'Studies in Contemporary Mentality', 'Pastiche: the Regional' and 'The Revolt of Intelligence', mount a cumulative argument against nationalism and its negative impact on intellectual culture. The argument began in 'Provincialism the Enemy' as a criticism of the German state and German *Kultur*, but over the course of the articles, American, English and, to a lesser extent, French culture was also targeted. By November 1919, when the first instalment of 'The Revolt of Intelligence' appeared, Pound's rallying call to intellectuals had become markedly more strident and politicised. 'European intelligence is "fed up"', he wrote, and 'there are men in Paris, there are men in other and smaller cities, already rejoicing in the number of *heimatlos*. [. . .] they regarded German Imperialism as but one of several infamies that the world would do well to be rid of.'[2] These articles have little to say about the visual arts, or indeed about literature: they are concerned with 'intelligence', rather than its product. But, as this chapter will explore, that shift from product to producer had important implications for Pound's interpretation of the visual arts during the 1920s.

The most immediate inspiration behind the revolutionary impulse of Pound's journalism was Gabriele D'Annunzio's seizure of the Adriatic port of Fiume on 12 September 1919.[3] Though Pound was by no means entirely

---

[1] 'Ur-Cantos: Autograph ms. and typescript'.
[2] 'The Revolt of Intelligence, [I]', *New Age*, 26 (1919), 21–2 (p. 21).
[3] See Alfredo Bonadeo, *D'Annunzio and the Great War* (Madison and Teaneck, NJ: Fairleigh Dickinson University Press, 1995), pp. 125–43, Michael A. Ledeen, *The First Duce: D'Annunzio at Fiume*

supportive of D'Annunzio, disliking in particular his famously rhetorical oratory, he was clearly encouraged by the sight of a writer as a political leader. 'In the main he represents art and literature', Pound wrote, and, deploying the opposition that was already central to the nascent cantos, he continued, 'he represents the individual human being, the personality as against the official card-index and official Globe-Wernicke system'.[4] While in 1915 the notion of an official state culture had been epitomised by Prussia, Pound now associated it with Woodrow Wilson, against whose allocation of Fiume to the new country of Yugoslavia D'Annunzio was rebelling. Though D'Annunzio had long been active in Italian politics promoting a vision of a greater Italy, and was only one of four figures approached to lead the insurrection (Mussolini was another), Pound chose to see his takeover as symptomatic not of Italian political unrest, but of a European-wide revolutionary impulse among intellectuals.[5] 'Fiume represents and precedes more important, if less melodramatic, conflicts between art, literature, intelligence, and card-index and officialdom', he claimed, and he concluded his article by pointing towards four 'symptom[s] of discontent': 'It may seem a far cry from Fiume to this blue pamphlet on painting [Lewis's *The Caliph's Design*], or to Parisians using a German term "heimatlos"; or to De Gourmont's pre-bellum query: "and when he comes to die, how will he be able to die if the registrar is not present to give him his death certificate?" Yet many small and scattered things serve to show the movement and direction of a current.'[6]

It was in the context of these concerns that Pound first explored the theories of the engineer-turned-economist C. H. Douglas. From 5 June to 7 August 1919, and 12 February to 5 August 1920, the *New Age* ran two series by Douglas, 'Economic Democracy' and 'Credit-Power and Democracy', which set out the basis of what would soon be known as Social Credit. Like many observers, including the Guild Socialists of the *New Age*, Douglas had come to regard the current economic system with suspicion: industrial expansion did not seem to have been accompanied by the economic prosperity expected, and financial power was becoming ever more concentrated in a few pockets. The central problem, Douglas claimed, was that prices did not match the total costs of production, as orthodox economists

(Baltimore, MD: Johns Hopkins University Press, 1977), and John Woodhouse, *Gabriele D'Annunzio: Defiant Archangel* (Oxford: Clarendon Press, 1998), pp. 315–52. For an influential contemporary response, see J. N. Macdonald, *A Political Escapade: The Story of Fiume and D'Annunzio* (London: Murray, [1921]).
[4] 'The Revolt of Intelligence, [I]', p. 21; 'The Net American Loss', pp. 205–14. Globe-Wernicke was an American company that specialised in filing equipment.
[5] Woodhouse, pp. 329–30.   [6] 'The Revolt of Intelligence, [I]', pp. 21–2.

believed, but were raised by the producers' use of bank loans at interest. The result was that purchasing power could not keep pace with production, so further loans were necessary, leading to progressive inflation. Thus the profits of industrial expansion were passed on to neither the workers nor the producers, but rather to those supplying loans to the producers – the banks. Douglas proposed a two fold solution: first, he advocated that the nation create enough capital to purchase its own goods in the form of a national dividend, thus creating a distinction between 'the obsession of wealth defined in terms of money' and 'real capital', which he defined as 'the collective potential capacity to do work'. Second, he recommended giving each item a fixed 'Just Price': 'the Just Price of an article, which is the price at which it can be effectively distributed in the community producing, bears the same ratio to the cost of production that the total consumption and depreciation of the community bears to the total production'.[7]

Douglasite economics did not have an immediate influence on Pound. Although he engaged with political and economic issues in 1919 and throughout the 1920s, Tim Redman and Leon Surette have shown that until 1931 his attention was largely restricted to topics that affected his own situation and that of his fellow artists. A 1919 article in the *New Age*, in which he responds to a French journal's announcement of a Federation Society of Arts, Letters and Sciences, is representative: 'In my younger days I also (in Arcadia) made out grandiose schemes in order that the world might be made safe for the arts', he remarks nostalgically. 'It will never be safe for the artist. Labour will always desire to kill him and the plutocracy will always want to turn him into a performing buffoon.' Rather than 'grandiose schemes', like those of the Federation, Pound proposes 'certain executive measures' that could improve life for the 'rare man of genius': 'protections of copyright, the abolition of obstructive tariff restrictions, the taxing of publishers who live exclusively on dead authors' brains, and the turning of the proceeds of such tax toward the training or relief of the living'. A month later, he made a point of distinguishing his promotion of intellectual culture from the economic debates in the *New Age*: 'Capital *v.* Labour is not the only conflict', he comments in 'The Revolt of Intelligence', 'there

---

[7] C. H. Douglas, *Credit-Power and Democracy with a Draft Scheme for the Mining Industry* (London: Palmer, 1920), p. 22; C. H. Douglas, *Economic Democracy* (London: Palmer, 1920), pp. 30, 77, 113–14, 134. See Redman, pp. 58–65, Alec Marsh, *Money and Modernity: Pound, Williams, and the Spirit of Jefferson* (Tuscaloosa, AL: University of Alabama Press, 1998), pp. 83–4, and Leon Surette, *Pound in Purgatory: From Economic Radicalism to Anti-Semitism* (Urbana and Chicago, IL: University of Illinois Press, 1999), pp. 28–30.

is also the endless conflict between the furnished and the half-furnished mind.'[8]

This is not to say, however, that there is no trace of Douglas's impact on Pound's writings before 1931. In 'Pastiche: The Regional', as early as the summer of 1919, the *New Age* discussions are clearly provoking Pound into thinking about the economic and political system which would favour the intellectual culture he is advocating, but his conclusions at this point run counter to those of Douglas and the Guild Socialists. Although he insists that he is not 'running counter to the policy of this paper, or sanctioning the "capitalist system"', the argument of this series is that 'wholly "unjust" concentrations of power (L.s.d.) have undoubtedly helped civilisation'. By October, Pound's engagement with Douglas's articles had become more explicit as he opposed his arguments to Douglas's key ideas: 'Whatever the "catch" in "over-production," it is the duty of a sane manufacturing system to over-produce every luxury which tends to increase the comforts and amenities of existence', he writes, and later in the same article he remarks dismissively, 'The fallacy of money is said to have been exposed by "the latest economists"; certainly only a doctrinaire can wax theological on "the even distribution of wealth"; no one cares a hang about even distribution of blank or stamped strips of paper.'[9]

While these references confirm that Pound was reading Douglas's articles in the *New Age* before they were published in book form, they also demonstrate that his initial reading was neither careful nor enthusiastic, and that he was sceptical about two issues fundamental to Douglas's argument and that of most other contemporary challenges to economic orthodoxy: overproduction and the arbitrary nature of credit, the key elements of all underconsumptionist economic theories.[10] However, by April 1920, only five months later, his opinion had evidently changed: he published positive reviews of *Economic Democracy* in the *Little Review* and the *Athenaeum*.[11]

The reviews suggest that Pound found the most persuasive aspect of Douglas's discussion to be his insistence on the 'supremacy of the individual, considered collectively', as opposed to the supremacy of either financiers or the State, in the guise of Fabianism and other forms of what Pound called

[8] '"Ésope," France and the Trade Union', *New Age*, 25 (1919), 423–4 (p. 423); 'The Revolt of Intelligence, [I]', p. 22.

[9] 'Pastiche. The Regional, IX', *New Age*, 25 (1919), p. 336; Pastiche. The Regional, II', *New Age*, 25 (1919), p. 156; 'Pastiche. The Regional, XV', *New Age* (1919), p. 448.

[10] Surette, *Pound in Purgatory*, p. 8.

[11] See also Pound's open letter of the same month to Harry Turner, editor of the Saint Louis-based journal, *Much Ado*: 'Am sending you Douglas' book and hope you will peruse and publicly digest it' ('A Letter from London', *Much Ado*, 10 [1920], 21–2 [p. 21]).

'disguised Prussianism'.[12] In both reviews Pound contextualises Douglas's economics by affirming the importance of individual freedom and delineating the various threats ranged against it by other political and economic possibilities: in this sense the reviews provide a fairly consistent extension of the arguments in 'The Revolt of Intelligence', and the several series that preceded it. The continuity with Pound's earlier articles is underlined further by the fact that in both reviews Pound discusses Douglas less as an economist than an intellectual, even an artist. Quoting Georges-Louis Leclerc, Comte de Buffon's famous axiom, he remarks, 'Le style c'est l'home [*sic*]; and a chinaman has written "A man's character is known from his brush-strokes." The clarity of some of Major Douglas' statements should show the more intelligent reader, and show him almost instantly, that he has here to deal with a genius as valid in its own specialty as any we can point to in the arts.'[13] Even more tellingly, Pound suggests that *Economic Democracy* has a worth extrinsic of the validity of its argument:

The author tries with undeniable honesty to solve the vicious-circle riddle; he writes with sufficient precision of phrase to command a certain respect for his mental capacity. Surrounded on all sides by confessions of helplessness and appeals to the better nature of abstract competitive bodies, one cannot abruptly reject the calculations of any man who has succeeded in convincing himself of the existence of a remedy; moreover the book, sound or unsound, is a mental stimulant.[14]

In 1920, then, Pound is far from persuaded by Douglas's economic theory, even though he is advocating his writings: the most he will say is that Douglas has 'trie[d]' to solve the 'riddle' of contemporary economics, that he has 'convinc[ed]' himself of the existence of a remedy'. But nevertheless, Pound still recommends what may be an 'unsound' theory on the basis of the 'mental capacity' demonstrated by Douglas's 'sufficient precision of phrase', and the resulting mental stimulation.

It is somewhat ironic that Pound should have fixed on Douglas's prose style as the most admirable aspect of the text, since A. R. Orage is widely believed to have been responsible for any virtues of clarity and readability it possessed. Even the most sympathetic commentators have found Douglas's writing infelicitous, especially in his later works, written without Orage's aid.[15] But Pound's equating of the text's value with the clarity of Douglas's

[12] Douglas, *Economic Democracy*, p. 5; 'J.L.', [Ezra Pound], 'Probario ratio', *Athenaeum*, 94 (1920), p. 445.
[13] '[Review of] *Economic Democracy* [by C. H. Douglas]', *Little Review*, 6.11 (1920), 39–42 (p. 40).
[14] 'Probario Ratio', p. 445.
[15] Frances Hutchinson and Brian Burkitt, *The Political Economy of Social Credit and Guild Socialism* (London: Routledge, 1997), pp. 12, 9.

style rather than with the validity of his argument shows the extent of his investment in a certain type of intelligence by 1920. This is the legacy of the individualist aesthetics Pound developed around imagism and vorticism, most forcefully stated in his assessments of Lewis and Gaudier, where the immediacy and clarity of their work was interpreted as an expression of their superior intelligence. Over the course of the last three years' *New Age* articles the connections between clarity and intelligence had hardened and Pound had started to extend these essentially aesthetic critiques into the political and economic realm. But the line of influence ran the other way, too: the economic also influenced the aesthetic, and Pound's early reading of Douglas sheds considerable light on his writing about art in the 1920s. Economics and aesthetics are, of course, easily linked; both are concerned with the assignment of value and the basis on which that assignment is made.[16] Moreover, as has been routinely observed, the Guild Socialist context ensured that Social Credit was more attentive to the economic contributions of artists and thinkers than capitalist economics had been.[17]

Pound does not discuss the place of artists in a Social Credit system, although he does respond to Douglas's statement that 'it is essential that the individual should be released [. . .] for other pursuits' by inventing the quotation "release of energy from routine in order that there may be more of it for invention and design" in an open letter to an American journal.[18] But of more interest to Pound at this time are Douglas's redefinitions of economic value and the distribution of credit, as is demonstrated by the quotations he chose for his *Economic Democracy* reviews. By the time he encountered Douglas's writings Pound had already realised that the circulation of ideas was as important as their production, but in the 1920s his aesthetics change to accommodate this. Douglas's definition of 'real capital' as the 'potential capacity to do work' and his definition of 'real credit' as 'the reserve of energy belonging to a community' suggest for Pound a way out of the cul-de-sac of commodification in which *Mauberley* seems caught.[19] As the underconsumptionist economist believes that production depends on consumption and the circulation of wealth, Pound might be said to

---

[16] See Barbara Herrnstein Smith, *Contingencies of Value: Alternative Perspectives for Critical Theory* (Cambridge, MA: Harvard University Press, 1988), John Guillory, *Cultural Capital: The Problem of Literary Canon Formation* (Chicago, IL: University of Chicago Press, 1993), Marc Shell, *The Economy of Literature* (Baltimore, MD: Johns Hopkins University Press, 1978).

[17] Hutchinson and Burkitt, p. 60, Kenner, *The Pound Era*, pp. 311–12.

[18] Douglas, *Economic Democracy*, p. 45; 'A Letter from London', p. 21. See Redman, p. 70, Hutchinson and Burkitt, p. 21.

[19] Douglas, *Economic Democracy*, pp. 113–14, 121.

develop an underconsumptionist aesthetics, in which the circulation of ideas is prioritised over the production of the artwork. Pound, like Douglas, locates value in potential, rather than achievement. As a result, Pound's approach to art changes in two fundamental ways: first, he redefines the work of art in very broad terms, as any contribution to civilisation, and, second, he evaluates art through an evaluation of the artist's intelligence, to the point where the artwork's value is primarily its ability to act as evidence of the artist's mental capacity. From this point, Pound's criticism noticeably shifts its attention from the artwork as a thing-in-itself, to the artwork as a record of the artist's thought.

Although this will enable Pound to appreciate works of art he had previously dismissed, there is also a strong line of continuity with his earliest aesthetic decisions. Douglas's concept of value is substantially indebted to Ruskin's economic theories, making it compatible with the Ruskinian shift in Pound's aesthetics described in the previous chapter. But in Douglas's assignment of value to the 'potential capacity to do work' as well as to production itself, Pound may also have heard an echo of Whistler's answer to Ruskin in the 1878 libel trial, when he stated that the price of *Nocturne in Black and Gold: The Falling Rocket* (1875) bought not the labour of two days, but 'the knowledge of a lifetime'.[20] This particular echo should alert us to the shortcomings of Pound's reinterpretation of the artwork. His transference of aesthetic value from artwork to artist does not, in fact, enable him to remove art from the capitalist economy. Instead, it merely reinforces one of the art market's most successful gambits, the institutionalisation of the artist as celebrity. Pound repeatedly demonstrated this misplaced confidence in the individual's ability to remove him- or herself from the capitalist system, as, for example, in his well-known remark in the *ABC of Economics* (1933): 'The minute I cook my own dinner or make the chair that I sit on I escape from the whole cycle of Marxian economics' because 'Marx deals with goods in the shop window or the shop basement' (*ABCE*, 53). As Douglas Mao has written of this passage, Pound's argument here is 'symptomatic of his neglect of Marx's insistence that exchange value arises from a total system of social relations, that capitalism in its very nature is not merely "dominant" in the usual sense of that term but pervasive and determining'.[21] While Pound's individualist politics and underconsumptionist economics appeared to offer a way of theorising art that could resist its commodification, in fact they obscured the extent to which the art market could control not only the artwork itself, but all aspects of its production

---

[20] Whistler, pp. 4–5.   [21] Mao, p. 147.

and dissemination. This miscalculation forms the basis of Pound's mature aesthetics, and it would come to structure his interpretation of all intellectual work.

In November 1919, three months after 'Economic Democracy' had concluded its serial run in the *New Age*, Pound composed an appreciation of Matisse in his 'Art Notes' column that demonstrates this new direction of his aesthetics:

> It is not necessary, either in the young or in the mature artist, that all the geometry of a painting be tossed up into the consciousness and analysed by the painter before he puts brush to canvas. *The genius can pay in nugget and in lump gold; it is not necessary that he bring up his knowledge into the mint of consciousness, stamp it into either the coin of conscientiously analysed form-detail knowledge or into the paper-money of words, before he transmit it.* A bit of luck for a young man, and the sudden coagulation of bits of knowledge collected here and there during years, need not for the elder artist be re-sorted and arranged into coin. This sort of lump-payment is not mediumistic or psychic painting; it is mastery, and Matisse displays it.[22]

Pound's increased interest in Matisse towards the end of 1919 was a response both to the exhibition of his work at the Leicester Galleries that provides the occasion for this review, and also to Lewis's praise in *The Caliph's Design*, published on 31 October, and read by Pound by mid-November at the latest.[23] More important than this shift in taste, however, is the logic of Pound's argument here. Matisse, he writes, should be appreciated as a genius, even though his work might not be finished in the traditional sense ('arranged into coin'): the 'coagulation of bits of knowledge' is still evidence of genius. Matisse's 'lump-payment' also has the virtue of being less susceptible to marketplace definitions of worth, which all too easily turn beauty into luxury. Both Peter Nicholls and Richard Sieburth have discussed this passage as one which 'casts much light on the early Cantos since it postulates an untraversable distance between monetary values and those of the artistic intelligence which cannot be absorbed into a system of prudent accumulation and exchange'.[24] What can be added to their astute analyses is an account of the new opportunities Douglas's reinterpretation of economic value offered to Pound's aesthetics. Pound had long understood money and art as antithetical, but what is new here is his valorisation of a

---

[22] 'Art Notes', *New Age*, 26 (1919), 60–1 (p. 60).

[23] Wyndham Lewis, *The Caliph's Design: Architects! Where is your Vortex?* (London: Egoist, 1919), pp. 49, 53–4. 'The Revolt of Intelligence, [I]', in which Pound's quotes from *The Caliph's Design*, was published on 13 November.

[24] Peter Nicholls, *Ezra Pound: Politics, Economics and Writing: A Study of* The Cantos (Basingstoke: Macmillan, 1984), p. 28, Richard Sieburth, 'In Pound We Trust: The Economy of Poetry/ The Poetry of Economics', *Critical Inquiry*, 14 (1987), 142–72 (p. 151).

kind of art that explicitly lacks the 'permanence' or 'certitude' he had prized previously.[25] It is precisely the inchoate nature of art that marks out the work of a genius here, as if completing the work would remove the complexity and integrity of the genius's knowledge. This new appreciation of a different kind of artistic work potentially opens up the category of art to works which do not have the aestheticist attributes of the beautiful art object, but rather portray an intelligence. It is this new sense of aesthetic value that becomes dominant in Pound's writing about the art he encountered in Paris.

'BUT WHY OH WHY THE DADAISTES?'

Pound's articles in the *New Age* had always been markedly, and controversially, francophilic, but during the post-war years the admiring references to French literature began to be accompanied by a more general appreciation of French intellectual culture, particularly for its proven ability to foment revolution.[26] After the extended stay in Toulouse in 1919 that inspired 'Pastiche: The Regional', and two visits to Paris in 1920 that gave rise to the 'The Island of Paris' series for Pound's new affiliation with the American *Dial*, the Pounds decided to move to France at the end of 1920.[27] At first they planned to spend a year in Paris, but by May the following year they were envisaging a more permanent residency: 'I daily ask myself why the hell I stayed in Eng. so long', Pound wrote to Ford (*L/FMF*, 57).

In Paris Pound saw an importance placed on the kind of international intellectual collaboration he was advocating in England; the aforementioned Federation Society of Arts, Letters and Sciences was only one example of the many proposals for cultural reconstruction that must have come to Pound's attention. In 1919, the recent Nobel Prize winner and well-known pacifist, Romain Rolland, had published a 'Fière déclaration d'intellectuels' in the socialist newspaper *L'Humanité* and made plans to hold an International Congress of Intellectuals. Pound was no admirer of Rolland, calling him a 'Bloomsbury fad' in a letter to the *Little Review* and preferring the more idealist intellectualism of his antagonist, Julien Benda.[28] But Rolland was a major influence on other writers Pound admired, such as those

---

[25] 'Exhibition at the Goupil Gallery', p. 109.
[26] 'Pastiche: The Regional, XVIII', *New Age*, 26 (1919), 48.   [27] Carpenter, pp. 372–9.
[28] Romain Rolland, 'Fière déclaration d'intellectuels', *L'Humanité*, 26 June 1919: see David James Fisher, *Romain Rolland and the Politics of Intellectual Engagement* (Berkeley and Los Angeles, CA: University of California Press, 1988), pp. 51–68; 'On the American Number [letter]', *Little Review*, 5.5 (1918), 62–4 (p. 64). For Pound on Benda, see 'B.L.' [Ezra Pound], 'Julien Benda', *Athenaeum*, 95 (1920), p. 62, 'The Island of Paris: A Letter', *Dial*, 69 (1920), [406]–11 (pp. 410–11), and *L/JQ*, 191. Pound obtained Benda's *Belphégor* for serialisation in the *Dial*, September-December 1920.

associated with the *Clarté* movement, which described itself as 'a league of intellectual solidarity for the triumph of the international cause'. Its steering committee included Henri Barbusse, Georges Duhamel, Anatole France, Thomas Hardy, Jules Romains and Laurent Tailhade, all writers Pound had praised over the last decade.[29] In February 1920, the critic Florent Fels began his journal *Action: Cahier individualistes de philosophie et d'art*, whose publication of Maurice de Vlaminck's poetry Pound praised in November 1920, and to which he contributed in May 1921.[30] *Action* published both the leaders of the individualist anarchist movement, Han Ryner, Maurice Wullens, Gabriel Brunet, Marcel Martinet, Tailhade, and Francis Vaud (and in its third issue, Dora Marsden), and the avant-garde writers and artists based around Max Jacob's *Nord-Sud* and Pierre Albert-Birot's *Sic*, including Blaise Cendrars, Jean Cocteau, Georges Gabory, Pierre Reverdy and André Salmon.[31] Such a positive union of avant-gardism and individualism made Paris extremely appealing to Pound.

Pound's 'The Island of Paris' series and its successor 'Paris Letter' were primarily concerned with the literary scene. In the first instalment, published in October 1920, Pound presented himself as having come to Paris 'seeking the triple extract of literature for export purposes; seeking a poetic serum to save English letters from postmature and American telegraphics from premature suicide and decomposition'. But these articles differ than their forerunners in 1913's 'The Approach to Paris' series: they lack the earlier articles' detailed analyses of individual poems and styles, and they pay greater attention to French cultural life in general, allowing Pound to move beyond the exclusively literary with some frequency. From the first Pound singled out the recent gathering of dadaist writers and artists as proof of the intellectual independence Paris fostered:

The young began in Zurich about two years ago, they have published papers which are very, very erratic in appearance, and which contain various grains of good sense.

They have satirized the holy church of our century (journalism), they have satirized the sanctimonious attitude toward "the arts" (toward the arts irrespective

[29] Nicole Racine, 'The Clarté Movement in France, 1919–1921', *Journal of Contemporary History*, 2.2 (1967), 195–227 (p. 201). For discussion of all the French writers bar Barbusse, see Pound's 'Approach to Paris' in the *New Age* in 1913; for Barbusse see '"Ésope," France and the Trade Union', p. 424 and 'On the American Number [letter]', p. 64; for Hardy, see Pound's articles on James in the *Little Review* in 1918.

[30] 'The Island of Paris: A Letter', *Dial*, 69 (1920), [515]-18 (p. 516); 'Ouvrages reçues', *Action*, 1 (1921), p. 56.

[31] Walter G. Langlois, 'Anarchism, *Action* and Malraux', *Twentieth Century Literature*, 24.3 (1978), 272–89 (p. 277).

of whether the given work of art contains a communication of intelligence). They have given up the pretense of impartiality. They have expressed a desire to live and to die, preferring death to a sort of moribund permanence [. . .].

They talk about "metallurgie" and international financiers whose names are never mentioned in the orderly English press.

They have as yet no capital sunk in works and they indulge in the pious hope that their remains will not be used to bore others [. . .].

Louis Aragon, Philippe Soupault, André Breton, Drieu La Rochelle contribute to *Littérature* and are published Au Sans Pareil. They are, I think officially, on good terms with Tristan Tzara, Picasso, Piccabia [*sic*].

One wonders, a little vaguely, how to introduce them, to a society where one is considered decadent for reproducing pictures by Cézanne [. . .].

Carrying on the satiric heritage of Laforgue, and of symboliste sonorities this group is already taking its place in the sun, by right of intelligence, more than by right of work yet accomplished.[32]

As the last sentence indicates, Pound understood the dadaist project as part of a genealogy of satire in which he also worked, a point underlined by the contribution of his recent exercises in satire, 'Moeurs Contemporaines' and the 'Yeux Glauques' section of *Hugh Selwyn Mauberley*, to dadaist publications: the *Le Pilhaou-Thibaou* issue of Francis Picabia's *391*, the dada issue of *Ca Ira!*, and Theo van Doesburg's *Mécano*.[33] But if Pound saw his recent satires as allied to dada's critique of contemporary culture, he also, this passage seems to suggest, read dada works as an alternative to the redundant aestheticism *Hugh Selwyn Mauberley* had ascribed to Mauberley and E.P. Where Mauberley produced a small but consistent body of work, the dadaists publish 'erratic' papers; where the poetry of E.P. and Mauberley aspired to the permanence of roses 'in magic amber laid', and the 'face-oval beneath the glaze', the dadaists desire impermanence for themselves and their works. Moreover, the dadaists have no 'capital sunk in works' and write, as Pound noted a year later, 'without an eye on any market whatsoever': their works are neither the 'mould in plaster' demanded by the modern age, nor the 'alabaster' which cannot resist the logic of the marketplace that turns art into luxury (*HSM*, 21, 28, 10).[34] Pound represents their art as part of an informed reaction against the global economy that his recent reading of Douglas had affirmed.

---

[32] 'The Island of Paris: A Letter', pp. 407–9.
[33] ['Moeurs Contemporaines', I–VIII], trans. Christian, *Le Pilhaou-Thibaou* [*391*, 15] (1921), p. [4], 'M. Staïrax, Clara, Soirée', *Ça Ira!*, 16 (1921), 110–11; 'Yeux Glauques', *Mécano*, 1 (1922), [n. pag.].
[34] 'Paris Letter', *Dial*, 71 (1921), [456]-463 (p. [456]).

By October 1920 Pound had already publicly signalled an association with the dadaists, which appears to have been inaugurated by his friendship with the painter and poet, Christian (Georges Herbiet).[35] In March 1920 he had appeared in *Dadaphone*, the seventh number of Tristan Tzara's *Dada* magazine, remarking that 'quelques jeunes hommes intelligents stranded in Zurich desire correspondence with other unfortunates similarly situated in other godforsaken corners of the earth'.[36] In the autumn he contributed a description of the English literary scene to *Littérature*, the magazine founded by the newly dadaist Louis Aragon, André Breton and Philippe Soupault.[37] Pound's correspondence reveals that during July he had been announcing his commitment to the dadaist project to English and American colleagues: on 12 July he told the *Dial*'s editor, Scofield Thayer, 'I particularly want this group represented' and on 28 July, Thayer received a letter from his co-owner of the magazine, James Sibley Watson, reporting that 'Pound writes that he has taken up with the Dadaistes' (*L/TW*, 71, 95). (The *Little Review*, whose individualist anarchist foundations were already providing fertile ground for American dadaist experiment, was to prove more receptive.)[38] On 29 July Richard Aldington wrote to Pound expressing his surprise at his new affiliation: 'why oh why the Dadaistes? Have they sane moments? The object of Dadaisme is to destroy all literature by discrediting it. You don't want to do that. You want to make literature a great force, which it

[35] Christian, 'Annales du Pélican', *Cahiers Dada/ Surréalisme*, 2 (1968), 185–97 and Poupard-Liessou, 'Christian, "Le Pérégrin dans l'ombre"', *Cahiers Dada/ Surréalisme*, 3 (1969), 20–1 are the sources followed by John Alexander, in 'Parenthetical Paris, 1920–1925: Pound, Picabia, Brancusi and Léger', in *Pound's Artists*, pp. 81–120 (p. 86) and Richard Sieburth in 'Dada Pound', *South Atlantic Quarterly*, 83 (1984), 44–68 (p. 49, n. 14). Michel Sanouillet asserts that Pound was introduced to the dadaists by Man Ray, who knew William Carlos Williams in New York. But Man Ray did not arrive in Paris until 14 July 1921, over a year after Pound had begun referring to his acquaintance with the dadaists, see *Dada à Paris* (Paris: Pauvert, 1965), p. 300, and also *L/MA*, 271, 273. The *Little Review* printed photographs of four untitled works by Christian, three paintings in the 'Picabia number' (Spring 1922), and a collage in the 'Miscellany number' (Winter 1922). The latter issue also contained Christian's brief story about his friendship with Pound in Paris, 'In the Minor Key of an Epoch', pp. 29–34. Pound refers to Christian's painting twice in *The Cantos* (80: 524, 105: 760). See Colin McDowell, '"In the Minor Key of an Epoch": Georges Herbiet', *Paideuma*, 22 (1993), 93–100.

[36] 'Dada No. 1', *Dadaphone* [*Dada*, 7] (1920), p. [7]. On the foundations of dada see Tristan Tzara, 'Memoirs of Dadaism', in Edmund Wilson, *Axel's Castle: A Study in the Imaginative Literature of 1870–1930* (London: Scribner, 1931), pp. 304–12, and also Dawn Ades, *Dada and Surrealism* (London: Thames and Hudson, 1974), pp. 20–1, William A. Camfield, *Francis Picabia: His Art, Life and Times* (Princeton, NJ: Princeton University Press, 1979), pp. 124, 134–7, Manuel L. Grossman, *Dada: Paradox, Mystification, and Ambiguity in European Literature* (New York: Pegasus, 1971), pp. 98–102, and their main source, Sanouillet, pp. 140–72.

[37] 'Lettre anglaise', *Littérature*, 16 (1920), p. 48.

[38] John Rodker, '"Dada" and Else von Freytag von Loringhoven [*sic*]', *Little Review*, 7.2 (1920), 33–6, see also Dickran Tashjian, 'From Anarchy to Group Force: The Social Text of *The Little Review*', in Naomi Sawelson-Gorse (ed.), *Women in Dada* (Cambridge, MA: MIT Press, 1998), pp. 263–91.

ought to be. You won't achieve that end by printing Soupault and Aragon. Aren't you a little too respectful of new things because they're new?'[39]

Aldington's objections are pertinent and indeed Pound would never share the cultural nihilism associated especially with Tzara. In later years Pound would credit the cultural innovations he encountered in Paris less to dada, as either movement or spirit, than to individual writers and artists, notably Picabia, Cocteau, Constantin Brancusi and Fernand Léger, of whom only Picabia had been a card-carrying dadaist. But in 1920 Pound was clearly drawn to the dadaists more generally, and not only 'because they're new'. While Pound may well have been 'looking beyond England for another group of which he could be a part', there was also a profound intellectual sympathy with this particular group, as his first description of them makes clear.[40] Pound points out their distrust of the press, of international finance and its relation to munitions, of the art market, and of what we would now, following Theodor Adorno, call the culture industry.

Paris, during and after the war, appeared to be maintaining an enviably avant-garde artistic culture, continuing to produce the new magazines and artistic manifestos that Pound thought the English establishment suppressed.[41] But recent research has demonstrated the extent to which the Parisian avant-garde absorbed and in some cases contributed to, the conformist ideology of wartime France. As in England, modernist culture in France came under attack from conservative critics during the war: cubism, just like vorticism, was condemned for its supposedly Prussian sympathies. In his ground-breaking study of the French wartime avant-garde, Kenneth Silver details how even the magazines that sought to defend modernist culture, like Cocteau's *Le Mot* and Amédée Ozenfant's *L'Élan*, did so through a repudiation of extreme experimentation accompanied by a rhetoric of equilibrium and intellectual order that intersected with the conservative and right-wing agenda. Cocteau published an ode in the eighth number of *Le Mot* dedicated to the figurehead of right-wing nationalism, Maurice Barrès. While other members of the avant-garde may not have nailed their colours so firmly to the mast, Silver's analysis persuasively portrays even the most left-wing members of the avant-garde's turn to classicism as part of a widespread patriotic affirmation of France's Latin cultural roots, emblematised in Picasso's self-transformation from cubist to interpreter of the legacy

[39] Richard Aldington, Letter to Ezra Pound, 29 July 1920, EPP, Beinecke, 1.28.
[40] Alexander, in *Pound's Artists*, p. 85.
[41] This previously hegemonic position is put forward by Roger Shattuck in his important *The Banquet Years: The Origins of the Avant-Garde in France, 1885 to World War I*, rev. edn (London: Cape, 1969), e.g. p. 326.

of 'the most public, confident, conservative, and quintessentially French of artists, Jean-Auguste-Dominique Ingres'.[42]

Before moving to Paris, Pound had read and extravagantly praised one critique of this stylistic shift: Lewis's *The Caliph's Design* had derided the 'reawakening of austerity' in the 'considerable cult' of Ingres, 'David, the stiffest, the dreariest pseudo-classic', and the related denigration of Cézanne in favour of Seurat, as 'fireworks of ingenious pseudo-scientific stunts, and ringing of stylistic changes on this mode and that'.[43] Although he characterised Picasso as 'one of the ablest living painters', Lewis criticised his recent work as 'rather equivocal and unsatisfactory in the light of present events', and ultimately condemned him as 'in the category of executants, like Paganini, or to-day, Pachmann, or Moiseivitch, where Cézanne is clearly a brother of Bach, and the Douanier was a cousin of Chardin'.[44] For Pound it was particularly this 'pitiless analysis of Picasso and of contemporary faddism' that made the tract itself a 'fine curative and purgative against all the titter of Frys, Bells, Lhotes, etc.'.[45] The invective against Fry and Bell is familiar, but it gains additional significance in the context of the reference to André Lhote, whose *Athenaeum* articles advancing a classicist cubism Lewis had disparaged, inspiring Pound to unfavourable remarks over the next months.[46]

Pound's now vehement anti-nationalism was at variance with this patriotic strain directing so much of France's cultural activity; in the sixth instalment of 'The Revolt of Intelligence' he had included 'La Patrie' in his criticism of 'narcotic' words and phrases so imbued with custom and superstition that they deflect analysis of the concepts to which they refer.[47] In the *Dial* articles, Pound set himself unequivocally against the right-wing nationalists; referring to Maurice de Vlaminck's work in the anarchist *Action*, he commented that 'Five lines of Vlaminck are worth all the forty

[42] Kenneth E. Silver, *Esprit de Corps: The Art of the Parisian Avant-Garde and the First World War, 1914–1925* (London: Thames and Hudson, 1989), pp. 8–12, 43–58, 268–83, 71; Jean Cocteau, 'La Grande Pitié des Victimes de France', *Le Mot*, 8 (1915), [2–4].

[43] Lewis, *The Caliph's Design*, pp. 46, 45, 70, 53. See Paul Edwards, 'Wyndham Lewis and the *Rappel à l'ordre*: Classicism and Significant Form, 1919–21', in David Peters Corbett, Ysanne Holt and Fiona Russell (eds.), *The Geographies of Englishness: Landscape and the National Past, 1880–1940* (New Haven, CT: Yale University Press, 2002), pp. 141–68. Silver discusses the reappraisal of Cézanne as a lowly naturalist, in contrast to Seurat, reappropriated as a classicist, pp. 336–9.

[44] Lewis, *The Caliph's Design*, pp. 55, 8, 56.   [45] 'Art Notes', *New Age*, 26 (1919), 96–7 (p. 96).

[46] See for example André Lhote, 'A First Visit to the Louvre', *Athenaeum*, 4660 (1919), 787–8, 'Cubism and the Modern Artistic Sensibility', *Athenaeum*, 4664 (1919), 919–20 and 'The Necessity of Theories', *Athenaeum*, 4668, 4670 (1919), 1039–40, 1126–7; Lewis, *The Caliph's Design*, pp. 56–7; 'Art Notes', *New Age*, 26 (1920), 159–60 (p. 159): 'M. Lhote's drawings (at the Chelsea Book Club) are as vacuous as his writing might lead one to expect.'

[47] 'The Revolt of Intelligence, VI', *New Age*, 26 (1920), 176–7 (p. 177).

volumes of Barrès; all the rhetoric that has been spouted during the past six years; all the official publications about the "land fit for heroes" and the safe place for democracy.'[48] He was similarly dismissive about the patriotic fashion for Ingres, and remarked that 'the mention of [Goya's] name ought probably to be enough to reduce the Ingres flurry to its proper place as a game of dealers and artistic philologers'.[49] In this intellectual climate, where patriotism had pervaded the range of the political spectrum and the pre-war avant-garde were turning to the national past for inspiration, the Paris dadaists were by no means a surprising affiliation for Pound, because they were widely perceived as its opposite: 'Extremists, revolutionaries, Bolsheviks, dadaists – same grain, same origin, same poison', proclaimed the far-right newspaper *Le Gaulois*:

> They have declared that [. . .] nothing which we consider reasonable, delicate, or beautiful interests them; that Greco-Latin culture and the French culture – *parbleu!* – that derives from it are finished. [. . .] Do you see what this deliberate craziness is directed at? Yes! Against everything that has hitherto established the French intellectual empire and that still does so today, thanks to the enquiring spirit, the clarity, the chain of ideas, logic, moderation, and taste. And it is the disgraceful love of chaos and anarchy that hides behind these clown masks.[50]

To Pound the avant-garde artists he once admired, such as Picasso, had become markedly less interesting as their consolidation of past styles moved them into the mainstream and hence the marketplace. Although in April 1921 Pound proposed a Picasso number of the *Little Review* (to follow Brancusi, Picabia and Lewis numbers), by November the following year, he wrote to Jane Heap that 'I can't be bothered to rowt out the stuff for Picasso number. The Duchamp wd. do just as well, and has been less done' (*L/MA*, 270, 288).[51] His critique of Picasso followed the dadaists' association of the cubists with 'odious commerce', and earlier that year he had remarked in the *Dial* that 'there is now nothing more to be said *about* a Bracque [*sic*] than about a [William] Nicholson picture; an abstract mode, or several abstract modes have been established and accepted. [. . .] The mark of the shop is upon a great deal of current production; Picasso experiments, but,

[48] 'The Island of Paris: A Letter', p. 518.
[49] 'On the Swings and Roundabouts: The Intellectual Somersaults of the Parisan vs. the Londoner's Efforts to Keep His Stuffed Figures Standing', *Vanity Fair*, 18 (1922), p. 49.
[50] Marcel Boulenger, 'Herr Dada', *Le Gaulois*, 26 April 1920, p. 1, qtd in and trans. by Silver, p. 305.
[51] Of these, only the Brancusi and Picabia numbers appeared, the former as the autumn 1921 issue (8.1), the latter as the spring 1922 issue (8.2). Pound's enthusiasm for Duchamp, and also Man Ray, with whom he associates Duchamp, is at its height during the winter of 1922–3. See in particular his 29 December 1922 letter to Margaret Anderson: 'Duchamp wd. be the most valuable collaborator you cd. get IF you can get him' (*L/MA*, 291).

lately, in the mode of Michael Agnolo [Michelangelo] or of Ford Madox Brown.' Therefore, he decides:

The main interest is not in aesthetics; certain main questions are up for discussion, among them nationality and monotheism. I mean that there is a definite issue between *inter*nationalist and *de*nationalist thought, and a certain number of people believe that it is a calamity to belong to *any* modern nation whatsoever. I suppose the present phase of the discussion began with the *heimatlos* in Switzerland, during the war.[52]

While Pound's tracing of contemporary debates about nationality to dada's birth in Zürich affirms his intellectual sympathy with the dadaists, it does not directly address the implications for interpretation of their art. His initial description of them in the *Dial* had suggested considerable interest, but also uncertainty about their achievement; their journals contained 'various grains' of good sense, he had remarked, and they were gaining attention 'by right of intelligence, more than by right of work yet accomplished'.[53] As Aldington rightly intuited, their bizarre performances, satirical jibes and found objects did not, of themselves, fall into Pound's category of art. After all, in June 1920 Pound published Canto 4, an example of poetic beauty that he found a necessary counterpart to the poem's satirical analysis. And earlier that year, he had made a hard distinction between contemporary satire and 'literature' in a discussion of Flaubert: 'literature is, however, concerned with the permanent elements of life', he had written, 'Bouvard is better than Salammbo, certainly; but "Coeur Simple" is not journalism; you cannot put a date on it'.[54] The problem these views create for Pound's appreciation of dadaist works is most explicitly addressed in the 'Paris Letter' of October 1921, when Pound quotes two Picabian witticisms and refers to the cover of the fourteenth number of Picabia's journal *391*, which showed a copy of a letter by Ingres, on which Picabia had written his own name 'Francis', in front of Ingres's signature. Pound decides, 'Neither the squibs not the photo can be "considered as literature"; any more of course than could the Xenia, the little two line tags which Martial made for saturnalia presents, be "considered as literature".' Then, however, he adds a qualification: 'not at least, as long as there are only a few dozen, but an accumulation of such wild shots ends by expressing a personality'.[55]

[52] Francis Picabia, 'Manifeste Dada', *391*, 12 (1920), p. 1, see Christopher Green, *Cubism and its Enemies: Modern Movements and Reaction in French Art, 1916–1928* (New Haven, CT: Yale University Press, 1987); 'Paris Letter', *Dial*, 72 (1922), [73]-78 (p. 74).
[53] 'The Island of Paris: A Letter', pp. 407–8.
[54] 'The Revolt of Intelligence, IV', *New Age*, 26 (1920), 139–40 (p. 139).   [55] 'Paris Letter', p. 458.

Whether 'expressing a personality' constitutes literature is not clear, but it is certainly implied, and in that qualification, we see Pound, perhaps unconsciously, revising his conception of art. By the 1920s, Pound is exerting extreme pressure on the artist's personality, increasingly seeing the revelation of intelligence as the prime criterion of artistic value and, as we saw in his reviews of *Economic Democracy*, even judging the validity of arguments on the basis of the author's writing style. Such is Pound's disillusion with '"Art" with the capital letter' that he shows in this period an increased tolerance for experiment, connoting intelligence, for its own sake. He praises Duchamp and Man Ray for 'carry[ing] their art to a point where it demands constant invention, and where they can't simply loll round basking in virtuosity'.[56] Dadaist experimentation is 'lump-payment', not knowledge 're-sorted and arranged into coin'. Its intelligence is affirmed and its integrity preserved by its repudiation of artistic finish and its consequent unsaleability. For Pound and the dadaists, at the moment experimentation turns into art, it becomes a commodity, a point made most succinctly by Duchamp's *Tzanck Check* (1919), an oversized hand-drawn cheque made out to Daniel Tzanck, a dentist, and signed by Duchamp, equating the artwork with a voucher that can be exchanged for cash.[57]

Apart from 'Moeurs Contemporaines' and 'Yeux Glauques', Pound's own contributions to dada periodicals were mainly 'squibs': the pseudo-announcement in *Dadaphone*, the 'Lettre Anglaise' in *Littérature*, a line about not being able to find a mistress in Paris in *Le Pilhaou-Thibaou* and, in the same publication, his most substantial offering, a page of jumbled quotations, references and polemic entitled 'Kongo Roux'.[58] The latter juxtaposes remarks about religion, finance and nationality, all issues surfacing in Pound's journalism of the period, and suggests that financiers and oil barons have so thoroughly corrupted national governments that a utopian denationalist town, 'Kongo Roux', should be built on the demilitarised left bank of the Rhine, where one could live in sexual and intellectual freedom ('On appellera ça KONGO/ ou Venusberg/ ou la nouvelle/ Athènes selon').[59] Although, as Richard Sieburth rightly notes, 'Kongo

[56] 'The Curse', p. 22; 'Paris Letter', *Dial*, 74 (1923), [273]-80 (p. 275).
[57] 'Art Notes', p. 60. See George Baker, 'The Artwork Caught by the Tail', *October*, 97 (2001), 51–90 (pp. 66–9).
[58] The translation of 'Moeurs Contemporaines', 'Kongo Roux', the line about the absence of a mistress, together with two satirical comments on dada published in the *Little Review*, were reprinted as appendices to the first serious consideration of Pound's relationship with the dadaists, Andrew Clearfield's 'Pound, Paris, and Dada', *Paideuma*, 7 (1978), 113–40. Pound was also quoted on the scatological cover of the July 1924 *391* responding to Léonce Rosenberg's question in *Bulletin de l'Effort Moderne*, 'Où va la peinture moderne?', with 'Aux chiottes!'
[59] 'Kongo Roux', *Le Pilhaou-Thibaou* [*391*, 15] (1921), p. 10.

Roux' 'anticipates the crackerbarrel logorrhoea of Pound's later wartime broadcasts', it is generically unique in Pound's œuvre, the moment when his journalism comes closest to his poetry, without being filtered into an identifiably poetic product.[60] The voice and subject matter of Pound's periodical articles are presented in an aesthetic form that is both verbally and visually innovative: the text deploys techniques of fragmentation and juxtaposition, and is arranged using experimental typography, but it repudiates the linguistic and metrical virtuosity characteristic of *The Cantos*.

The underlying principle of Pound's acceptance of the dadaist squib, that intellectual power is manifested in radically compressed and defamiliarized forms, had also been present in Pound's readings of vorticist art, especially of Lewis's paintings and designs.[61] By 1915, when Pound was considering vorticist art as a potential model for *The Cantos*, he associated both Lewis's and Gaudier's work with the ability to mobilise contemporary critique with an immediacy his own work lacked. But the important difference between vorticist and dadaist works was that only the latter carried their critique into the very materials they used, rejecting the traditional paint or stone for the materials of mass production. Though this departure from traditional materials was not an innovation Pound championed, or even seems to have recognised as significant, the particular circumstances of his cultural interests combined with his new economic theories enabled him to read dadaist works as deliberately confounding the capitalist transformation of painting, sculpture and music into luxury or kitsch. For Pound, works such as Duchamp's *Fountain* (1917), Man Ray's *Obstruction* (1920) and Picabia's *L'Oeil Cacodylate* (1921) did not have 'the mark of the shop' upon them and were therefore able to mount an independent critique of their context, renouncing the traditional autonomy of the aesthetic artefact, parcelled off from life.[62] Here, the terms of Pound's appreciation for dada come surprisingly close to the influential 1970s and 80s analyses of dada and surrealism as 'the historical avant-garde'. Like Peter Bürger, Pound reads dada as 'an attack on the status of art in bourgeois society', a 'practical' art that 'directs itself to the way art functions in society, a process that does as much to determine the effect that works have as does the particular content'.[63]

---

[60] Sieburth, 'Dada Pound', p. 60.
[61] See Pound's reproduction of two designs in 'Wyndham Lewis', and the comment: 'Maestria is evident in small works as in great ones. If you cannot see the control and skill and power in these two designs, God help you' (p. 233).
[62] 'Paris Letter', p. 74.   [63] Bürger, p. 49.

The logical conclusion of dada's critique was the disintegration of the category of 'art' as it had been previously defined: as Thierry de Duve observes, it became 'legitimate to be an artist without being either a painter, or a poet, or a musician, or a sculptor, novelist, architect, photographer, choreographer, or filmmaker. A new "category" of art appeared – art in general, or art at large – that was no longer absorbed in traditional disciplines.'[64] From 1920 Pound's career embraces this concept of 'art in general', or conceptual art, furthering the interdisciplinary elements already present in his criticism and his poetry, and enabling continuities to be drawn between an extremely wide range of artworks that would not only include his own poetry, Joyce's novels, Lewis's painting and Gaudier-Brzeska's sculpture, but also Douglas's economic treatises, George Antheil's compositions and Mussolini's speeches. His attempt to account for Picabia's significance takes exactly this form.

In a 1921 article for the Literary Review of the *New York Evening Post*, Pound wrote:

> To begin with, Picabia is not a bad painter. He is perhaps not a painter at all? Take away the painting and there would still be nearly all of Picabia; Picabia, the man who, in ten lines and an almost photographic drawing of a wheel or a valve will dissociate, or satirize, or at any rate expose "all the formal thought or invention" that a salon painter or secondary cubist employs in a "picture" [. . .]. I do not present Picabia as a master painter; nor as a master sculptor in the sense that Brancusi is a sculptor, or Picasso a master draughtsman, or Matisse a beautifully gifted manipulator of color; but Picabia does, on the other hand, work in a definite medium, to which one may give an interim label of thought. In his beautiful and clear pictures, which cannot be reproduced by half-tone blocks, there is perhaps not a sign of visual sensitivity, or at least of that kind of visual *receptivity* which underlies the nervous outlines of a Picasso, but there is a very clear exteriorization of Picabia's mental activity; of a mental sensitivity of a kind, let us say, which distinguished Dante's discrimination of the qualities of brightness in the *Paradiso* from the thicker emotional qualities of the *Inferno*.[65]

While this passage presents Pound as an early advocate of conceptual art, it also indicates where he parts company with the dominant interpretations of dada. According to Benjamin's influential reading, 'the Dadaists attached much less importance to the sales value of their work than to its uselessness for contemplative immersion [. . .]. What they intended and achieved was a relentless destruction of the aura of their creations, which

---

[64] Duve, p. 95.
[65] 'Parisian Literature', Literary Review, *New York Evening Post*, 13 August 1921, p. 7.

they branded as reproductions with the very means of production.'[66] While Pound acknowledges that not all dada works are able to sustain contemplation, the 'aura of their creations' remains intact: it is simply transferred from artwork to artist. His interest in dada is enabled by a lessening of attention to individual works of art in favour of the oeuvre, which can be read as an index of the artist's intelligence. It is indicative that Pound's vorticist art criticism frequently named favourite works, but his art criticism after 1920 names very few.

Pound's essay in the *Evening Post* also demonstrates that there were some dadaist works that were less challenging to his taste. Although, characteristically, he does not name particular works by Picabia, his first reference in this article, to 'an almost photographic drawing of a wheel or a valve', marks his appreciation for Picabia's well-known 'mechanomorphic' style, in which Picabia worked in 1915 (inspired, he said, by his stay in New York that year) and from 1917 to 1919.[67] The 1915 drawings, such as *Le Saint des Saints* and *De Zayas! De Zayas!*, were executed in ink on paper.[68] The works from 1917 to 1919 were more varied in their use of materials, and included some watercolours and oils, such as *Prenez garde à la peinture* (ca. 1919) (fig. 5) and *L'Enfant carburateur* (1919). When the *Little Review* produced a Picabia number in 1922, following Picabia's appointment as foreign editor, Pound picked out twenty-one works for reproduction. His choice gave a fair representation of Picabia's career and included watercolours from 1903 as well as recent dadaist works. But the order in which the works were reproduced gave clear priority to the machine-inspired designs: the first eight plates were examples of this style.[69]

Pound's description of Picabia's mechanomorphic works employs categorically different terminology from that used to describe his 'squibs'. The rhetoric of experimentation is relinquished in favour of a vocabulary and frame of reference that suggests a more permanent significance for

[66] Benjamin, pp. 239–40.
[67] 'Mechanomorphic' is Camfield's term: see pp. 77–90, 99–100. For Picabia's commentary on these works see 'French Artists Spur on an American Art', *New York Tribune*, 24 October 1915, pt. iv, p. 2.
[68] See Barbara Zabel, 'The Constructed Self: Gender and Portraiture in Machine-Age America', in Sawelson-Gorse, pp. 22–47.
[69] Pound recalls choosing the works for reproduction in 'D'Artagnan Twenty Years After', *Criterion*, 16 (1937), 606–17 (pp. 615–16). The works reproduced were (in order of reproduction): *Les yeux chauds* (1921), *Petite solitude au milieu des soleils* (1915), *Prenez garde à la peinture*, (ca. 1919) (fig. 5), *L'Enfant carburateur* (1919), *Fantaisie* (1915), *Le Saint des Saints* (1915), *Révérence* (1915), *Cette Chose est faite pour perpétuer mon souvenir* (1915–16), *Révérences* (c. 1913), *Force comique* (1913), *Chose admirable à voir* (c. 1913–14), *New York* (1913) *L'Oeil Cacodylate* (1921), *Danse de Saint-Guy* (1922), a page of typography labelled *The News From Russia* [*Titre inconnu*] (c. 1920), *Le Fou* (1903), *Portrait de Camille Pissarro* (1903), unidentified watercolour portrait (1903), watercolour of a toreros (1902), and *Torse nu* (1909).

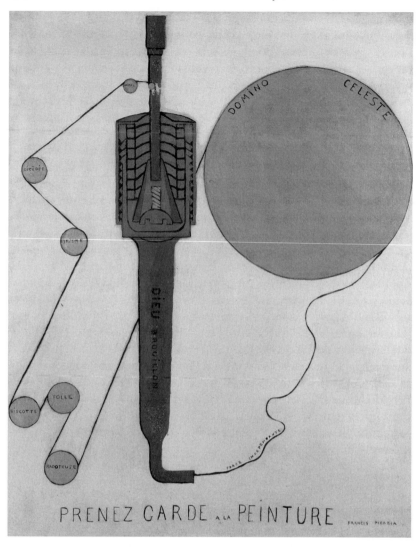

5 Francis Picabia, *Prenez garde à la peinture* (c. 1919)

the works. Their value is still in their 'exteriorization of Picabia's mental activity', but the introduction of terms like 'beauty' and 'clarity', and the comparison with Dante, place Picabia's artworks in a more conventional aesthetic frame. This rhetoric recurs in Pound's subsequent criticism of Picabia: in October 1921, for example, he described Picabia as 'having gradually effaced all colour, all representation, nearly all design in his love for the absolute', and praised his 'hyper-Socratic destructivity'. Though these phrases are clearly descended from well-established elements of Pound's criticism – the scientific and mathematical analogies, the formalist rhetoric of 'arrangements' and 'planes', the preference for design over colour – the Paris years see a new emphasis on art as a process of clearing and cleaning and a heightened appreciation for art that foregrounds clarity of design.[70] In this, Pound was adopting the prevalent critical vocabulary of the post-war years, carried over from the literal imperative, particularly deeply felt in France, to clear away the debris of the war in preparation for reconstruction. The dadaists used this vocabulary to describe their own project: in the 'Dada Manifesto 1918', for example, Tzara had proclaimed that 'there is a great negative work of destruction to be accomplished. We must sweep and clean. Affirm the cleanliness of the individual after the state of madness.'[71] But this vocabulary was more strongly associated with the *rappel à l'ordre* of the neoclassicists, whose reinterpretation of classicist art entailed a new commitment to the laws of architecture, and to the related simplicity of drawing.[72] It imbued the 'purism' of Ozenfant and Charles-Edouard Jeanneret (Le Corbusier), who began their 1918 manifesto, *Après le cubisme*, with the statement, 'The War over, everything organizes, everything is clarified and purified.'[73] Thus, although Pound had deliberately sought an association with the avant-garde group that had set itself most firmly against the order and rationality of this post-war classicism, the works he praised most highly were those that could be assimilated to the conservative aesthetic values of post-war Paris. What is more, his praise is framed in terms that echo those of the conservatives pursuing a nationalist political agenda, the very people, like Barrès, he was simultaneously disparaging.

[70] 'Paris Letter', p. 457.

[71] Tristan Tzara, 'Manifeste Dada 1918', *Dada*, 3 (1918), [1–3], (p. [3]). English translation Tzara, 'Dada Manifesto 1918', in Robert Motherwell (ed.), *The Dada Painters and Poets: An Anthology* (Boston, MA: Hall, 1981), pp. 76–82 (p. 81).

[72] See Silver, especially chapters 6, 7, 8. The phrase 'rappel à l'ordre' is usually attributed to André Lhote, writing in *Nouvelle Revue Française* on 1 June 1919, though Jean Laude notes that the painter Roger Bissère used it to describe Georges Braque's work in *L'Opinion* on 29 March and 26 April 1919. See Laude, *Le Retour à l'ordre dans les arts plastiques et l'architecture, 1919–1925* (Paris: Université de Saint-Étienne, 1975) pp. 15–19.

[73] [Amédée] Ozenfant et [Charles-Edouard] Jeanneret, *Après le cubisme* (Paris: Édition des Commentaires, 1918), p. [11], English translation Ozenfant and Jeanneret, 'After Cubism', trans. John Goodman, in Carol S. Eliel, *L'Esprit Nouveau: Purism in Paris, 1918–25* (Los Angeles, CA and New York: Los Angeles County Museum of Art/ Abrams, 2001), pp. 129–68 (p. 132). See Silver, pp. 227–32, and Susan L. Ball, *Ozenfant and Purism: The Evolution of a Style, 1915–1930* (Ann Arbor, MI: UMI Research Press, 1981), pp. 32–3, 34–55.

BRANCUSI AND UTILITY

It was in his writing about the Paris-based Romanian sculptor, Constantin Brancusi, that Pound's new classicist vocabulary was deployed most influentially.[74] Pound had encountered Brancusi's work in London: his sculptures were first shown in England at the 1913 Allied Artists' Association, at which Pound had met Gaudier, and both Epstein and Gaudier were profoundly influenced by his work.[75] Yet in a letter to the *Little Review*'s editor Margaret Anderson in September 1917, Pound had called Brancusi's work 'sperm untempered with the faintest touch of intelligence' (*L/MA*, 124). His animosity is remarkable: it was Epstein's and Gaudier's most Brancusian pieces that Pound had admired, John Quinn had been collecting Brancusi's work since 1914, and by 1916 large circulation magazines like *Vanity Fair* were praising Brancusi's 'austere influence [. . .], which helps those who realize the true beauty of line and form, to escape from convention, prettiness and all sorts of compromise', terms which echoed Pound's praise for Gaudier.[76] Soon after he arrived in Paris, however, Pound changed his mind: on 21 May 1921 he wrote to Quinn, 'From what I have seen I think he is by far the best sculptor here' (*EPVA*, 246); James Sibley Watson reported that when Pound took him to meet Brancusi a year later he witnessed Pound 'chittering and apologizing and kowtowing' to Brancusi (*L/TW*, 244); and Ford Madox Ford reported that Brancusi had inspired Pound to take up sculpture himself: 'He acquired pieces of stone as nearly egg-shaped as possible, hit them with hammers and then laid them about on the floor.'[77]

Pound's interest was immediately translated into action. In a letter to Margaret Anderson written from 29 April to 4 May 1921, Pound suggested, 'hav[ing] talked the year's issue over with Picabia', that the *Little Review*

---

[74] In *The Final Sculpture*, Michael North discusses the influence of the Parisian post-war classicists, especially Brancusi, on Pound's conception of 'the work a culture does to maintain a tradition' (p. 173). The following discussion traverses some of the same ground, but is particularly concerned with exploring how Pound's appreciation of Brancusi's work, in which he appears to return to a pre-*Mauberley* aestheticism, can be brought to terms with his engaged critique of dadaist works.

[75] Silber, *Gaudier-Brzeska*, pp. 107, 124, 287.

[76] Ann Temkin, 'Brancusi and His American Collectors', in Bach, Rowell and Temkin, pp. 50–73 (p. 53); 'Brancusi Carries Simplification Further', *Vanity Fair*, 7.3 (1916), p. 75. One adverse reaction to Brancusi that may have influenced Pound was Hulme's: Hulme grouped Brancusi with Gauguin and Maillol as post-impressionists: see Hulme, *Collected Writings*, p. 277.

[77] Ford Madox Ford, *Memories and Impressions*, ed. Michael Killigrew (Harmondsworth: Penguin, 1979), p. 326. Pound described his sculpture as a reaction against the work of the American sculptor, Paul Rudin: see *L/WCW*, 168–70. It is now in the possession of Mary de Rachewiltz, and is reproduced as 'Self-Portrait' in *Ezra Pound e le arti: La bellezza è difficile* (Skira: Milan, 1997) p. 63. For a very positive, if somewhat inaccurate, account of the relationship between Pound and Brancusi by a friend of the sculptor, see V. G. Paleolog, 'Brancusi and Ezra Pound', *Romanian Review*, 8 (1988), 69–73.

produce a whole Brancusi number, with twenty illustrations and an essay
by Pound, as the first in a series of special artists' numbers. The Brancusi
number was to be the inaugural issue of the *Little Review*'s new larger,
quarterly format, and Pound saw it as a means of responding defiantly to
the recent censorship of the journal's publication of *Ulysses*: 'the ANSWER
is to come out at least in appearance three times as solid, complete new birth,
full of guts'. He included twenty-two photographs of Brancusi's sculpture
with the letter, with strict instructions for their reproduction, 'Please keep
the order marked on back, print them as PLATE I, Plate II. etc. without
the concession of titles [. . .]. I can't over emphasize the importance of
getting the best possible reprods. of the photos. and getting them as large
as the page will hold.' He insisted that 'it is worth publishing them all, not
as an expense but as an investment, this number shd. be a permanent bit of
property for you and counts as my contribution to the upkeep of the L.R.
for the year' (*L/MA*, 270–3).

The Brancusi number was published as the autumn 1921 issue, with
twenty-four photographs of Brancusi's sculpture.[78] Pound's essay on Brancusi opened the striking blue-and-white striped volume: it is one of his
most important writings on art, a serious and imaginative engagement
with Brancusi's sculpture, in fact 'the first substantive essay on the sculptor
to appear in English', and, indeed, highly influential.[79] The essay was not
only significant in building Brancusi's reputation; Pound took the opportunity to set out a far fuller statement of aesthetics than he had allowed
himself since his 1916 memoir of Gaudier. He presents Brancusi's sculpture
as expressing a coherent aesthetics, an 'approach to the infinite *by form*, by
precisely the highest possible degree of consciousness of formal perfection;
as free of accident as any of the philosophical demands of a "Paradiso"
can make it'. As the use of the Italian suggests, the paradise Brancusi is
working towards is Dante's paradise, and Pound's essay draws on over a
decade of reading, thinking and writing about Dante and Tuscan poetry in
the context of Neoplatonic philosophy. In his 'Paris Letter' of the following
January he is even more explicit: 'Brancusi has created an universe, a *cielo*,

[78] Photographs of the following works were reproduced: *Mlle Pogany* [II] (bronze) (1920), *Plato* (1919–20), *Mlle Pogany* [II] (1919), Study for *The Kiss* (1919), *Endless Column* (1918), *Madame L.R.* (1914–17), *Yellow Bird* (1919), *Chimera* (1915–17/18), *Danaïde* (bronze with black patina) (c. 1913), *Leda* (1920/21), *Three Penguins* (1911–12), *The First Step* (1913–14), *Golden Bird* (1919/20), *Caryatids* (1908), *The Kiss* (1909), *Prodigal Son* (1914/15), *Little French Girl* (1914–18), *Cup* [II] (1917–18), *Timidity* (1917), *Sleeping Muse* [I] (1909–10).

[79] Temkin, p. 57. Anna C. Chave provides a compelling alternative account of Brancusi's work, explicitly rejecting Pound's influence: see *Constantin Brancusi: Shifting the Bases of Art* (New Haven, CT: Yale University Press, 1993), pp. 1–3, 14.

a Platonic heaven full of pure and essential forms.'[80] For Pound, Brancusi's is a classicist art, characterised by beauty, order, clarity, and permanence.

The terms of Pound's admiration for Brancusi seem, therefore, to be entirely at odds with those he had used to explain his involvement with the dadaists. In a 1921 article for William Carlos Williams's and Robert McAlmon's *Contact*, he had stated unequivocally that 'the symbolist position, artistic aloofness from world affairs, is no good now', and his emphasis on the political engagement of the dadaists had seemed a positive response to that verdict.[81] But his analysis of Brancusi's sculpture appears to rescind this decision, as does the other article he contributed to the Brancusi Number, 'Historical Survey', in which he wrote that 'the work of art is not a means. The work of art is an end. It is the result of an act or actions committed to please the artist and for *no* other reason.' The search for an engaged art appeared to have been abandoned, and in January 1922 Pound described 'the serene sculpture of Brancusi' as 'above or apart from the economic squabble, the philosophic wavering, the diminishing aesthetic hubbub'.[82] As Richard Masteller understandably concludes in his illuminating essay on Brancusi's American reception, Pound's essay in the *Little Review* transmitted an 'astringent modernism': 'Pound's demand that much of contemporary culture be erased – no derivative representationalism, no "idiotic ornamentation" – bespoke a growing hostility toward the world of his audience.'[83] Brancusi's art appears to take no more account of the 'march of events' than Mauberley's (*HSM*, 9).

Pound's interpretation of Brancusi's sculpture is less astringent than it first appears. The last paragraph of 'Brancusi' (from which Masteller's quotation is taken) indicates that Pound has not, after all, abandoned his recently adjusted aesthetics; there, he addresses the social importance of Brancusi's sculpture by turning to the subject of domestic architecture and design, the focus of so much aesthetic discussion in the post-war years:

But if we are ever to have a bearable sculpture or architecture it might be well for young sculptors to start with some such effort at perfection, rather than with the idea of a new Laocoon, or a "Triumph of Labour over Commerce." (This suggestion is mine, and I hope it will never fall under the eye of Brancusi. – But

[80] 'Brancusi', *Little Review* [8.1] (1921), 3–7 (p. 7); 'Paris Letter', p. 76. See Leon Surette, 'Cavalcanti & Pound's Arcanum', in *Ezra Pound and Europe*, ed. Richard Taylor and Claus Melchior (Amsterdam: Rodopi, 1993), pp. 51–60.

[81] [Review of] *Credit Power and Democracy*, by Maj. C. H. Douglas and A. R. Orange [*sic*]', *Contact*, [4] [1921], p. [1].

[82] 'Historical Survey', *Little Review* [8.1] (1921), 39–42 (p. 42); 'Paris Letter', p. 75.

[83] Richard N. Masteller, 'Using Brancusi: Three Writers, Three Magazines, Three Versions of Modernism', *American Art*, 11 (1997), 47–67 (p. 61).

then Brancusi can spend most of his time in his own studio, surrounded by the calm
of his own creations, whereas the author of this imperfect exposure is compelled
to move about in a world full of junk-shops, a world full of more than idiotic
ornamentations, a world where pictures are made for museums, where no man has
a front-door that he can bear to look at, let alone one he can contemplate with
reasonable pleasure, where the average house is each year made more hideous, and
where the sense of form which ought to be as general as the sense of refreshment
after a bath, or the pleasure of liquid in time of drouth or any other clear animal
pleasure, is the rare possession of an "intellectual" (heaven help us) "aristocracy."[84]

The fundamental ideas here are not new: Pound's aversion to sculpture
with narrative content repeats his long-held belief that 'every concept, every
emotion presents itself to the vivid consciousness in some primary form'.[85]
The argument that the early twentieth century's supposed lack of a 'sense of
form' has had an adverse impact on its built environment is similarly well
established in Pound's criticism.[86] But the significance of this statement in
1921 is that Pound draws here on a pre-war commitment to abstract form, a
commitment that in 1921 was extremely unpopular, yet he argues that it can
be 'useful' in the sense required by post-war reconstruction narratives. His
last sentence, with its explicitly populist agenda, indicates that he stands
by his anti-elitist polemics of the previous year.

 Pound's reading of Brancusi's sculpture was not simply a return to his
earlier aestheticist position, but rather an attempt to retain the privileged
place for art that was a feature of that position, within an aesthetics now
characterised by social responsibility. The implications of this become more
explicit in Pound's writing about Brancusi later in the 1920s, during and
after the famous case Brancusi brought against the United States Customs
in 1928. Brought to New York for Brancusi's solo exhibition at the Brummer
Gallery, import duty had been charged on Brancusi's bronze *Bird in Space*
(1924) (fig. 6), on the basis that it was a manufactured metal object of utility
and therefore taxable, rather than an original work of art, which was not
subject to import duty. Like the Whistler vs. Ruskin trial that had taken
place fifty years before, the Brancusi vs. United States trial confronted the
difficulty of establishing a legal definition of art.[87]

---

[84] 'Brancusi', p. 7.   [85] 'Vortex. Pound', p. 154.
[86] See 'Art Notes: Building: Ornamentation!', *New Age*, 23 (1918), 320, 'Art Notes: Super-Fronts!', *New Age*, 23 (1918), 414, 'Art Notes', *New Age*, 26 (1919), 96–7.
[87] See *Brancusi vs. United States: The Historic Trial, 1928* (Paris: Société Nouvelle Adam Biro, 1999), Laurie Adams, *Art on Trial: From Whistler to Rothko* (New York: Walker and Company, 1976), pp. 35–58, Temkin, pp. 61–2, Pontus Hultén, Natalia Dumitresco and Alexandre Istrati, *Brancusi* (London: Faber, 1986), pp. 174–86, Chave, pp. 198–249.

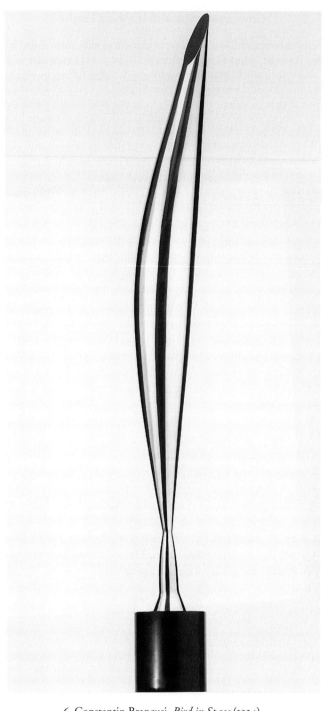

6 Constantin Brancusi, *Bird in Space* (1924)

In order to prove that *Bird in Space* was an original work of art, Brancusi's lawyers had to overturn a precedent judgement of 1916 that stated that sculptures were 'imitations of natural objects in their true proportions of length, breadth, and thickness, or of length and breadth only'. It was relatively straightforward to establish that Brancusi was a respected sculptor, rather than a producer of 'table, household, kitchen, and hospital utensils', but the attempts to define the sculpture on its own terms were frustratingly circular. When asked why he considered *Bird in Space* a work of art, Epstein, appearing as a witness for Brancusi, replied, 'Well, it pleases my sense of beauty, gives me a feeling of pleasure, made by a sculptor it has to me a great many elements but consists in itself a beautiful object [*sic*].' Such subjective testimony could be easily countered, both by the witnesses for the State's defence, the sculptors Robert Ingersoll Aitkin and Thomas H. Jones, who responded, 'I don't think it has the sense of beauty', and by the defence attorneys themselves who asked if 'a brass rail, highly polished, curved in a more or less symmetrical and harmonious circle [. . .] would be a work of art'. Epstein was cornered into the unconvincing reply that 'a mechanic cannot make beautiful work'. Nevertheless, the judge, Associate Justice Waite, was either sufficiently acute or impatient to dismiss much of the defence's attempt to establish the legal impossibility of abstract sculpture. Unlike Sir John Huddleston, the judge in the Whistler case, Waite was able to conceive of art as a necessarily contingent sociological category: although *Bird in Space* did not meet the 1916 legal definition of sculpture, he concluded that 'under the influence of the modern schools of art the opinion previously held has been modified with reference to what is necessary to constitute art within the meaning of the statute'. Accordingly, he found in Brancusi's favour: 'although [*Bird in Space*] has neither feet nor feathers portrayed in the piece, it is beautiful and symmetrical in outline, and while some difficulty might be encountered in associating it with a bird, it is nevertheless pleasing to look at and highly ornamental, and as we hold under the evidence that it is the original production of a professional sculptor [. . .] we sustain the protest'.[88]

The taxation of Brancusi's sculpture and the trial by both the legal system and the press exerted a particular pressure on Pound's aesthetics. The American press took the opportunity to restate their commitment or aversion to modern art, and when the radical left-wing *New Masses* published a review of the Brummer Gallery exhibition in January 1927, it elicited a letter from Pound that sheds considerable light on the system of aesthetics he was

[88] *Brancusi vs. United States*, pp. 115, 71, 28, 65, 28, 114–15.

constructing. The review, by the Marxist artist Hugo Gellert, asked questions that echo those Pound had asked himself earlier in the decade. Antagonised by one of Brancusi's aphorisms printed in the catalogue, 'When we are no longer children, we are already dead', Gellert inveighed against its Rousseauist position: 'It is about time the artist – like every other human being – grew up. Imagine the builder of the Brooklyn Bridge announcing "I am a child".' Gellert argued for an engaged art, demanding the artist acknowledge 'that Art is bound to time and space'. Drawing attention to the date of Brancusi's marble *Princess X*, exhibited at the Brummer as *Portrait* (1916), Gellert wrote: 'what is [*sic*] that Brancusi worked upon in 1916 during the War in Paris? What had he to say? He cut a huge phallus into marble – that is what he had to say! Men are slaughtered, men are crazed. The artist, the divine, toys with the phallus . . . It is Art, it is pure, it is above good and evil. Hurrah! Long live Art.'[89]

Pound's reply was published in the March issue. He began by asking 'Why the HELL should Brancusi, a roumanian peasant by birth, take sides in a war between German empire [*sic*] and two capitalist arms firms?' and concluded that art 'has no political opinion', but, for him, this did not consign Brancusi's sculpture to aestheticism: 'there never was an artist less addicted to "art for arts sake" than Brancusi. The mystical residue, or "fonds" in him is a great embarrassment to his aesthete admirers', he writes. Perhaps thinking of Brancusi's aphorism, 'the arts have never existed for themselves. Throughout the ages, they have only been the adjunct of religion', Pound understands Brancusi's 'mystical residue' as antithetical to aestheticism and having an importance akin to scientific invention: 'Do you heave rocks at every electric light bulb, just because Edison don't paste a Bolshevik label on each one?', he continues. 'Brancusi is trying to save the world by pure form. You may disapprove of messiahs; but you shouldnt [*sic*] mistake 'em for aesthetes.' The editor's reply to Pound's remark about Edison crystallised the point: 'What funny notions you have got. Why should I throw rocks at anything *useful*?'[90] To Pound, Brancusi's art, because of its mystical residue, *was* useful.

Pound's somewhat strained argument was put under further pressure by the terms of the trial itself. Since the law understood a defining quality of art to be its lack of utility, Brancusi's witnesses repeatedly testified that *Bird in Space* had no useful purpose. Pound's writing about Brancusi during this period has quite a different emphasis. He wrote to Brancusi

[89] Hugo Gellert, 'O + .I. = BRANCUSI', *New Masses*, 2.3 (1927), p. 25. On the sculpture as phallus, see Bach, Rowell and Temkin, p. 140 and Chave, pp. 92–8.
[90] 'Pound vs. Gellert [letter]', *New Masses*, 2.5 (1927), p. 25; Hultén, Dumitresco and Istrati, p. 232.

expressing outrage and offering help, lobbied the US Customs and the House of Representatives, and he discussed the case in two essays of 1928, the posthumously published 'Brancusi and Human Sculpture' and 'Article 211' in his short-lived magazine, the *Exile*.[91] In 'Brancusi and Human Sculpture' he explains the utility of Brancusi's work at length: 'Brancusi's *L'Écorché* (*The Skinned Man*) is not only in the Art Museum in Bucharest', he writes, 'but it is in the Roumanian academy of medicine, so the medical students can learn where the muscles are.' In what could well be a direct response to Gellert's accusations, Pound addresses 'the bright-eyed calves who tell me what ISN'T in Brancusi's work. And, naturally, not having known anything about Europe in 1910 they don't know why it happened.' Emphatically placing Brancusi's sculpture in its post-war context, he comments 'When all France (after the war) was teething and tittering, and busy, oh BUSY, there was ONE temple of QUIET [. . .]. There was one place where you cd. take your mind and have it sluiced clean [. . .]. I mean there was this white wide intellectual sunlight at 5 francs taxi ride from one's door'. In this essay, it is no longer Brancusi's 'mystical residue' that is the locus of the sculpture's utility ('no mystic shilly shally, no spooks, no god damn Celtic Twilight, no Freud, no Viennese complex'), rather, Brancusi's importance lies in his ambition to 'get all the forms BACK into the one form'. To rephrase in the aesthetic rhetoric of the period, Brancusi's sculpture aimed not at analysis but synthesis, not dadaist critique, but classicist reconstruction. 'The effect of Brancusi's work is cumulative. He has created a whole universe of FORM', Pound continued. 'You've got to see it together. A system. An Anschauung. Not simply a pretty thing on the library table' (*EPVA*, 306–8).[92]

This statement gives some indication of how Pound can bring his admiration for Brancusi's sculpture to terms with his commitment to the dadaist experiment. Brancusi, like the dadaists, is interpreted through the discourse of artistic genius. But while the dadaists' genius is expressed by their continual experimentation, their refusal to make art that can be assimilated

---

[91] Hultén, Dumitresco and Istrati, p. 183; George. W. Ashworth, Letter to Ezra Pound, 21 November 1927, Letter to George W. Ashworth, 18 January 1928, J. D. Nevius, Letter to Ezra Pound, 12 March 1928, Mary E. Nulle, Letter to Ezra Pound, 21 August 1928, EPP, Beinecke, 5.237; 'Brancusi and Human Sculpture', *EPVA*, 306–9: internal evidence suggests a date of December 1928 or possibly early 1929 for this essay; 'Article 211', *Exile*, 4 (1928), 20–3. In the letter to Ashworth and 'Article 211', Pound relates the trial to the recent decision to categorise the Nassak diamond as a work of art, and therefore let it into the US without the payment of import duty, a decision that was eventually reversed: see Ian Balfour, *Famous Diamonds*, 4th edn (London: Christie's, 2000), p. 191.

[92] 'Chronology', in Bach, Rowell and Temkin, p. 373: in 1903 *L'Écorché* 'is purchased by the Ministry of Education, and four plaster casts are made to be used by students at medical schools in Bucharest, Craiova, Jassy, and Cluj'.

to either the art market or the nationalist cause, Brancusi's genius appears to produce eminently saleable objects that partake of the classicist agenda. Pound, however, does not locate Brancusi's genius in individual artworks, but in his 'system', his outlook ('Anschauung'). It is not the sculptures that hold Pound's attention, but their cumulative effect. In Brancusi's studio the groups of sculptures and carved bases, together with the hand-crafted or customised furnishings and appliances, form a vision of a perfected world, a whole environment of visual stimulation and refreshment, absolutely distinct from a collection of ornamental items produced for sale. Brancusi's studio gave Pound a glimpse of art playing the social role he, like so many other turn-of-the-century intellectuals, envisioned. As Michael North has remarked, Brancusi's studio and sculpture are a major model for the paradise described in *The Cantos*, with its 'forest of marble', and 'arbours of stone –/ marble leaf, over leaf' (17:78).[93] But this paradise was for Pound a real, as well as an ideal, place, and its form, to which Pound would allude in his writing for the rest of his career, is one of the most significant legacies of his aesthetic and ideological education in Paris.

FERNAND LÉGER, ARCHITECTURE, AND MACHINE AESTHETICS

Pound's dominant concern on his arrival in Paris was to find or establish an intellectual centre unmarred by post-war nationalism; by the time he left in October 1924, his major preoccupation was the construction of what he called a 'universe of FORM' (*EPVA*, 308). The transition can be dated from December 1922, when Pound turned his attention to the appearance of the post-war world, in the process of being reconstructed, with an intensity and a level of practical detail lacking from his previous sporadic comments on architecture. In hindsight, three motivating factors can be isolated: his study of the church of San Francesco in Rimini, which would form the focus for cantos 8–11; his awareness of the proposed reconstruction programmes of Mussolini's fascist government; and, most immediately, the reconstruction project in France and the emergence there of a modernist architecture, associated particularly with Charles-Edouard Jeanneret, now calling himself Le Corbusier, whose treatises were being translated by the former vorticist Frederick Etchells for John Rodker's press. The earthly paradise Pound envisions during the 1920s is no medieval ideal; he embraces modern technology with a confidence inspired by Douglas's critique of

---

[93] North, p. 160.

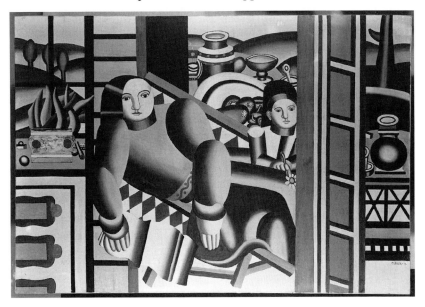

7 Fernand Léger, *La Femme et l'enfant (la mère et l'enfant)* (1922)

anti-mechanisation, his sense of it as a specifically American contribution, and the contemporary currency of a machine aesthetic that had been inaugurated by Italian Futurism, extended by the dadaists, and in the early 1920s was finding one of its most articulate exponents in a figure close to Le Corbusier, Brancusi and, to a lesser extent, the dadaists: Fernand Léger.[94]

  Pound's friendship with Léger appears have become closer in the second half of 1922. On 20 August, he mentions Léger in a letter home ('Leger's doing interesting painting'), and Léger's *La femme et l'enfant* (1922) (fig. 7) and *Fumées sur les toits* (1910) were reproduced in the *Little Review*'s winter 1922 'Miscellany number'.[95] Pound was pleased: 'The Leger comes up so damn well, I think we ought to use more of him', he wrote to the editors, and seven more works were reproduced in the 'Exiles number' of spring

[94] Douglas, *Economic Democracy*, pp. 44–5; *MA*, 78. In the following discussion I am indebted to Alec Marsh's unpublished paper, 'Pound, Léger, Le Corbusier: Machine Aesthetics', presented at the 118th MLA Convention in New York on 29 December 2002.
[95] Letter to Isabel Weston Pound, 20 August 1922, EPP, Beinecke, 60.2684. The painting reproduced as fig. 7 is a slightly different version of *La femme et l'enfant* from that reproduced in the *Little Review*.

1923 (*L/MA*, 296).[96] A cubist before the war, Léger had returned from the front with a new artistic lexicon that rejected the conventional cubist reper- toire in favour of simplified geometric forms given a distinctive solidity he attributed to his analysis of machinery. By 1922 his initially 'dissonant, dis- integrated approach to painting and to modern life' had given way to a close engagement with the classicism that dominated the work of the Parisian avant-garde. In his still authoritative study of Léger and the avant-garde, Christopher Green traces the point of conversion to 1920, specifically to the painting of *Le Mécanicien*, 'an image of the machine-man, which com- bined the precise balance of the Purist approach to man and the machine with the uncompromising dignity of a figure style from the past'. By the following year, Léger had become closely associated with Ozenfant and Jeanneret's purism, and by the mid-1920s his industrial aesthetic doctrine was widespread.[97]

Pound's most extended consideration of Léger's contribution to post-war aesthetics occurs in a 'Paris Letter' for the January 1923 issue of the *Dial*:

Fernand Leger is industrious. Taking his work retrospectively one knows of the time he stopped painting and for some years puzzled over the problem of ideal machines, three-dimensional constructions having all the properties of machines save the ability to move or do work. This is a perfectly serious aesthetic problem; Leger comes to a provisional answer in the negative, not convinced, but wondering whether the *objêt*, the real machine, won't in the end be more interesting to look at, and *better aesthetically*.

The struggle is interesting, at least as a symptom of sensitivity, and an evidence of his being aware of the much discussed and deplored gap between "art and life" in our time.

Leger returns to painting and finds the easel picture a constriction. Many of his designs only become effective when one imagines them forty feet by sixty, instead of the twelve by fifteen demanded by studio limits. Ghirlandaio wanted to paint the town walls of Florence. Leger would be perfectly happy doing the outside of a railway terminal, or probably doing an ad on the slab side of the sky-scraper.

Through it all is the elegy, the lament that we lack a "*chef d'orchestre*"; that painting ought to be part of architecture; that there is no place for sculpture or painting in modern life; that painters make innumerable scraps of paper. This is true. The stuff is vendible or non-vendible, it is scraps, knick-knacks, part of

[96] *Fumeurs* (1911) (titled *The Two Smokers* in the *Little Review*), *Les maisons sous les arbres* (1913) (*Painting* in *LR*), *L'homme au chien* (1921) (*Landscape* in *LR*), *Le Grand déjeuner* (1921) (*The Breakfast* in *LR*), Curtain design for the Ballets Suédois ballet *Skating Rink* (1921), *Le Compotier de poires* (1923) (*The Dish of Pears* in *LR*), and *Le Pont* (1923) (*The Bridge* in *LR*, reproduced in reverse). Léger also designed the cover of the issue.

[97] Christopher Green, *Léger and the Avant-Garde* (New Haven, CT: Yale University Press, 1976), pp. 6– 7, 109–10, 114–17, 222–3, 209–10; Matthew Affron, 'Fernand Léger and the spectacle of objects', *Word and Image*, 10 (1994), 1–21 (pp. 6–7).

the disease that gives us museums instead of temples, curiosity shops instead of such rooms as the hall of the Palazzo Pubblico in Siena or of the Sala di Notari in Perugia.[98]

Components of this argument are familiar from Pound's earlier writings: the commitment to the real, rather than idealised, object, the belief that 'painting ought to be part of architecture', that the sale of artworks automatically debases them, and the allusions to Quattrocento architecture. But the interest in machinery for its own sake, rather than for inspiration and adaptation as in vorticism, is new, and it may be attributed to Pound's friendship with Léger. When Léger published a lecture he had given later the same year at the Collège de France, 'L'Esthétique de la Machine', in the *Little Review*, he drew attention to the continuity between Pound's ideas and his own by dedicating the essay to Pound. Though there are clearly parts of the lecture with which Pound would have disagreed, such as Léger's praise for window-dressing shopkeepers as 'artisan-creators', there is also much common ground. Like Pound, Léger argues against 'the hierarchy of the arts' which trains people to appreciate form only when it is discovered in an art gallery or a museum: 'Why do they go to gaze upon a poor imitation of a landscape hanging on a wall when a beautiful electric meter is at hand which they do not see?', he asks. The answer is notably Poundian: the cause is 'bad visual education' and 'excessive specialization' that 'has made men afraid to step out of their own narrow fields'.[99]

In 1923–4 Pound and Léger stepped out of their narrow fields to collaborate with Man Ray, Antheil and an American filmmaker, Dudley Murphy, on their own piece of machine art: the film *Ballet Mécanique* (1924). Judi Freeman's meticulous essay on the background to its production demonstrates that although the participants gave differing accounts of their individual contributions, Murphy and Léger were primarily responsible for the film itself, Man Ray's contribution 'was restricted to the shooting of imagery in the earliest phases of the project', and Antheil was solely responsible for the score. Pound was involved in the project from its inception: he introduced Léger, Antheil and Murphy to each other, and, according to his own and Legér's account, he and Murphy applied the vortographic system of fragmenting the image to cinematography. 'We took a few metres of interesting and highly

---

[98] 'Paris Letter', *Dial*, 74 (1923), [85]-90 (pp. 87–8).
[99] Fernand Léger, 'The Esthetics of the Machine: Manufactured Objects, Artisan and Artist', *Little Review*, 9.3 (1923), 45–9, 9.4 (1923–4), 55–8 (pp. 48–9, 56, 45).

unsatisfactory film', wrote Pound, 'Man Ray with his brilliant record and long experience produced something infinitely better; Murphy combined with Léger and got some interesting results'.[100]

For Léger, the 'purely cinematographic' elements of the film medium, especially the close-up, 'the only cinematographic invention', enabled one to direct aesthetic attention to the 'plastic *possibilities*' of the man-made object. *Ballet Mécanique*'s means of achieving this, he told readers of the *Little Review*, was to have 'no scenario – Reactions of rhythmic images, that is all'.[101] This focus on 'pure' cinema was representative of the views of the avant-garde film makers and critics, such as René Clair and Jean Epstein, who were part of Léger's milieu, and Murphy, too, testified that that 'the film was based on a belief that surprise of image and rhythm would make a pure film'.[102] But despite the evident correlation between Léger's and Murphy's purist interpretation of cinema and the classicist rhetoric of Pound's art criticism, Pound's remarks on Abel Gance's film *La Roue* (1922), on which Pound's and Léger's friend, Blaise Cendrars, had worked, showed that his opinion of cinema had not improved. While characteristically 'laud[ing] the experiment' and welcoming its 'publicity for cubism', the film, he thought, 'very probably' 'settle[d] the question [. . .] once and for all that the cinema is no use as art'.[103] By 1927, in a draft for Canto 27, he dismissed all 'machine made art':

> machine made art
>   ROT
> always the automatic
>   part
> the part not penetrated
> by intelligence
> / even in M. Ray
> Coburn. / M. Ray
> The automatic part – still
>   further reduced?[104]

---

[100] Judi Freeman, 'Bridging Purism and Surrealism: The Origins and Production of Fernand Léger's *Ballet Mécanique*', in *Dada and Surrealist Film*, ed. Rudolf E. Kuenzli (Cambridge, MA: MIT Press, 1996), pp. 28–45 (pp. 31–3); *MA*, 76.

[101] Fernand Léger, 'Ballet Mécanique', in Léger, *Functions of Painting*, ed. Edward F. Fry (London: Thames and Hudson, 1973), pp. 48–51 (pp. 49, 50, 48); Fernand Léger, 'Film by Fernand Léger and Dudley Murphy[,] Musical Synchronism by George Antheil', *Little Review*, 10.2 (1924–5), pp. 42–4 (p. 43).

[102] Green, *Léger and the Avant-Garde*, pp. 279–81; Dudley Murphy, 'Murphy by Murphy' (1966), unpublished ms., qtd in Freeman, p. 31.

[103] 'Paris Letter', p. [273].

[104] 'Cantos "XXV–XXX" [i.e. 24–8]: autograph ms. notes and typescripts', EPP, Beinecke, 72.3240.

Uncompromising as they are, these lines were written at the high point of Pound's investigation into the machine aesthetic, and though 'machine made art' is rejected here, Pound continued to maintain that machines themselves were aesthetically significant.

That significance is explored at length in 'Machine Art', an extended essay which began life as a contribution to a special issue on American art in *This Quarter*: the Pound archive at Yale holds seven letters from Pound to his parents, written between June and December 1925, which ask them to obtain 'photos. of machinery and spare parts', not 'harbour cranes WITH ROMANTIC CLOUDS IN THE BACK SIDE'.[105] However, one of *This Quarter*'s editors died before the issue appeared, and the material was returned to Pound. In 1927, Pound sent the photos he had collected and the manuscript of 'the Machine book' to Pascal Covici, the publisher of his journal the *Exile*, who would also bring out the American edition of *Antheil and the Treatise on Harmony* later that year. After a delay of over a year, Covici pulled out of the arrangement due to the lack of financial return on Pound's previous publications. Pound lightly revised the manuscript in 1930, but he did not attempt to publish it again, although he sent a brief summary of the ideas with fifteen of the photographs to Samuel Putnam's *New Review* in 1931.[106]

Although Léger's name is entirely absent from the 1927 text, and confined to a footnote on his experiments with '"ideal" machines' in the 1930 version, 'Machine Art' is a close companion of Léger's writings (*MA*, 70–1).[107] The central argument reprises that of Léger's lecture: that the form of a machine can be as interesting as, or more interesting than, that of a sculpture or a painting, and that modern life could be improved by harnessing this knowledge: 'when we get to the Bliss Press we have [. . .] something to comfort us in an age filled by political villainies and confusions', Pound writes, 'the architect's best lesson may very possibly lie in the machine' (*MA*, 59, 72). That latter point is a central precept of purism.

But Pound also extends Léger's argument. Léger claimed that 'the more the motor [of the automobile] perfects its function of utility the more

---

[105] Letter to Isabel Weston Pound, 10 June [1925], EPP, Beinecke, 60.2689; Letter to Homer Loomis Pound, 11 August [1925], EPP, Beinecke, 60.2690.

[106] See Donald Gallup, *Ezra Pound: A Bibliography* (Charlottesville, VA: University Press of Virginia, 1983), pp. 449–50, and 'Machines', *New Review*, 1 (1931–2), pp. [291]-92. The 1927 version of the typescript was published in *Ezra Pound e la scienza: Scritti inediti or rari*, ed. Maria Luisa Ardizzone (Milan: Scheiwiller, 1987), pp. 103–51, and the 1930 version was published in *MA*, pp. [57]-83. References are to the 1930 text unless otherwise indicated.

[107] Ardizzone reproduces the endnote as part of the main text (*MA*, 70–1), but in the ms. the anecdote is marked '# footnote to p. 10': see 'Machine Art', pp. 10–10a, EPP, Beinecke, 111: 4705.

beautiful has it become', but he cautioned 'we must not conclude from this example that perfection of utility necessarily implies the perfection of beauty'.[108] Pound, however, concludes just that, judging the utility of machines on the basis of their appearance: 'I am not so sure about the Kearsage crane, I chose it as an illustration of "Gothic" form', he remarks. 'I dislike the Gothic, and I believe, on perhaps the too flimsy basis of hearsay, that the Kearsage crane does not work to complete satisfaction [. . .]. I suspect that the better a machine becomes as a machine, the better it will be to look at.' Although Pound acknowledges that 'this is perhaps a wild guess, and need not be taken as an essential part of my argument', in fact it is precisely the logical conclusion of his argument: beauty is coextensive with utility. This assumption is necessitated because, unlike Léger who was primarily concerned with the machine as aesthetic object, Pound is interested in the machine's inventor. Just as Brancusi's sculpture and Picabia's squibs and designs are primarily significant to Pound as evidence of their creators' intelligence, so the machine is interesting only in so far as it is the product of 'the inventor's thought, or more probably the thought of a whole series of inventors': 'These single parts and the foci of their action', he writes of pieces of a drill grinder, 'have been made by thought over thought; by layer on layer of attention' (*MA*, 69, 57, 59). The beauty and the utility of the machine is testimony to the process of intelligent thinking that produced it. It is the product of 'the knowledge of a lifetime', to use Whistler's formulation, or the 'cultural heritage', to use Douglas's.[109]

As we have seen, Pound's shift of focus away from the artwork towards the artist paved the way for a new comprehension of 'art in general', one of the earliest expressions of which was his advocacy of dadaist experimentation. In 'Machine Art', Pound's appreciation of 'art in general' enables a breadth of reference that instructively maps out the trajectory of his interests during the 1920s. The text begins with a section entitled 'The Plastic of Machines', an unusual phrase in Pound's lexicon, but a common one in Léger's; it then distinguishes between 'machine plastic and the plastic of architecture'; and the major part of the essay is concerned with the 'the acoustic of machinery'.[110] If 'Machine Art' had its intellectual origins in avant-garde painting and sculpture in Paris, it was also conceptually compatible with Pound's growing interest in avant-garde music: he had been promoting the work of George Antheil intensively since the winter of 1923–4. By the

---

[108] Léger, 'The Esthetics of the Machine', pp. 46–7.
[109] Whistler, pp. 4–5, C. H. Douglas, *Social Credit* (London: Palmer, 1924), p. 56.
[110] See Léger, 'The Esthetics of the Machine', pp. 45, 46; *MA*, 57, 70, 72.

mid-1920s he had established a set of critical concepts that could be applied across the arts. His concept of 'absolute rhythm', first defined in 1910, and the related theory of the 'Great Bass', first mentioned in an article on Antheil in 1927, are analogous to his statements on the 'formal perfection' of Brancusi's sculpture; indeed, he explicitly related them in his *Little Review* essay on Brancusi.[111] And, as he had in describing Brancusi's studio, Pound uses the classicist rhetoric of purism to think through the social benefits of musical form: 'the main effect is *restful,* namely all this clatter and clangor is brought into order, is put under some sort of control', Pound writes of Antheil's music, 'and after the first shock or exacerbation there succeeds a feeling of calm, and of, if you like, the mind or will of the composer producing this order' (*MA*, 79).

The hero of 'Machine Art' is not the composer, however, nor is it the 'artisan' of Léger's lecture; it is the engineer. For Pound, as for Le Corbusier, 'the engineering mind is about the most satisfactory mind of our time' (*MA*, 77).[112] Like his judgement about the inefficiency of the Kearsage crane, Pound's faith in the engineering mind is an unsubstantiated intellectual leap, a notion whose truth could only be metaphorical, although its application would be literal: 'the practice of engineering seems to me less stultifying than most other contemporary practices. It does not seem to me, and I do not see how it can be, built up by layer after layer of bunk.' This statement draws on Pound's admiration for the former engineer C. H. Douglas's intelligence, of course, but as Pound continues it becomes clear that 'the engineering mind' will not only be recommending economic programmes: 'when the engineering mind tackles the problem of the utter uselessness of many alleged government officials, the utter needless obscurantism and obstructionism of their "functions," it seems to me that the engineering mind will clear away a good deal of this superstition. It will experiment. It will come clear-headedly to perceptions unclogged by fixed ideas.'[113] But in what situation could 'the engineering mind' have authority over government officials? 'It seems to me that the engineering

[111] *GC*, xxi: this introduction is dated 'November 15 1910'; 'Workshop Orchestration', *New Masses*, 2.5 (1927), p. 21; 'Brancusi', p. 4.

[112] Compare Le Corbusier-Saugnier, *Vers une architecture* (Paris: Crès, [1923]), pp. [3], 6: 'The Engineer's Æsthetic, and Architecture, are two things that march together and follow one from the other: the one being now at its full height, the other in an unhappy state of retrogression [. . .]. Our engineers are healthy and virile, active and useful, balanced and happy in their work. Our architects are disillusioned and unemployed, boastful or peevish', English translation Le Corbusier, *Towards a New Architecture*, trans. Frederick Etchells (London: Rodker, 1927), pp. 7, 18.

[113] In the 1927 text this paragraph is significantly shorter and concerns governments, not government officials: 'when the engineering mind tackles the problem of many (alleged) governments, it will find many of them wholly useless' ('Machine Art', in *Ezra Pound e la scienza*, p. 136).

mind, even a little released from immediate problems, or given that much extra leisure for "invention and design" might lead to a sort, and a very sane sort of Confucianism; non-interference and order.' 'The engineering mind', then, is to be in the position of directing the very organisation of the State:

> When this happens, a lot of public nuisances, passport officials, customs officials, in fact about 85% of all "functionaries" will be sent to the scrap. I don't mean they will of necessity be killed off or starved. But it will be found to be cheaper, more expeditious, more efficient, to pay them to live in complete idleness than to allow them to interfere in any way with the active and productive private members of the community [. . .].
>
> The tyrant is biologically preferable to the bureaucrat, at least he has in him some principle of life and of action. The bureaucracy is mere rust and fungus, all the more dangerous because of the imperceptible pace of its ravages. (*MA*, 77–8)

The 'hero engineer' was a familiar figure of machine age utopianism, especially in the United States, as Cecelia Tichi and Sharon Stockton have shown. 'Individuals like Henry Ford, Frank Lloyd Wright and Herbert Hoover', writes Stockton, 'represented the convergence of individual vitality and authoritarian principles that many Americans believed could lead the United States into a still more efficient, dynamic future.'[114] With Herbert Hoover's election to the presidency in 1928, the nation gained an engineer as its head of state, an engineer, moreover, whose characterisation of his profession bore a marked comparison to Pound's. 'With engineers there is the fascination of watching a figment of the imagination emerge through the aid of the sciences to a plan on paper', wrote Hoover. 'Then it moves to realization in stone or metal or energy. Then it brings jobs and homes to men. Then it adds to the necessities and comforts of homes. That is the engineer's high privilege among professions.'[115] Though Hoover is not mentioned in 'Machine Art', Pound's praise for Henry Ford affirms the importance of the essay's American context. However, in its admiration for a hero engineer who is a tyrant, the quotation above points back to Europe.

---

[114] Sharon Stockton, 'Engineering Power: Hoover, Pound and the Heroic Architect', *American Literature*, 72 (2000), 813–41 (p. 814); see also Cecelia Tichi, *Shifting Gears: Technology, Literature, Culture in Modernist America* (Chapel Hill, NC: University of North Carolina Press, 1987), pp. 97–170 and Tim Armstrong, *Modernism, Technology and the Body: A Cultural Study* (Cambridge: Cambridge University Press, 1998), pp. 63–4.

[115] Herbert Hoover, *America's Way Forward* (New York: Scribner's, 1939), p. 65, see Stockton, pp. 816–17.

THE MALATESTA CANTOS AND THE EFFICIENT TYRANT

The trajectory of Pound's Paris writings about the visual arts goes a long way towards accounting for these remarkable and sinister lines, helping to explain Pound's admiration for the most notorious engineer-tyrant of the period, Benito Mussolini. In the first instance, however, it sheds light on his attraction to a much earlier tyrant: Sigismondo Malatesta, the fifteenth-century ruler of Rimini. This is not to suggest that Pound's admiration for Mussolini and Sigismondo (or Sigismundo, as Pound referred to him) can be separated entirely: Lawrence Rainey has shown that the positive impression Pound formed of members of the Fascist party during his research for the Malatesta Cantos 'related directly to his writing about Sigismondo and later sparked his favorable view of Benito Mussolini and Fascism's effects in everyday life'.[116] Sigismondo and Mussolini were, to a certain extent, read through each other. But both were also read through the complex of ideas Pound developed over the course of his stay in Paris, a complex developed above all in relation to the visual arts.

Pound had stopped working on *The Cantos* around December 1919, apparently frustrated by his inability to find an equivalent of Browning's approach to the epic, capacious enough to represent the 'modern world', yet characterised by an immediacy and vigour that could engage twentieth-century readers and carry them through potential obscurities. But he returned to the poem in late spring 1922, inspired by Joyce's and Eliot's approaches to related challenges in *Ulysses* and *The Waste Land*, and having found a subject that embodied the poem's ideals. That subject was Sigismondo Malatesta, particularly for his reconstruction of the church of San Francesco, which Pound saw for the first time in May. On his return to Paris at the beginning of July, Pound worked on the drafts and notes he had begun in Italy and completed a draft of the four cantos by January 1923. He travelled to Italy again at the beginning of January, and undertook further research in Italian libraries and archives between 16 February and around 20 April. Back in Paris, he sent the finished 'Cantos IX to XII of a Long Poem' (8–11 in the present editions) to Eliot in May for publication in the *Criterion*, where it appeared in July 1923.[117] Pound's satisfaction with his work was borne out by the speed with which he continued working on

[116] Rainey, *Institutions of Modernism*, p. 109.
[117] Lawrence S. Rainey, *Ezra Pound and the Monument of Culture: Text, History, and the Malatesta Cantos* (Chicago, IL: University of Chicago Press, 1991), pp. 229–30.

the poem, completing five more cantos and revising the earlier ones by the autumn of 1923.[118]

San Francesco, inaccurately referred to since the nineteenth century as the Tempio Malatestiano, has been the subject of extensive scholarly attention as the first known architectural project of Leon Battista Alberti, who encased the existing thirteenth-century church in a façade and side panels of 'a style more overtly classical than that of any Renaissance building constructed up to that time'.[119] Although the remodelling of the interior of the church by Matteo de' Pasti and Agostino di Duccio is richly ornamental and Gothic in style, the exterior is characterised by a restraint and precision that refers to the nearby ancient Roman Arch of Augustus.[120] Such a building, not simply built, but *re*built in a classical style, must have been particularly striking in the post-war period, especially to Pound, living in France, which had borne the brunt of the war damage, and well aware of the aesthetic and ideological debates surrounding its reconstruction. Indeed, Pound's first visit to San Francesco occurred as the classicism he favoured was starting to lose ground architecturally in France. 'If the historical traditionalism, composure, and balance embodied by neo-classicism stood as the cornerstone of the *rappel à l'ordre* during the immediate postwar years, this was no longer true after 1923,' Romy Golan has argued. 'When it came to reconstruction, it was not the master narrative of modernist urban architecture but the far less epic idiom of regionalism that prevailed during the 1920s. In contrast to the machine aesthetic which stood for internationalism and modular standardization as a way of reshaping the present, regionalism stood for the particularities of the vernacular as a way of reviving the past.' Even at the 1925 Paris Exposition Internationale des Arts Décoratifs et Industriels Modernes, since remembered for the presence of Le Corbusier and Ozenfant's *Pavillon de L'Esprit Nouveau*, regionalism dominated the French section: the best plots were given to the pavilions of regional France, with their limewashed walls, pitched roofs and gables, and craft-filled interiors.[121]

[118] Myles Slatin, 'A History of Pound's Cantos I–XVI, 1915–1925', *American Literature*, 35 (1963), 183–95 (pp. 189–93), Bush, pp. 239, 252, Carpenter, p. 423.

[119] Joanna Woods-Marsden, 'How quattrocento princes used art: Sigismondo Pandolfo Malatesta of Rimini and cose militari', *Renaissance Studies*, 3 (1989), 387–414 (p. 396), Helen Ettlinger, 'The Sepulchre on the Façade: A Re-evaluation of Sigismondo Malatesta's Rebuilding of San Francesco in Rimini', *Journal of the Warburg and Courtauld Institutes*, 53 (1990), 133–43 (pp. 133–4); Charles Hope, 'The Early History of the Tempio Malatestiano', *Journal of the Warburg and Courtauld Institutes*, 55 (1992), 51–154 (p. 51).

[120] See Robert Tavenor, *On Alberti and the Art of Building* (New Haven, CT: Yale University Press, 1998), pp. 27, 51–2

[121] Romy Golan, *Modernity and Nostalgia: Art and Politics in France Between the Wars* (New Haven, CT: Yale University Press, 1995), pp. 9, 23, 58–60. Golan adds: 'The gradual distancing from

Pound related San Francesco directly to the reconstruction work in France. He deplored most of the new architectural design: 'the softness of the Paris stone invites every abortion; the boudoir and the curves of domestic plumbing seem to have set the Beaux Arts ideal of form', he complained. He was not opposed to modern architecture (he imagines the 'fun to be had in planning twenty-eight stories in place of the old three to six'), but thought that the 'new aesthetic of reinforced concrete' was 'mostly botched, incomplete, unaccomplished, unrealized by constructors'. Neither was he impressed by Paris's neoclassicist monuments: 'For the ass who built the Madeleine and the nincompoops who imagined that mere multiplication of some "classic" proportion would make a larger building more [. . .] imposing, rather than more of an imposition . . . there is nothing but contempt.' Nevertheless, classicism is clearly Pound's preferred style: he is pleased to find in his recent reading of Alberti's treatise *De Pictura* (1435) the view that the architect is influenced by the painter, which supports his oft-repeated wish that architects would employ sculptors and painters. Deploying Alberti's analogies between musical harmony and architecture, he insists that the proportion of windows to doors in a house front 'can attain "the qualities of music," it does in any number of *palazzi* in Verona'; and his specific examples of good architecture are the Virginia State Capitol Building, modelled on the Maison Carrée at Nîmes on Thomas Jefferson's instructions, and the church of San Francesco.[122]

Yet San Francesco hardly presented an ideal pattern for a modern building project: work on the church had ceased in 1461 after Sigismondo fell from power, and according to recent interpretations, even if the work had been completed it 'would certainly have been a curious combination of Gothic and Renaissance elements, as indeed it is today'.[123] This church was neither the 'masterly, correct and magnificent play of masses brought together in light' Le Corbusier was advocating, nor was it the 'temple of QUIET' Pound found in Brancusi's studio, both of which could be understood by Pound as socially useful in their aspirations towards formal perfection. San Francesco, on the contrary, was characterised by its 'beautiful inutility'.[124] Nevertheless, by 1922 there was a place for such a building in Pound's

neo-classicism, an aspect of the French call to order unanimously overlooked by art historians, may well have reflected France's wish to disassociate itself from an increasingly violent fascist regime in Italy' (p. 9).

[122] Leon Battista Alberti, *On Painting and On Sculpture*, ed. and trans. Cecil Grayson (London: Phaidon, 1972), pp. [60–1]; 'Paris Letter', p. 90; Tavenor, p. 74.

[123] Hope, p. 148.

[124] Le Corbusier-Saugnier, *Vers une architecture*, p. 16, English translation Le Corbusier, *Towards a New Architecture*, p. 29; 'Paris Letter', p. 90; *EPVA*, 307.

aesthetics. While it is hard to imagine Pound as responsive to this unfinished, inconsistent building had he seen it during his years in London, his
reading of Douglas and his involvement with the Parisian avant-garde rendered San Francesco legible. In a markedly parallel line of reasoning to his
rationalisation of Picabia's 'squibs' ('an accumulation of wild shots ends by
expressing a personality'), Pound states that 'If the Tempio is a jumble and
junk shop, it nevertheless registers a concept. There is no other single man's
effort equally registered' (*GK*, [i]).[125] San Francesco, like dada collages and
found objects, is a work of conceptual art.

Consequently, although Pound actively related the materiality of San
Francesco to his thinking and writing about contemporary architecture,
the building's more important and long-term impact was as evidence of
Sigismondo's force of character and his ability to establish conditions that
enabled artistic creation. 'In a Europe not YET rotted by usury, but outside the then system, and pretty much against the power that was, and
in any case without great material resources, Sigismundo cut his notch',
Pound famously wrote in *Guide to Kulchur*. 'He registered a state of mind,
of sensibility, of all-roundness and awareness' (*GK*, 159). Pound is therefore relatively uninterested in the individual works that filled the Tempio.
Agostino di Duccio's bas reliefs and Piero della Francesca's fresco, for example, are not mentioned in the Malatesta Cantos; the important point for
Pound is not Sigismondo's collection of art, but his creation of a 'civilisation' in Rimini that was 'carried down and out into details' such as 'the
little wafer of wax', the seal he reproduces as the frontispiece to *Guide to
Kulchur* (*GK*, 159, [2]).

Sigismondo is most significant for Pound, then, as a patron in a broad
sense, and indeed Pound begins the first Malatesta Canto with a long quotation from Sigismondo to Giovanni de' Medici, which offers a lifetime's
salary to a painter, presumed by Pound (probably erroneously) to be Piero
della Francesca, 'So that he can work as he likes,/ Or waste his time as he
likes/ [. . .] never lacking provision' (8: 29).[126] As a number of critics have
remarked, Pound's admiration for Sigismondo's patronage was sharpened
by the fact that only two months before first seeing San Francesco he had

---

[125] 'Paris Letter', p. 458.
[126] Pound described this letter as: 'to Giovanni dei Medici, presumably re/ Pier Francesca; and says
he wants the master painter for life, with a set provision, security to be given'. See letter to Henry
Allen Moe, 31 March 1925, EPP, Beinecke, 25.1081. On the identity of the painter, see Franco Borsi,
Leon Battista Alberti: The Complete Works, trans. Rudolf G. Carpanini (London: Faber and Faber,
1989), p. 92.

launched his own patronage scheme, 'Bel Esprit'.[127] By the time he wrote about the scheme in November 1922's *Dial*, Sigismondo was marshalled as evidence for the success of patronage, and specifically the return on its 'risks': 'questions of whether they, the writers, will go on producing when "freed" are almost irrelevant. [. . .] There was once a man in a small town who had Pisanello, Pier Francesco, and Mino da Fiesole all working for him at one time or another. They might have turned out bad jobs, but they didn't.' Bel Esprit's patronage was different from Sigismondo's, however, because it was spread across a number of subscribers: in the modern world 'few of us can afford to keep up a dozen or even one artist'. Subscribers, therefore, would not own works of art or, in this case, manuscripts, in the way that Sigismondo, or for that matter, John Quinn did.[128] While the scheme aimed to support individuals and to produce art, its rhetoric emphasised a larger end in view: an 'organized or coordinated civilization', like Sigismondo's Rimini (*L*, 172).

Although 'Bel Esprit' was based in Paris, and had arisen, Pound explained, from interest generated by one of his reviews of Douglas's *Credit Power and Democracy*, the article in the November *Dial* shows him starting to look towards Italy as a potential site for his 'coordinated civilization'. London is 'a decadent wallow', Paris is 'an enervated centre', America is 'inchoate', but Italy, Pound thinks, is 'reawakening'. Evidence is provided in the article's review section, which gives a dismissive account of recent French literature and then turns 'with relief' to consider D'Annunzio's recently published prose poem *Il Notturno*. Recalling his fascination with the spectacle of D'Annunzio as political leader in 1919, Pound remarks, 'In the fury of Fiume, in the general bewilderment of manifestos, aeroplanes, bombs, *fascisti*, et cetera, together with memories of vast verbal emprise, one had forgotten – if one ever had – a critical estimate of the "poet hero" as a writer.' The critical estimate turns out to be markedly positive: D'Annunzio, Pound says, has 'some sort of vigour, some sort of assertion, some sort of courage, or at least of ebullience that throws a certain amount of remembered beauty into an unconquered consciousness', and he writes of 'the things that make life bearable'.[129]

---

[127] 'Credit and the Fine Arts', *New Age*, 30 (1922), 284–5; A. D. Moody, 'Bel Esprit and the Malatesta Cantos: A Post-*Waste Land* Conjunction of Pound and Eliot', in Taylor and Melchior, pp. 79–91, Timothy Materer, 'From Henry James to Ezra Pound: John Quinn and the Art of Patronage', *Paideuma*, 17.2&3 (1988), 47–68 (pp. 61–4), Rainey, *Institutions of Modernism*, pp. 108–9; Rainey, *Ezra Pound and the Monument of Culture*, p. 70.
[128] 'Paris Letter', *Dial*, 73 (1922), [549]-554 (p. 551).   [129] 'Paris Letter', pp. [549], 552–4.

We should note the date of this 'Paris Letter' carefully. Although published in the November issue of the *Dial*, Pound dated his article 'October 1922': Pound wrote this advertisement for a reawakening Italy and the poet who had since been adopted as a fascist hero in the month of Mussolini's March on Rome. As we know from Rainey's important research on Pound's Italian contacts during his years in Paris, Pound was socialising with D'Annunzio's former mistress, Luisa Casati, during August 1922, and he first used the term 'fascist' in his correspondence on 25 August when he wrote to Dorothy Shakespear that '[Casati's] fascisti have taken her back to Italy'. A month after writing the *Dial* article, Pound attended a talk by the American journalist Lincoln Steffens which included a notably positive account of Mussolini. During his research on Sigismondo in Rimini in March 1923, he was assisted by the manager of his hotel, Averardo Marchetti, a founder member of the Rimini branch of the Fascist party, 'a noble fascist', Pound called him. By August 1923 Pound was asking his friend Nancy Cox-McCormack, who had recently sculpted the first bust of Mussolini, to find out 'if the dictator *wants* a *corte letteraria*; if he is interested in the procedure of Sigismundo Malatesta in getting the best artists of his time into Rimini, a small city with no great resources. I know, in a general way, the fascio includes literature and the arts in its programme; that is very different from being ready to take specific action.'[130] Pound's ambitions for his programme of patronage had thus become much greater during his stay in Paris, and it was particularly in his writing about the visual arts that this had become apparent. While he had arrived in Paris in 1920 admiring the 'denationalist' dadaists with 'no capital sunk in works', by January 1923 he was quoting Léger on the limitations of 'easel painting' and the desire to paint 'the outside of a railway terminal', if only there was a *chef d'orchestre* to organise the 'place for sculpture or painting in modern life'.[131] Pound envisioned a systematic approach that would place writers and artists closer to the ruling powers, which would literalise his description of Brancusi as a messiah, 'trying to save the world by pure form'.[132] In a return to the revolutionary rhetoric of 1919, Pound calls for a 'list of the resolute, of the half-thousand exiles and proscripts who are ready to risk the *coup*'.[133]

---

[130] Rainey, *Institutions of Modernism*, pp. 138–9, 129, 140. See also Nancy Cox-McCormack, 'Ezra Pound in the Paris Years', ed. Lawrence S. Rainey, *Sewanee Review*, 102 (1994), 93–112.

[131] 'Paris Letter', p. 74; 'The Island of Paris: A Letter', p. 408; 'Paris Letter', p. 88.

[132] 'Pound vs. Gellert [letter]', p. 25.

[133] 'On Criticism in General', *Criterion*, 1 (1923), 143–56 (p. 143).

A full account of Pound's attraction to Italian fascism is beyond the scope of this book: that story has been told elsewhere.[134] However, it is relevant to emphasise that Pound's aesthetic interests and affiliations supported his positive impression of Mussolini's regime, and certainly no longer acted as a prophylactic against it, as they might have done ten years earlier. In the context of his post-war writings, it is not difficult to understand Pound's attraction to a regime that at an early stage of its rule held a Congress of Institutions of Fascist Culture, issued a 'Manifesto of the Fascist Intellectuals', and made a priority of establishing cultural institutions.[135] While in hindsight, one can see that Mussolini's invocation of art and culture was the strategic use of a powerful ideological weapon, and his cultivation of intellectuals masked the anti-intellectualism and brutality of his regime, to Pound they seemed long-overdue recognition of the political importance of the cultural elite.

Pound's proximity via Léger to the purists, and their legacy in his thinking about architecture, also contributed to his positive evaluation of Mussolini's regime. Pound's high regard for the engineering mind as tyrant in 'Machine Art' is anticipated by Le Corbusier's esteem for the town planner as despot in his *Urbanisme*, written the previous year. Below an engraving of Louis XIV approving the plan for the Invalides, Le Corbusier wrote, 'Homage to a great town-planner. This despot conceived immense projects and realized them. Over all the country his noble works still fill us with admiration. He was capable of saying "We wish it," or "Such is our pleasure".'[136] The post-war years appeared to present the opportunity to create a new civilisation, and the dream of a ruler with the power and will to put their ideas into practice pervades the Utopian visions of many during the period; Lewis's Caliph is another such town-planning autocrat.[137] Reconstruction on the massive scale conceived in this context readily becomes an index of the commitment and efficiency of the ruler, and, indeed, for Pound the fascist

---

[134] See Robert Casillo, *The Genealogy of Demons: Anti-Fascism, and the Myths of Ezra Pound* (Evanston, IL: Northwestern University Press, 1988), and 'Fascists of the Final Hour', in *Fascism, Aesthetics and Culture*, ed. Richard J. Goslan (Hanover, NH: University Press of New England, 1992), Andrew Hewitt, *Fascist Modernism: Aesthetics, Politics, and the Avant-Garde* (Stanford, CA: Stanford University Press, 1993), Redman, Rainey, *Institutions of Modernism*, pp. 107–45, Paul Morrisson, *The Poetics of Fascism: Ezra Pound, T. S. Eliot, Paul de Man* (New York: Oxford University Press, 1996).

[135] See Edward R. Tannenbaum, *Fascism in Italy: Society and Culture, 1922–1945* (London: Lane, 1972), p. 326 and Richard A. Etlin, *Modernism in Italian Architecture, 1890–1940* (Cambridge, MA: MIT Press, 1991), pp. 379–83.

[136] Le Corbusier, *Urbanisme* (Paris: Crès, [1925]), p. [285], English translation Le Corbusier, *The City of Tomorrow and Its Planning*, trans. Frederick Etchells (London: Rodker, 1929), p. 302. See Silver, p. 389.

[137] Lewis, *The Caliph's Design*, p. 11.

regime's construction programme acted as concrete evidence of the wisdom and effectiveness of Mussolini's rule. 'No one denies the material and immediate effect', he wrote in *Jefferson and/or Mussolini* (1935), '*grano, bonifica, restauri*, grain, swamp-drainage, restorations, new buildings' (*J/M*, 73). In 1936 Pound proposed that a 'Casa Littoria' be constructed in Rapallo, based on a plan by the late Antonio Sant'Elia, whose futurist designs had been taken up by Italian architects as prototypes for a fascist architecture. The building, Pound explained, should house a 'library accessible to foreigners, either dilettantes or tourists, to help them understand the new Italy'. This education in fascist Italy was not only to be transmitted through reading matter, but through the building itself: 'this building, if inspired by a project of Sant'Elia, would open the eyes and probably the mind to the contemporaneous [situation] of the nation'. Pound discussed the project with Marinetti, who responded, 'Glory to Antonio Sant'Elia glory to fascist Italy so well architectured by Benito Mussolini.'[138]

As early as January 1924 Pound wrote to Nancy Cox McCormack about Mussolini as urban planner:

CAN you get a few choice words from Muss. exclusively for [Ford Madox Ford's journal] the Transatlantic, one or two pages, or as much more as he likes on his scheme of restoration of Rome [. . .] Get Muss to write a line on new building in Rome, new paving, etc. (possibly as link in revival of Italian intellectual life – that leads on to our other affair) [. . .]. The Transatlantic is a free international avenue of communication. Muss wd. reach the PENSEURS partout; and they "make the opinion of next week".[139]

Mussolini's notorious, never fully realized, five-year programme for the reconstruction of Rome was designed, as the dictator himself said, to 'liberate all of ancient Rome from mediocre disfigurements' and 'create the monumental Rome of the twentieth century'.[140] As Le Corbusier had written in his 'Lesson of Rome' chapter of *Vers une architecture* (1923), 'Rome's business was to conquer the world and govern it. Strategy, recruiting, legislation: the spirit of order.'[141] Rome was a symbolic idea, a means of uniting Italy

---

[138] 'L'arte di Sant'Elia a Rapallo', *Il Mare*, 29 (1936), p. [1], English translation Esther da Costa Meyer, *The Work of Antonio Sant'Elia: Retreat into the Future* (New Haven, CT: Yale University Press, 1995), p. 202; Filippo Marinetti, Letter to Ezra Pound, 12 July 1936, EPP, Beinecke, 33.1377. See also Diane Ghirardo, *Building New Communities: New Deal America and Fascist Italy* (Princeton, NJ: Princeton University Press, 1989).

[139] Letter to Nancy Cox-McCormack, c. 5 January 1924, qtd in Rainey, *Institutions of Modernism*, pp. 40–1.

[140] Benito Mussolini, 'Per la cittadinanza di Roma' (21 April 1924) in *Opera Omnia di Benito Mussolini*, ed. Edoardo and Duilio Susmel (Florence: Fenice, 1951–63), xx: 234–6 (p. 235), English translation Etlin, p. 391.

[141] Le Corbusier-Saugnier, *Vers une architecture*, p. 124, English translation Le Corbusier, *Towards a New Architecture*, p. 154.

through a reappropriation of the past: Mussolini envisaged a Rome that was 'vast, ordered, mighty, as it was in the days of the first empire of Augustus'.[142] Pound's letter demonstrates just how precisely he could relate Mussolini's display of fascist power to his own post-war efforts to 'restart civilisation' (*L*, 173). Here, Pound thought, was a leader who could write effectively, who was interested in communicating with 'thinkers', whose frame of reference was international, and who could understand the connection between architectural construction and intellectual life. Here, in short, was an 'artist', in the expanded sense Pound had been employing since 1920. As Rainey comments, 'the affair is not without touches of the comic [. . .] or even the absurd, as we are left to contemplate an issue of the *Transatlantic Review* that might have contained the first sections of what became *Finnegans Wake* alongside writings by Pound, Ernest Hemingway, Gertrude Stein, and Benito Mussolini'.[143] But this is no brief moment of self-delusion on Pound's part; this is the well-reasoned product of Pound's post-war criticism, in which the artist, the maker of 'art in general', will regenerate civilisation through his intellectual efficiency and his perception of form. As Pound famously wrote in *Jefferson and/ or Mussolini*, 'I don't believe any estimate of Mussolini will be valid unless it *starts* from his passion for construction. Treat him as *artifex* and all the details fall into place. Take him as anything save the artist and you will get muddled with ccontradictions' (*J/M*, 33–4).

Although Pound was far from alone in thinking along these lines, by 1933 this interpretation entailed a considerably selective reading of Mussolini's biography. But even during the early 1920s, it is striking how the post-war climate's cult of efficiency enabled the fascists' routine use of violence to be rationalised. A collection of Mussolini's lectures published in 1923 by the mainstream publishers J. M. Dent (in London), and E. P. Dutton (in New York) was framed by an unashamedly partisan introduction that described how 'it was not possible [. . .] for the Fascisti to deal with the Communists otherwise than by using violence, as normal means would have been entirely inadequate', and celebrated the 'rigorous discipline' of military organisation under the fascists, summed up by their motto '"No discussion, only obedience"', facilitating 'the sudden mobilisations and demobilisations carried out, often at a few hours notice'.[144] Although *The*

---

[142] Benito Mussolini, 'La nuova Roma' (31 December 1925), in *Opera Omnia di Benito Mussolini*, XXII: 47–9 (p. 48), English translation Etlin, p. 392.

[143] Rainey, *Institutions of Modernism*, p. 141.

[144] Barone Bernado Quaranta di San Severino, 'Introduction: A Note on Italian Fascismo', in *Mussolini as Revealed in his Political Speeches*, ed. and trans. Barone Bernado Quaranta di San Severino (London: Dent, 1923), pp. ix–xix (pp. xi, xv).

Times' coverage of the March on Rome was marked by its lack of decision in 1922, they commemorated it on 31 October 1923 by saying 'it is beyond question that Italy has never been so united [. . .]. Fascism has abolished the game of Parliamentary chess; it has simplified the taxation system and reduced the deficit to measurable proportions; it has vastly improved the public services, particularly the railways; it has reduced a superfluously large bureaucracy without any very bad results in the way of hardships or unemployment; it has pursued a vigorous and fairly successful colonial policy.'[145]

The Malatesta Cantos demonstrate Pound's similar rationalising of a violent rule for the sake of expediency. In Canto 8 Pound describes a scene at the General Council of Ferrara-Florence, convened from 1438–45 to reunite the Latin and Greek churches, and attended by Sigismondo. The Neoplatonic philosopher, Georgios Gemistus Plethon, who was part of the Byzantine delegation, tells the story of Plato's failed attempt to educate the young Dionysius II of Syracuse:

> And the Greek emperor was in Florence
>   (Ferrara having the pest)
> And with him Gemisthus Plethon
> Talking of the war about the temple at Delphos,
> And of POSEIDON, *concret Allgemeine,*
> And telling of how Plato went to Dionysius of Syracuse
> Because he had observed that tyrants
> Were most efficient in all that they set their hands to,
> But he was unable to persuade Dionysius
> To any amelioration   (8: 31)

In accepting the invitation to advise Dionysius, Plato had envisaged establishing an ideal state under the rule of a benevolent tyrant, and in his last work, the *Laws*, he describes the efficiency of that form of government, as Pound notes.[146] In recounting this story here, Pound suggests Sigismondo is the efficient, well-educated despot Plato had hoped Dionysius might become. The anecdote also alludes to the fact that Sigismondo later looted Plethon's ashes during a military expedition in the Peloponnesus, and had them buried in San Francesco, an act that, far from deploring,

---

[145] See 'Mussolini: A Character Sketch', *Times*, 30 October 1923, p. 11, col. c, 'The Meaning of Fascismo: From Anarchy to Tyranny', *Times*, 30 October 1922, p. 14, col. c; 'Achievements of Fascismo. A New Italian Unity. Mussolini's Power', *Times*, 31 October 1923, p. 13, col. a.

[146] The main source for information about Plato's visits to Dionysius II of Syracuse is the seventh epistle, see Plato, *Timaeus, Critias, Cleitophon, Menexenus, Epistles*, trans. R. G. Bury (London: Heinemann, 1929), pp. 476–565; Plato, *Laws*, 2 vols., trans. R. G. Bury (London: Heinemann, 1926), 1: 268–81.

Pound admired as evidence both of Sigismondo's recognition of Plethon's importance, and of the efficiency of tyrannical action.

Canto 8 not only advocates the efficiency of the tyrant, it experiments with a literary equivalent. It is in this canto that Pound changes his method of literary production, transferring historical documents into the poem in extended quotations, without revising them into poetic form. This expedient, much praised by critics who have seen it as 'one of the decisive turning-points in modern poetics', bears scrutiny once again since it has traditionally been read as the point where the literary text enters modernist visual culture – as a collage.[147] Marjorie Perloff, for example, makes the much-quoted observation that 'Pound's basic strategy in the *Cantos* is to create a flat surface, as in a cubist or early dada collage, upon which verbal elements, fragmented images, and truncated bits of narrative, drawn from the most disparate contexts, are brought into collusion.'[148] Has Pound, almost ten years after proposing to 'write to paint', found another method of bringing the vitality he associated with vorticism into *The Cantos*?

While describing *The Cantos* as a collage is immediately striking, eloquently expressing the visual shock produced by the dense, foreign material embedded in the Malatesta Cantos, it is misleading. What the analogy suggests, of course, is that the poem is avant-garde, collage being the strategy by which the dadaists and surrealists, and, to a lesser extent, its 'inventors', the cubists, expanded and critiqued the institution of art, in particular its self-definition through discourses of originality and purity. But there is no record of Pound praising collage techniques in the visual arts, and *The Cantos* is a collage only in so far as it fails, as Michael André Bernstein has succinctly remarked. The resulting 'liberating fragmentation [. . .] in effect transforms *The Cantos* from a totalitarian ideogram into an open-ended *grand collage*. And it is exactly in this incomplete form that *The Cantos* has proved so fruitful a model for subsequent writers.'[149] The Malatesta Cantos do not anticipate the poem's failure, however; rather their importation of extra-poetic material is a gesture of supreme self-confidence in the individual's constructive powers, whether those powers belong to Pound,

[147] Bernstein, *The Tale of the Tribe*, p. 40.
[148] Marjorie Perloff, *The Poetics of Indeterminacy: Rimbaud to Cage* (Princeton, NJ: Princeton University Press, 1981), p. 181. See also Perloff, 'Ezra Pound and "The Prose Tradition in Verse"', in *The Futurist Moment*, pp. 162–93, Charles Altieri, 'Picasso's Collages and the Force of Cubism', *Kenyon Review*, 6.2 (1984), 8–33, Clearfield, p. 143, James Laughlin, *Pound as Wuz: Essays and Lectures on Ezra Pound* (Saint Paul, MN: Graywolf, 1987), p. 107, and Jacob Korg, 'The Dialogic Nature of Collage in Pound's *Cantos*', *Mosaic*, 22 (1989), 95–109.
[149] Michael André Bernstein, 'Robert Duncan and the Individual Tradition', *Sagetrieb*, 4 (1985), 177–90, (p. 189).

Sigismondo, or Mussolini. Thus, while the poem is a product of the avant-garde's invention of 'art in general', drawing its material from beyond art's traditional boundaries, it also argues for the primacy of the individual artist. These cantos are a work of synthesis, not analysis. Although today these terms are used relatively neutrally to describe the formal trajectory of cubism specifically, the qualitative force of their broader early twentieth-century use is directly relevant here.[150] The Malatesta Cantos emphatically repudiate the analytical mode of the pre-war avant-garde, the mode in which the poem was begun, and join the synthetic *rappel à l'ordre* of the post-war classicists. Analysis to synthesis is, indeed, the trajectory that Pound himself retrospectively mapped out in *Guide to Kulchur*: 'the nineteen teens, Gaudier, Wyndham L. and I as we were in *Blast*', 'the 1920's' characterised as 'the sorting out, the *rappel à l'ordre*', and finally 'the new synthesis, the totalitarian' (*GK*, 95).

[150] Silver, pp. 345–9.

Afterword

The trajectory from analysis to synthesis is the trajectory not only of *The Cantos*, but of modernism itself. It would be a mistake to see Pound's career as unrepresentative of his era, or his tragedy as the result of egotism and eccentricity: his decisions are explicable and comprehensible. Moreover, they illuminate an important passage in our own literary history. The rhetoric of unity, coherence and synthesis was as much a part of the mid-twentieth century's literary critical project as it was Pound's, and the course of its development was not dissimilar. As recent re-evaluations of the New Critics have demonstrated, the formalist literary criticism in which modernist studies was forged was not, at least initially, 'merely an aesthetic hedonism'; rather, for the New Critics, 'the value of form was the extent to which it offered a critique of the rational content' of a work.[1] Pound's formalism was developed for similarly critical ends: first to rebut philology's utilitarianism, and subsequently to register art's engagement with political and ethical concerns. Vorticist form, Pound thought, enabled one to articulate political threats to individual autonomy; dadaist experiment could undermine the nationalist appropriation of art history. It was in this way that visual culture shaped the formalism of literary modernism; this early formalism by no means entailed the excision of content.

Nevertheless, in his determination to establish continuities between the poetry and criticism of the imagist period and that written after his move to Italy twelve years later, Pound inevitably minimised the contexts that determined his intellectual decisions, and over-emphasised formal correspondences. Allusions to visual artists and art works provided a convenient shorthand for stylistic continuity, but they simultaneously simplified the role of visual culture in his poetic development. The immediacy Pound

[1] Mark Jancovich, 'The Southern New Critics', in *The Cambridge History of Literary Criticism: Modernism and the New Criticism*, ed. A. Walton Litz, Louis Menand, and Lawrence Rainey (Cambridge: Cambridge University Press, 2000), pp. 200–18 (p. 205). See also Jancovich, *The Cultural Politics of the New Criticism* (Cambridge: Cambridge University Press, 1993).

hoped to harness for his earliest criticism through allusions to contemporary painting, the poetics of beauty he developed to combat the limitations of language, the realist satire he modelled on Lewis's work, the 'historical method' he transferred from Gaudier's 'Vortex' manifesto, and the resistance to the art market he admired in dada – these diverse reactions to the challenge of contemporary art were retrospectively rationalised in the 1930s to create a genealogy for Pound's new ideological commitments. From the mid-1920s, the visual arts function in Pound's oeuvre less as inspiration than as illustration.[2]

Pound continued to take an interest in contemporary visual art: in the early 1930s he became compelled by the work of the surrealists, especially that of Salvador Dali and Jean Arp, in 1934 he supported the sculptor Heinz Henghes, and in the 1950s his principal muse was Sheri Martinelli, who was 'the first', he wrote in 1956, 'to show a capacity to manifest in paint or in la ceramica what is most to be prized in my writing'.[3] There is still important research to be done on Pound's aesthetic interests in these later years. But evidence of such new enthusiasms is comparatively rare in Pound's later writings: the later references to the visual arts more typically take the form of reiterated endorsements of the work of Lewis, Gaudier and Brancusi and continued admiration for Quattrocento sculpture and architecture.[4] Pound ceased to respond to the visual arts as a challenging model and even the new artists he encountered entered his writing only within already established parameters: thus models for the work of the surrealists are found in the Middle Ages, Henghes is measured against Gaudier, and Martinelli's painting is compared to Botticelli's.[5] It is appropriate, then, that his privileged analogy for the composition of *The Cantos* is not collage, but stone

---

[2] The most obvious example of this, which regrettably falls outside the scope of the present study, is Pound's conception of Henry Strater's illustrated capitals for *A Draft of XVI. Cantos* (Paris: Three Mountains Press, 1925) as a visual analogy for the poem's classicist values and its specific arguments. See *L*, 188, Michael Culver, 'The Art of Henry Strater: An Examination of the Illustrations for Pound's *A Draft of XVI. Cantos*', *Paideuma*, 12 (1983), 448–78, McGann, *The Textual Condition*, pp. 129–41 and *Black Riders: The Visible Language of Modernism* (Princeton, NJ: Princeton University Press, 1993), pp. 77–80, Rainey, *Ezra Pound and the Monument of Culture*, pp. 198–209.

[3] On Dali and Arp, see 'Our Contemporaries and Others', *New Review*, 1 (1931), [149]-152, '[Review of] *The Quattro Cento* by Adrian Stokes', *Symposium*, 3 (1932), 518–21 (p. 521), 'The Coward Surrealists', *Contemporary Poetry and Prose*, 1 (1936), p. 136; on Henghes, see Laughlin, pp. 13–14, *L/JL*, 31–2, 'Notes for 1934 article', EPP, Beinecke, 104.4356, and the Pound/ Henghes correspondence, EPP, Beinecke, 22.961; on Martinelli, see 'Introduction', in *La Martinelli* (Milan: Scheiwiller, 1956), pp. 5-[12] (p. 11), and the Pound/ Martinelli correspondence, EPP, Beinecke, 33.1389–93.

[4] See Letter to Douglas Fox, 27 October 1939, EPC, HRHRC, 7:2, Letter to Peter Russell, [4 February 1952?], EPC, HRHRC, 8.7, Letter to Peter Russell, 1 September [no year], EPC, HRHRC, 8.8, 'Introduction', in *La Martinelli*, p. 6.

[5] 'The Coward Surrealists', p. 136; 'Notes for 1934 article'; Sheri Martinelli, Letter to Ezra Pound, 21 December 1958, EPP, Beinecke, 33.1392.

carving, with its rigorous distinction between carving subject and carved object. That analogy, for all the beauty that Pound associates with it, is ideologically conservative, summarising the stream of binary oppositions upon which the poem's argument comes to depend.[6] It is an analogy whose very pervasiveness indicates the extent to which Pound's engagement with the visual arts has become evacuated of its history, existing only as a repository of analogies to be manipulated at will. Thus, in 1934, listening to Mussolini 'speaking very clearly four or five words at a time, with a pause, quite a long pause, between phrases, to let it sink in', Pound is reminded of Brancusi's sculpture: 'The more one examines the Milan Speech the more one is reminded of Brancusi, the stone blocks from which no error emerges, from whatever angle one look at them.'[7] Three decades of theorising the relationship between politics and the visual arts are submerged in this close reading. But the reading has become too close: it registers the form of the textual object, but lacks the critical distance to interpret its content and context. Captivated by formal perfection, this reading can analyse neither the artist's role in the creative act, nor the argument of the work. This is reading as looking; apprehension imagined as so immediate it can bypass language – and thought – altogether. By 1934, not only Pound's aesthetics, but also his politics are founded on this optical optimism, this fantasy of the innocent eye. This book has sought to describe the genealogy of that fantasy, the effects of its application, and, of course, its impossibility.

[6] See Davie, *Ezra Pound: Poet as Sculptor*; Kenner, *The Poetry of Ezra Pound*, p. 314, Richard Read, 'The Letters and Works of Adrian Stokes and Ezra Pound', *Paideuma*, 27.2–3 (1998), 69–92, 'The Unpublished Correspondence of Ezra Pound and Adrian Stokes: Modernist Myth-making in Sculpture, Literature, Aesthetics and Psychoanalysis', *Comparative Criticism*, 21 (1999), 79–127.

[7] '1934 in the Autumn [letter]', *Criterion*, 14 (1935), 297–304, rpt. in *Jefferson and/ or Mussolini* (New York: Liveright, [1936]), pp. vii–ix.

Index

391, 164, 169

Aaronson, Lazarus, 103
Action, 163, 167
Action Française, 97
Adams, Laurie, 179
Ades, Dawn, 165
Adorno, Theodor, 166
aestheticism, 7, 12–24, 27–9, 36, 43–8, 50, 109, 115, 145, 152, 164, 171, 182
Affron, Matthew, 186
Agar, Patricia A., 15
Agassiz, Louis, 1
Duccio, Agostino di, 194, 196
Albert-Birot, Pierre, 163
Alberti, Leon Battista, 195
Aldington, Richard, 85, 98, 165, 169
Alexander, John, 165, 166
Allied Artists' Association, 68, 75, 100, 104, 176. *See also* Rutter, Frank
Alma-Tadema, Lawrence, 98
Altieri, Charles, 5–7, 113, 203
American Art Association, 21
American Society of Painters in Water Color, 20
anarchism, 65–6, 80–99, 114, 168. *See also* individualism, anarchist
Anderson, Margaret, 168, 176
Angelico, Fra (Guido di Petro), 39, 41, 42–3
Ankenbrand, Frank, Jr, 29
Anshutz, Thomas, 25, 26, 28
Antheil, George, 37, 172, 187, 190–1
Antliff, Mark, 57, 72, 81, 86, 91, 93
Aragon, Louis, 164, 165, 166
architecture, 5, 30, 51, 144, 147, 178–9, 184, 186, 189, 193–6, 199–201
　fascist, 199
　New York, 71
　Parisian, 195
　Italian Renaissance, 75, 134, 206
　Roman, 75

of Taj Mahal, 84. *See also* Le Corbusier; reconstruction
Ardis, Ann L., 3, 4, 89, 96
Ardizzone, Maria Luisa, 189
Aristotle, 34
Armory Show (New York), 70, 79–80
Armstrong, Tim, 192
Arnold, Matthew, 18
Arp, Jean, 206
Art Club of Philadelphia, 29
Art Institute of Chicago, *see* Chicago Academy of Fine Art
Ash Can School, 25, 76
Ashworth, George W., 183
avant-garde, 3, 9, 78, 152–3, 163–75, 186, 203–4

Bach, Friedrich Teja, 76, 182, 183
Bach, Johann Sebastian, 136
Bacon, Francis, 34
Baker, George, 170
Bakunin, Mikhail, 66
Baldick, Chris, 4
Balfour, Ian, 183
Balkin Bach, Penny, 24
Ball, Susan L., 175
Balla, Giacomo, 126, 131
Ballet Mécanique, 187–8
Barbizon School, 21
Barbusse, Henri, 163
Barclay, Florence, 11
Barnhart, Richard M., 60
Barrès, Maurice, 166, 168, 175
Baudelaire, Charles, 65
Baumann, Walter, 5
Beardsley, Aubrey, 53
beauty, 8, 12–17, 18–19, 28, 33, 36, 38, 39–41, 42–8, 50, 84, 93, 121, 125, 147, 149–51, 161, 169, 174, 178, 190
Beckett, Jane, 140
Beddoes, Thomas Lovell, 43

208

Picabia, Francis, 5, 164, 166, 168, 169, 171, 172–5, 176–9, 190, 196
Cette chose est faite pour perpétuer mon souvenir
Chose admirable à voir, 173
Danse de Saint-Guy, 173
De Zayas! De Zayas!, 173
L'Enfant carburateur, 173
Fantaisie, 173
Force comique, 173
Le Fou, 173
Mouvement Dada, 173
New York, 173
L'Oeil Cacodylate, 173
Petite solitude au milieu des soleils, 173
Portrait de Camille Pissarro, 173
Portrait de Guillaume Apollinaire, 173
Prenez garde à la peinture, 173–4
Révérence, 173
Révérences, 173
Le Saint des Saints, 173
The News From Russia [*Titre inconnu*], 173
Torse nu, 173
Les Yeux chauds, 173
Picart-le-Doux, Charles, 72
Picasso, Pablo, 5, 9, 67, 72, 77, 86, 87, 112, 125–6, 130, 131, 141, 145, 164, 166–9, 172
Exhibition of Drawings by Pablo Picasso (London), 67
Mandoline et le Pernod, La, 85
Piero della Francesca, 68, 196, 197
Pierpont Morgan, John, 21
Le Pilhaou-Thibaou, see 391
Pisanello, 1, 197
Pissarro, Camille, 77
Plarr, Victor, 148, 149, 150
'To a Greek Gem', 148
Plato, 84, 202
Platonism, 105, 177–8, 202
Plethon, Georgios Gemistus, 202–3
poetry: appeal to the visual sense, 15–16, 52–8
as mathematical equation, 51, 53, 54
as science, 83–5
as sculpture, 148–9
Japanese, 55
perceived as anarchist, 80
poetics of beauty, 39–48, 206
Poetry, 73, 81, 82, 134, 145
Poets' Club, 55
pointillism, 93
Pondrom, Cyrena N., 55
Poore, Henry Rankin, 38
popularisation, 8, 11–17, 136–52, 179
Porter, Eleanor H., 11

post-impressionism, 8, 50, 62–81, 86, 94, 106, 114, 115
Exhibition of Pictures by Paul Cézanne and Paul Gauguin (London), 67
Exhibition of the Work of English Post Impressionists, Cubists and others (Brighton), 68, 97
Manet and the Post-Impressionists (London), 61, 64–6, 70
Post-Impressionist and Futurist Exhibition (London), 68, 69, 76
Second Post-Impressionist Exhibition (London), 66–7, 73, 79
Twentieth-Century Art: A Review of Modern Movements (London), 68.
See also Fry, Roger *and* Bell, Clive
Pound, Dorothy Shakespear, *see* Shakespear, Dorothy
Pound, Ezra:
at college, 26–39
attempts painting, 28
attempts sculpture, 176
attitude towards Great War, 113–20
begins *Cantos*, 118–28
develops interest in contemporary art, 69–78
knowledge of Renaissance art, 134
launches imagism, 78, 81–3
publishes first art criticism, 49, 55, 94–102
publishes first literary criticism, 11–14
self-fashioning, 13, 18–19, 27–9, 37, 49
writes first art criticism, 29–39
Works:
poetry: 'Albâtre', 148
The Cantos, 6, 7, 8, 43, 112–13, 118–34, 136, 147–53, 154, 161, 165, 171, 184, 193–6, 204, 205, 206–7
Canto 1, 121, 127–8
Canto 2, 130
Canto 3, 132
Canto 4, 119, 123, 169
Canto 27, 188
Canto 45 ('Usura Canto'), 131, 133
Canto 46, 131
Canto 49 ('Seven Lakes Canto'), 131
Canto 110, 131
Hell Cantos (Cantos 14–15), 151
Malatesta Cantos (Cantos 8–11), 131, 184, 193–6, 202–4
The Pisan Cantos (Cantos 74–84), 131
'Three Cantos' (*Poetry*), 119, 123, 124, 131–3
'Three Cantos, I', 112, 122–3, 125–7, 131
'Three Cantos, II', 126, 132
'Three Cantos, III', 127
unpublished *Cantos* drafts, 9, 111, 118–28, 133, 188

218

Index